REMEMBERING HEAVEN'S FACE

A STORY OF RESCUE IN WARTIME VIETNAM

JOHN BALABAN

THE UNIVERSITY OF GEORGIA PRESS   *Athens*

Published by the University of Georgia Press
Athens, Georgia 30602
© 1991 by John Balaban
Preface © 2002 by John Balaban
All rights reserved
Designed by Edith Fowler
Printed and bound by Creasey Printing Services

The paper in this book meets the guidelines for
permanence and durability of the Committee on
Production Guidelines for Book Longevity of the
Council on Library Resources.

Printed in Canada

06   05   04   03   02   P   5   4   3   2   1

Library of Congress Cataloging-in-Publication Data

Balaban, John, 1943–.
Remembering heaven's face : a story of rescue in
wartime Vietnam / John Balaban.
p.   cm.
Originally published: Remembering heaven's face.
New York : Poseidon Press, 1991.
ISBN: 0-8203-2415-9 (pbk. : alk. paper)
1.Vietnamese Conflict, 1961–1975—Personal narratives,
American. 2.Vietnamese Conflict, 1961–1975—
Conscientious objectors—United States. 3.Vietnamese
Conflict, 1961–1975—Children. 4. Balaban, John, 1943–
—Journeys—Vietnam. 5.Vietnam—Description and
travel. I. Title.

DS559.5 .B35 2002
959.704'3373—dc21   2002023075

Originally published as *Remembering Heaven's Face:
A Moral Witness in Vietnam* by Poseidon Press.

For DAVID LANE GITELSON
1942–1968
"The Poor American"

CONTENTS

PREFACE

Nearly thirty years ago in Huế, I glimpsed an odd event that has lingered with me. By then, I had already completed two years of alternative service as a conscientious objector to the war, first as a teacher at a Vietnamese university, then as a field representative for a group that treated war-injured children. I had learned Vietnamese. I had been wounded in the Tet Offensive. When my selective service obligations were over, I left the war behind and went home to teach English at Penn State. But in less than a year, as the war still raged, I was back, traveling alone with a tape recorder, collecting on tape and translating the oral poetry that Vietnamese had been singing for hundreds, perhaps thousands, of years.

That day in the old imperial capital, a Vietnamese friend was trying to help me understand the notion of *mặt trời*, "sun," but literally "face of heaven," which he said meant the countenance of Ông Trời, Mr. Sky, also known as Ông Xanh, or Mr. Blue, who watches our affairs and constantly reassesses our fates. The face of heaven, he said, can be seen in those mirrors, engulfed by ceramic flames, that top royal buildings in the imperial city, but, he added, Heaven also appears in the humblest of homes as the mirror placed on family altars. On the mirror's face, Vietnamese paint the names of their ancestors; then they cover the mirror with a red cloth.

I was still curious about the mirror and its red cloth, and so, several days later, my friend took me to a balcony that looked down into the courtyard of a nearby home. "Be very careful, Mr. John," he said, as we crouched behind the thick, colonial balustrades, "if they see us, we have big trouble."

There below, beneath the terracotta roof of an old house whose entrance gate still displayed a mandarin's insignia on the portal, some old men were standing in the dusty court-yard. One of them, a man with thinning white hair, began to play a wooden flute. Huddled on the balcony, we watched as, one by one, each took a red cloth, draped it over his face, leaned back to tilt his face skyward, and then began to dance in slow whirls, arms extended, palms up, wheeling in glides that seemed filled with rapture.

That mysterious dance holds elements of all of my memo-ries of Vietnam. In always varying proportions, they con-tain a secret witnessing of a strange event, some bewilder-ment at what I was seeing, and some threat of violence—all tinged with a sense of the human spirit reaching toward Heaven, of that spirit being watched by Heaven, where, in the Taoist-Buddhist continuum, our moral efforts are judged and weighed.

I volunteered to go to Vietnam, but as a conscientious ob-jector to war. Like the millions of young men who bore arms, I came home filled with memories that sometimes seem more real than my present life, even now at middle age. Then, as a civilian engaged in alternative service, traveling alone on public buses, on river boats, or hitchhiking on choppers and planes, talking to farmers, recording their poetry in the evening while a firefight might spring up on the opposite riverbank, I often saw a Vietnam that other Americans missed. *Đi ra một ngày, về một sàng khôn* is one of the proverbs I learned from peasants in the Mekong Delta: "Go out one day and come back with a basket full of wisdom." Leave the safe, unsurprising village, the proverb says, take to the road, dis-cover something new. Bring it home. When I started to write this account, I opened up notebooks that I had taped shut for decades for fear of what was in them ... and then found myself on that bright, perilous road once again.

While most of the following events took place in the midst of war, this is not exactly a story about the war, but a story of rescue. Most of the children I helped save—scalped, burned, blasted, or shot when I found them—are now adults, parents or even grandparents themselves. Most were returned home to their families. But some, orphaned or paraplegic, stayed in the U.S. and started new lives. One little girl even became a banker in California. The poetry I recorded is still being sung in the countryside of Vietnam and the culture that sustained that poetry for four thousand years is still alive today. And while many of my funny, wise, reckless, young American friends of those days are dead, what they did and what they learned is not. It is as if all of us were being watched, all of us journeying under a brilliant blue sky that is the face of heaven.

PART ONE

GOING OUT
ONE DAY

INTERNATIONAL VOLUNTARY
SERVICES

CHINA

Red River

Black River

Dienbienphu

HANOI

Haiphong

GULF OF TONKIN

LAOS

Vinh

SOUTH CHINA SEA

17th Parallel - - - - Demarcation Line

Hue

Danang

THAILAND

Quang Ngai

Kontum

Pleiku

VIETNAM

CAMBODIA

Mekong River

Dalat

Cam Ranh Bay

PHNOM PENH

Tay Ninh

HO CHI MINH CITY (SAIGON)

Long Xuyen

Cao Lanh

Vung Tau

My Tho

MEKONG RIVER DELTA

Can Tho

0   50 100 km

0   50   100 miles

1

CAPTURED

Early in August of 1967, only two weeks after I had arrived in Vietnam, I was walking along the road from the remote provincial capital of Cao Lanh to its tiny airstrip. The road was a dusty red swath, running through a tin-roofed settlement along a fouled canal, and cutting, farther away from town, through rice fields, and through groves of papaya and coconut palms whining with cicadas. As I ambled by, flocks of lorikeets screeched in the palms. In the dusty yards, children stopped their play to chase off mynah birds pillaging rice set out to dry in flat baskets. When they saw me, the children were struck mute at the uncommon spectacle of an American taking a walk alone; then they started shrieking *"Mỹ! Mỹ!"* ("American! American!") as if a strange dog had just strayed past the malodorous ditch that separated me from their yards.

While I trudged along under a "heavy sun," as the Vietnamese say, sandals and toes and ankles coated with red dust, the dust in my hair and nose and staining the collar of my white shirt, my head was swimming with excitement. I was happy. Never mind that in Vietnamese "red dust" is a phrase for the mutable world and that I was taking a walk in a war zone. I was seeing the place for the first time without American intermediaries. For the first time since leaving the United States three weeks earlier, I felt I was really in Vietnam. At least, at last, *finally*, I thought, I was out in the country and free to sort out the rightness or wrongness of my volunteering to come here. Now—for the length of my walk, at any rate—I was free of my burdensome colleagues in the International Voluntary Services, the Peace Corps–like private organization that had brought me to Vietnam and to which I was obligated for two years under the Selective Service Act.

In a nearby paddy, peasants—their heads wrapped in the checkered scarves of the Delta or protected by conical hats—bent knee-deep in itchy muck as they weeded seedlings, the sun glinting off their black pajamas. These farmers paid me no attention, but closer by a soldier in fatigues, who was hunting rats with a long bamboo pole tipped with a sharp trident, gave me a wave as he stalked along the paddy dike. I waved back. I could see the gold in his teeth when he smiled. Not far behind him, a little boy in shorts and flipflops, perhaps nine or so, probably his son, had slung the soldier's carbine over one shoulder while over the other he gripped a burlap bag sagging with rats.

I suppose I knew the walk was ill advised. I was free because our Vietnamese-language teacher had yet again failed to show up in Cao Lanh because, as he had confessed over the phone to our team leader, he thought our small town of seven thousand too insecure, too close to the Cambodian sanctuaries of the Viet Cong. Didn't we know, he had asked across the scratchy phone line from the Danang Bureau de Poste et Télégraphe, that on the American Fourth of July, just before we arrived, the whole place had been mortared?

It was a long walk to the Cao Lanh airstrip, which was the only place I knew outside of town except the Green Beret camp. I figured Americans would be at the airfield and I could hitch a ride the six or so miles back into town. I had qualms, however, about riding with American soldiers. The week before, agonized by jock itch and athlete's foot, I had gone to see a teenaged Navy medic who gave me some antifungal cream, and—in the way boys show one another their pet frogs and jackknives—showed me a "VC" ear he kept in a jar of formaldehyde. Though I kept my views to myself, especially around soldiers, who thought being a Peace Corps type suspicious enough (what kind of person would *volunteer* to go to Vietnam?), I was after all a conscientious objector to military service. Somehow I wanted Vietnamese to know this, as if they would appreciate the moral difference which I distinguished between my presence and that of the 500,000 other young Americans who were pouring into the country: I had come not to bear arms but to bear witness.

A small convoy of ARVN (Army of the Republic of Vietnam) trucks churned up the road and swept past me. I stood in a dust cloud as the air horns blasted hellos, and I looked into the open backbeds at small men in big helmets, some laughing and pointing as they held up their M-16s, others raising their hands in the peace sign. Clinging to the railings were their wives and children, all hurtling along the bumpy road to a base camp somewhere off in the nowhere, to be mortared by the Viet Cong.

Somewhere past the last corrugated roof, past the last refugee shack walled with flattened Budweiser cans, out in the country, where the road cut into green rice fields crisscrossed by mud dikes, I noticed a little building roofed in terra-cotta tiles and topped by two recoiling ceramic dragons. A temple, I thought. I saw no harm in taking a look at a temple so close to the main road.

I crossed over a cement pipe that bridged a drainage ditch. The temple was on a shady little island engulfed by flooded paddy. To reach it, I had to take a path that doglegged among some thatched houses clustered under coconut palms and edged by pepper plants and melon gardens. It was mid-afternoon and hot as a steam bath. Nearby some children fished in the dirty water until they pulled out a decaying magazine with a toddler's face wadding off the sopping cover. When the children looked up and saw me, they ran down the dike path to the thatched houses. Now they watched me as I approached.

Before I got very far into the hamlet, a group of men came out from the houses and stood across the dike, blocking my path. The way they just stood and stared tripped a little flare of alarm in my stomach. I stopped. I realized I had no choice but to stay on the dike, for on my one side was the tiny village and on the other the flooded fields where running was impossible. So, while not exactly whistling a happy tune, I kept walking and said hello in Vietnamese as I approached them.

They said nothing in reply, but parted to let me pass through, as I kept my eyes glued on the temple, hoping that would explain why I was there. I was nervous, but relieved, and then I saw, farther ahead, another group coming from behind a house to block the path. Now my path was blocked both before and behind me. Without much choice, I kept approaching this new group. No guns, I noted.

Again they said nothing as I said hello. I regretted that no one back in Cao Lanh knew I was on this hike, and hoped that maybe these men were just pissed off at the presumption of my sauntering off the road right into their hamlet. I could hear chickens nearby, a pig grunting in a yard, but loudest of all was the blood singing in my ears, noisier than locusts, as I walked the last few steps. No one moved.

This time a man reached out and put his hands on my shoulders, spun me around, then nudged me forward. With a few shoves more, as the others surrounded me, he prodded me off the path and into an open doorway. Inside was a dirt floor, a chair (where they sat me down), a table, a polished wooden bench, a calendar that had a picture of a girl holding a rose against her cheek, and, high up in a corner by the door, a little altar with some photos of old people, in front of which burned a tiny kerosene lamp and a stick of incense. Behind a doorway in a wall of woven bamboo strips was the rest of the house, but it didn't seem that anybody was there.

About twelve men had come in with me. They wore the baggy black dress of farmers, some turbaned with the scarves common in the South, especially in the formerly Cambodian Mekong Delta. Children, for whom I was suddenly grateful—I didn't think the men would hurt me in front of children—were gawking through the one window and the open door, some whispering and others staring wide-eyed as they chewed on stalks of sugarcane. I did not understand one word of what was being said. At that point, my entire Vietnamese vocabulary was little more than "hello," "boiled water, please," and *không,* "no." Anything useful, like the word for "antiwar" or "civilian," was beyond me. I did, however, know the word for "teacher," *giáo-sư,* and said it. Someone laughed. I grinned as if it seemed like a good joke to me too. Then a man who thought he spoke French, but really did not, started making Gallic noises at me. I tried to respond in French, saying I was a schoolteacher, a civilian, a noncombatant, but the man simply did not understand. Another, older man to whom the others deferred was telling my interrogator what to ask. Nothing was getting through. Meanwhile, my interrogator, whose face was pitted with smallpox scars and blotched, I began to suspect, from booze, was getting embarrassed and angry. Some of the men had started laughing at him. He began shouting, as if volume would increase my understanding. Someone reached over my left shoulder and took out from my shirt pocket my ballpoint pen and little notepad. I realized I had to try to stop things before they got worse and, with my chest ready to explode, I jumped to my feet with a loud "No!"

All, including me, blinked and seemed surprised.

Someone from behind patted my shoulder to quiet me down and that gave me heart enough to say, in pointlessly clear and calmer English, that I had better get back to town. I even glanced at my Timex, as if I were late for something. Then, along with everybody else, I took a look at the man who seemed to be in charge, at his tanned and deeply creased face, his thick gray crewcut, his crowfooted, studious eyes with the whites a bit yellowed from the liver disease that accompanies a life in the tropics.

He examined me with a look that was more scientific than unfriendly. In fact, I thought I detected some mirth hidden in his composure. As the seconds ticked by, I watched him weigh my fate; my stomach flared with terror once again. Finally, he made a shooing motion with one hand, as if to a fly, or a dog, or a child.

Giving a whoop that startled me, the children rushed in and pulled me out of the room. As the kids began chattering like birds, one boy yanked my hand toward the path; others felt at the magical hair on my arms. I looked back and nodded a bewildered goodbye to the men, who were already turning back into the house.

I hitched a ride to Cao Lanh in an Army jeep, but didn't tell the two GIs up front anything about what had just happened. I wasn't sure what had happened. Had I just met the Viet Cong? If I had been kidnapped, why was I now free? No ordinary farmers would take such liberties with an American. Americans were walking death. Any Vietnamese in the country would know that as soon as I returned I could report the event to authorities who at the least would organize a sweep of the hamlet or, if it struck the whim of the Vietnamese in charge or his American adviser, they might call in an air strike that would mulch the entire hamlet—men, women, children, pigs, chickens, chili and melon gardens, and the mysterious little temple that led me there. Americans, to country people, were walking hellfire. Was I imagining things?

When I got back, the IVS girls were baking up a Betty Crocker cake mix that the Public Safety Officer next door had gotten at the commissary downriver in Sadec. "Boy, are you sunburned!" one of them said, flour caking her hands and dusting her nose, on which her glasses drooped. Chi Hoa, our housekeeper, who was irritated at their taking over her kitchen, used my arrival to complain in almost intelligible English about working in a house that doesn't burn incense, but what could she do, etc. The world was none the worse for my experience. I decided to say nothing. Whoever those men were, they had let me go.

Two days later, while fishing the tiny ponds behind our house, I had some of the mystery cleared up, some of it increased, when Mr. Sanh, a former company commander who now worked for the American Public Safety Officer, joined me with a pot of tea and his English-conversation book as I sat angling for little silvery chubs. One of Mr. Sanh's underlings had fetched me a bamboo pole and a string from the market. Sanh did small favors for me so I would help him practice his English, his ticket to a better job with Americans. Pouring us both a cup of tea, he tried out his English on his favorite topic, the depredations of the Viet Cong. The year before, his company of ninety-six men had been reduced to sixteen in a single battle. His son, a medic with the company, had been killed. The perpetually grinning flunky who had just gotten me my fishing gear had lain wounded in a sugarcane field for a night and a day and hadn't been in his right mind since. When the company was retired, Mr. Sanh was employed by the United States Agency for International Development (USAID), which was training him and his sixteen cosurvivors to be policemen and guards.

"I teh you 'bout VC, Mr. John," he said, opening his book to a vocabulary list and revealing the bullet hole that pierced the bottom half of its pages.

I nodded politely. The grasshopper I was trying to fix on my hook wriggled its legs and spat tobacco juice on my fingers.

"Some week ago, they blow up school and bridge near Hong Ngu."

"Anybody hurt?" In our house nearby, Chi Hoa had just rinsed the breakfast plates and some rice grains were now tumbling out of the drain that emptied into the pond. I could see ripples of fish and cast my line over, plunking the grasshopper right in the middle of the scurry. Nuoi, the deranged guard, bobbed his head and clapped his hands with delight.

"No. They cowar'. Hit at nigh', so no chilren there. *Similarly,*" he added, to introduce a word from his vocabulary list, "bridge empty."

"Oh!" I had a strike. The grasshopper disappeared under the pond surface which twirled in smoke-blue and bright manila streaks of phenol.

"But, Mr. John, last nigh' they ambush some American soldier on road to airport."

I handed my pole to Nuoi and looked at Sanh. Overhead a propaganda plane was circling low over the market across from the ponds, blaring its loudspeakers at the crowd of conical hats milling below. "Anybody hurt?"

"Oh, driver he shot up number ten. Other GI just break leg in crash."

"Where on the road did it happen?"

"What you say?"

"Where on the road was the ambush?"

"Maybe, 'bout . . ." Sanh paused as he put together the sentence. ". . . halfway. You know *miéu* on lef' of road?"

"What's a *meeou?*"

"It like small temple or, what you say, *shrine?*"

Sanh's words had a disorienting effect on me that was almost physical. Confusions that had grown in me like vertigo since I had left the United States only a month before, now prospered wildly in my head. A month earlier, wearing a white linen suit, fancying myself a kind of diplomat of conscience, I left Dulles Airport with a planeload of young IVS volunteers. It was my first real trip outside the United States. Jet-lagged, as if in a dream, I watched train guards in Tokyo use sticks to shove the rush-hour crowds into subway cars. Looking at those commuters packed into the cars, their faces jammed against the windows and doors like wall-eyed sardines staring back from an opened can, I realized that I didn't have a clue as to their emotions. In Hong Kong, our group's next stop, I read in a newspaper that three young men had bashed another to death on the street because he had "stared at them." From the same paper I had clipped a story about a Mr. Lau Sik-yan, forty-four, who leapt to his death from a hundred-foot ledge "after dancing and performing for twenty minutes as hundreds watched. Lau," the paper said, "crawled onto the ledge ten minutes after a seventeen-year-old Chinese girl had thrown herself to death from the same spot. There is no known connection," the clipping read, "between the two."

In Kowloon Harbor, I was shouted at by an emaciated stevedore who caught me watching his skeletal brethren smoking opium amid the packing crates on the wharf. As I walked the streets, I was overwhelmed by the hundreds of thousands of hopeless people piled in the government housing projects, their massed lives as anonymous as those of the jellyfish that littered the foul harbor and beached the shore, their human selves seeming as discardable as the broken baskets, bottles, and household debris sunk in the tidal mud. I couldn't fathom how values like freedom, justice, and individual dignity—values that I had fixed as universals in my young American mind—could mean anything for such people. If the face of heaven were a bright mirror, then those Chinese faces stacked in housing flats and factories—like the Japanese faces squeezed cheek to jowl in the Tokyo subway cars—were the faces of hell.

I had carried this spiritual jet lag with me into Vietnam where it only intensified. On the ride into Saigon from Tan Son Nhut Airport in the backbed of an IVS truck, in heat that I did not think possible on this planet, my silly white suit was grimed with crankcase oil as the truck fer-

ried sixty of us new volunteers and our luggage to a suf-
focating dormitory on the outskirts of town. From dusk
to dawn in the curfewed city, small-arms fire riddled our
sleep as jittery soldiers—patrolling bridges and barbed-
wire barricades—popped shots at dogs, or tumbling tin
cans, or palm fronds floating in the filthy rivers. Bombs
thumped on the evening horizons. *Không* was the first
word I learned in Vietnamese: "no." The distant bombs
sounded like that: *không; không.*

Later that evening in Cao Lanh, still reeling from the
thoughts set off by Mr. Sanh's revelation, I walked alone
by the ponds, listening to the base howitzers open up their
evening harassment of the countryside, their random shells
probably exploding on grazing water buffalo and on anything else too innocent to take cover. I considered the
meaning of Mr. Sanh's report. The GIs had been ambushed
at the spot where I had waved goodbye to the hamlet
children, near the shrine that had lured me off the road.
One of the soldiers was critically wounded. Perhaps my
silence had caused his injury and that of his companion
whose leg had been smashed. How was I *not* part of this
war?
Beside the ponds, where women were dipping fishnets,
stood some weathered tombs. High above, two F-105s
were zooming through the edges of arriving thunder-
clouds. One of the Green Berets had told me the Viet Cong
sometimes slid the tops off such tombs and hid there during
air attacks. During the last flood, he said, when his hy-
droplane unit thought they could catch the VC out in the
open, away from their flooded hideouts, the Green Berets
had skimmed across submerged rice fields and reed plains
but found no one except farmers and livestock stranded
on hillocks. Then, by chance, as the Americans took a
break, two young Viet Cong burst up from the muddy
water near the idling hydroplanes. They had been hiding
there, breathing through reeds. Even their faces were cov-

ered with leeches; they must have been in the cold water for hours, as were their comrades throughout the flooded Delta. That was the enemy.

The jets were now delivering an air strike, darting through the clouds above the old, decaying tombs chiseled in *nôm* characters, the ancient script of Vietnam from centuries before. A scrawny mutt was snuffling a pile of feathers and chicken bones atop one of the crypts. I knew the Vietnamese buried their relatives near the family fields, as if their very flesh, returned, rendered, would nurture their descendants. When rice is cooked, Vietnamese say they can tell by the odor of the steam in what riverine silt that rice had been grown.

A schoolteacher had told me that during the last Indochina war the Viet Minh had a stronghold here, near the Thap Muoi Canal. Ho Chi Minh's father was supposed to be buried somewhere nearby. ("Nothing is more precious," his famous, revolutionary son had said, "than independence and freedom.") Before the American war, the Vietnamese had fought the French, the Japanese, the Chinese, the Chams, and here in the Mekong where their historical Southern migration had led them, the Khmers. For two thousand years, they had waged wars against foreigners. Despite the initial sense of dislocation I'd felt in the cities, here I began to see that Vietnamese lives were lived not on a Spenglerian trash heap of history but, rather, in a dense spiritual and physical continuum in which ancestors guided them and history reflected destinies cast in heaven. A continuum in which individuals, like the weathered man who was in charge of my captors, were empowered to make life-and-death decisions. Next to this antiquity and preposterous resolve, the jets diving on the horizon seemed like so many gnats.

What was my role in this, I wondered? What moral use, if any, could I have in Vietnam? As I stood by the ponds, watching the air strike, recoiling from Mr. Sanh's news, my conscientious objection seemed like so much vain posturing. I was the merest spectator, a proverbial cricket that might be crushed where tigers and elephants fight. If Mr. Sanh's account was accurate, those men who had detained me had probably been planning the ambush when I blundered upon them. How did they have the nerve to release me? How could they know I would not report the incident? Had I become part of that ambush when the children took me back to the road? How was I *not* a part of this war?

2

WHY I WAS IN VIETNAM

For all the confusion that engulfed me as soon as I arrived in Vietnam, I had come with clear conviction. I was opposed to the taking of human life. I was opposed to all war and, in particular, opposed to this war. It seems odd to me now that I could have developed such notions in the late fifties and early sixties, especially growing up as I did in a rough housing project rife with violence. My childhood memories include a ten-year-old girl running by my back porch with a dart in her back; a boy that other boys had hoisted off his feet by a rope noosed around his neck and slung over an oak limb; a girl whose forehead was gashed by her brother's machete; children beaten by their alcoholic parents; a playmate who had cracked his drunken father's ribs with a hammer; a ten-year-old buddy shooting me in the stomach with a hunting arrow; a boy down the street struck dead by an O'Boyle's ice-cream truck; and a man getting hauled off by the cops because he was starting fistfights in a line outside a house where he was wailing, "I ought to be next. I'm her husband!"

Skinny, asthmatic, given to talking with imaginary creatures, as a child I cringed at this violence while admiring intensely my older brother who learned to survive within it: at seventeen, he sometimes toted a nickel-plated .32

revolver; his last day in school was when he punched a
teacher down the school steps. Yet, somehow, all that violence propelled me in the opposite direction.

In high school, one of my best friends was a Quaker.
Despite my father's military career, my parents' Eastern
Church, Romanian heritage, my neighborhood violence,
and my brother's example, I found myself attending
Quaker meetings, picketing the Army's biological-warfare
center at Fort Dietrick, Maryland, and trying to take on
in debate—at the local John Birch Society, of all places—
the legal counsel for the House Un-American Activities
Committee.

My father—once a lieutenant in the U.S. Cavalry before
it was mechanized and armored—disapproved of my be-
havior and talked of patriotic duty. But even as he did, I
remembered his old uniform musty in a closet, his sword
rusting in its scabbard, his dried-out, creaky leather riding
crop with its lead-weighted pommel; remembered that he
had been cashiered and almost court-martialed after
whacking a superior officer on the head with the hard end
of that riding crop when the fool, grasping for insults with
a weak sense of Romanian and Hungarian history, had
called my dad a "dirty Hunky."

It was what my father did by instinct rather than what
he said that took hold in me. Neither of us realized, as we
argued, that what moved us both was a sense of injustice.
Even in his ever-failing American dream, where his business ventures never reached solvency and where bill col-
lectors kept my mother in tears, I remember him—with
his European degrees and accent, his starched white shirts,
thin bow ties, and overly formal English—trying to shape
up our shabby neighbors, rousting drunks from the summer's dewy lawns, chastising and kicking them up until
they stumbled into their houses to sleep. And, still later,
when the government sold the whole coal-burning, ram-
shackle mess, I remember my dad's hapless attempt to
organize these same people into a cooperative that would

allow them to buy their own homes for fifty dollars each, cash down, through a benevolent collective mortgage offered by federal lawyers.

By the time I was sixteen, our arguments had become frequent and violent. One day he swung a haymaker at me and I blocked it. He broke his thumb. Within minutes I had shoved two dollars into my blue jeans and was out the door, running across the snow-covered field behind our house. Six-foot drifts edged the highway. In the dead of winter in 1960, I was running away from home.

I had no idea where to go, so I hitchhiked up the road to say goodbye to one of my high-school teachers. The plan I hatched in the time it took me to get there was to head out for California. That, however, was the entire plan and, luckily for me, I never got far with it. Instead, I stayed the year with the teacher and her husband, driving to school with her each day, cutting firewood and doing chores in the afternoons. I saw my parents at my June graduation for the first time in months.

In that odd half-year, I joined the Southampton Monthly Meeting of Friends. Sitting in the silence of the Quaker meeting with those kind strangers, waiting, as they say, for the "still, small voice" to speak, I found a refuge, a way against violence.

The next year, as a freshman at Penn State, I fell in with two classmates in Beginning Latin, Andy Stapp and Tim Reussing. At first I was the more politically aware, joining the 1963 civil-rights march on Washington where, standing among the hundreds of thousands before the Lincoln Memorial, I heard Martin Luther King speak his famous dream and was powerfully confirmed in a sense of another, possible society. Back at Penn State, I exhorted Stapp and Reussing to get involved. Stapp was largish, gap-toothed, and sloppy. He talked and ate a lot, told very funny jokes, liked to be right, and was generally a good-natured wise guy. Our good-looking, more mainstream friend, Reussing, was—except for his interest in Greek classics—a typ-

ical frat rat, more concerned with sorority mixers than
with the Gulf of Tonkin. In the normal course of things,
Andy would have gone on to finish a Ph.D. in classics and
Tim would have become a business executive with literary
interests. But these possibilities were eliminated one week-
end in 1965 when Andy, who was increasingly aroused by
the war, boarded a bus chartered for an antiwar march in
Washington, where he was clubbed, arrested, stripped, and
handcuffed naked to a pole in a D.C. detention room. He
said he saw cops dragging a girl by her long red hair down
a corridor in the station. Whole hanks of hair had been
pulled from her scalp.

It was one of the first marches to turn ugly. Earlier in
that day, when the police charged the demonstrators who
had linked arms and plunked down on some government
lawn, Andy recalled seeing a kid, who had been wearing
a helmet, standing helmetless, dazed, his nose dribbling
blood as he stared down into an open palm where one of
his eyes lay.

None of us was the same after that, but Andy *really* got
radical, joining campus chapters of the May 2nd Movement
and the Progressive Labor Party, both far-left groups on
the Attorney General's List. Reussing tagged along with
him. I shied away, put off by Stapp's relentless tirades and
talk of violence. Finally, when Andy burned his draft card
in one of the first incidents of that kind, the FBI came after
him. Then he and Reussing fled on Tim's motorcycle,
heading for Cuba and getting as far as New Orleans, never
to return to college. "FUGITE. FUGITE. FABIUS BITHYNIUS
INSPECTUS INVENIT" was my last message to them, a telegram I wired them with fifty bucks after being grilled by
the FBI myself: "Flee. Flee. The FBI is coming." With my
friends gone, I spent my senior year in an isolation of
books, in reading Marvell and Donne and Yeats. I won a
Woodrow Wilson Fellowship that took me to Harvard.

As the first person from my neighborhood ever to have
gone to *any* college, I was mindful of my incredible good

fortune at attending Harvard's graduate school for free. I studied hard, happily immersed in Chaucer, Ovid, *Beowulf*, and the Scottish poets of the later Middle Ages. I kept my social conscience only barely alive by joining the Students for a Democratic Society; I never found time to go to a meeting. As the war droned on and Vietnam was filling up with American troops, I would have been content occupying myself with the literature of past centuries if it had not been for Robert Strange McNamara, Lyndon Johnson's Secretary of Defense, who brought the war home to me one warm spring afternoon in 1967.

As I was returning to my apartment from Widener Library, plodding along with a heavy bookbag, eyes itchy in the unfamiliar sunlight and shoulders stooped from too much hunkering over books in the dingy stacks, I came across a large crowd outside of Lowell House. They were students mostly, and they were waiting to speak to McNamara, who was inside as a guest of the new Kennedy Institute, talking to a small group of undergraduates. At that time, the Johnson administration was still getting away with saying very little about the actual conduct of the war, although rumors of napalmed civilians had filtered into the press. During his Cambridge visit, McNamara had been petitioned to speak to the Boston academic community, with its many colleges and junior colleges. To make his acceptance easier, some of his fellow guests at the Kennedy Institute offered to share a platform with him. He refused.

When I got to Lowell House, perhaps five hundred persons were milling about. An SDSer was haranguing the crowd with a bullhorn, but generally it was pleasant and amiable. Far down Mt. Auburn Street, someone had hung a bedsheet with an illegible protest from a third-story window. From the same window, the blurry tune and some of the words of "Mack the Knife" floated toward the crowd.

When McNamara did emerge from Lowell House, it

was through a side exit into a narrow street; the crowd rushed over and, at first unintentionally, blocked his car. The Secret Service agents looked menaced and started pushing students out of the way. I thought it might get rough, so I stood behind an ABC camera team and looked in at the Secretary as he sat in his car. After a few minutes, I saw him lean over to say something to an agent and then get out. Another agent helped him up onto the roof of the shiny Buick. The roof buckled with a crumpling sound that McNamara ignored. Even standing there on the roof of the car—in his dark-blue suit, white shirt, dark tie, wire-rimmed glasses, strands of thinning hair brushed straight back—McNamara looked formidable. The crowd quieted as he began to speak.

He said, "I'll give you four minutes; then I must leave."

The crowd hushed.

"When I was a student in California," he began, "I was as radical as you."

The crowd groaned, but kept its peace.

"But there was one difference. . . ."

Dead silence.

"I was more polite."

It was as if he had clobbered an enormous cow. Huge boos bellowed out from the students. Someone yelled, "Fuck you!" Another, "Murderer."

Just in front of me, the ABC camera whirred to a stop. The cameraman shot a look at the sound man, who gave him a we-got-it wink. Then McNamara, his four minutes done, was helped down and driven off through the hooting youngsters.

The next day, Harvard apologized in the press.

That moment of public insolence—I mean McNamara's—made me suddenly ashamed of my books, my university, and the safety of my student deferment. (Stapp, now drafted into the Army in reprisal for his card-burning, was at that moment being court-martialed at Fort Still.) I was ashamed too of the impotence of the crowd outside

Lowell House. Even the antiwar demonstrations that were now marching in big cities across the country (100,000 in New York on April 15; 20,000 in San Francisco that same day) seemed to have no effect on Johnson or Congress. It occurred to me that the only place to learn anything, to *do* anything about Vietnam was in Vietnam, where the U.S. buildup had now reached 400,000 troops. So, a week later, I began dickering with my Pennsylvania draft board about trading in my student deferment for a conscientious objector's. They advised against it. I demanded a hearing.

When I finally had my hearing in late spring, the draft board, which had the power to order me to prison, seemed to be just a bunch of old men frightened that I might make a speech. A veritable Moose Lodge. None of them would look me in the eye, not even the jittery old duffer who held out a Bible for my swearing in. The only thing they asked me was if I really intended to do alternative service in Vietnam. The hearing was about as long as McNamara's baiting of the crowd outside Lowell House. I was crushed. I had prepared answers regarding the sanctity of life. I was ready to state that the Supreme Deity, which the Selective Service Act required me to believe in, was a kind of goodly energy permeating the universe. I was ready to quote Martin Luther King, Mahatma Gandhi, and George Fox's declaration of 1660 to Charles II ("we utterly deny all outward wars and strife"), but they didn't ask me anything except if I would agree to serve my alternative service in Vietnam. I had no intention of carrying bedpans in a VA hospital, or of serving as a medic, or, worse, of going to jail. I saw no obligation to let the State abuse me. I found my antiwar views altogether moral, even patriotic, certainly not cowardly, and saw no reason why I should be punished or humiliated for them. I told them I was going to Vietnam whether or not they approved my status as a CO.

I was then told that the hearing was concluded. That was it. At first I thought they had turned me down out of hand. I can imagine now how they must have laughed over that one: the kid who really *forced* them to send him to Vietnam.

So, two months after my draft-board hearing, I was sitting in my new linen suit on top of my luggage in the greasy backbed of the International Voluntary Services truck that took us from Tan Son Nhut to the Agricultural Ministry dorm. Most of the new volunteers were kids from small Midwestern colleges. The boys, many of them right off the farm, were signed up for ag work with peasants or for something called Rural Development; the girls, and one or two other males besides me, were to teach English. Because of my new Harvard degree, I had been promised an assignment at the university in Can Tho, the capital of the Mekong Delta. For most of us, this was our first big trip away from home. Perched on our bags, jet-lagged, stunned by the heat, we gaped at the Honda packs that swirled past our truck, at jeeps mounted with .50-caliber machine guns, at all the Americans and Vietnamese in uniform, their pistols, their shotguns, their M-16s.

The first week was like some weird fraternity hazing or summer camp gone awful. In our dormitory, the floor of the common bathroom was slippery green with fungal scum where urine and shower water backed up from the clogged drains. All of us soon had some kind of crotch rot and diarrhea; one girl's face became infected from bedbug bites. Children hooted at us and pelted us with rocks when we walked to the restaurant where IVS had arranged for our meals. Inside, we'd find bits of stone and dead ants in the rice. Outside the restaurant, a Vietnamese woman whose whole face was a mass of noodly bags, so that only her eyes could be made out, begged at the door. After the first few days, even the farm boys were complaining. One guy just packed his bags and flew home.

The International Voluntary Services liked to rough it. We had to learn, we were told, to live like Vietnamese. One old IVS hand told me he wished he could *be* a Vietnamese.

IVS, with its 250-some volunteers (I was the only CO at the time; maybe the only civilian CO in Vietnam, although a handful more appeared later and the military had its CO medics) was the largest agency on contract to USAID, whose officials, of course, did not live like Vietnamese. They were the new colonials, inheriting all the accoutrements of their French predecessors. During that week of Saigon orientation, we got invited for drinks at AID villas—renovated three-story French-colonial affairs, fully air-conditioned and maintained by Vietnamese servants and armed guards. Talking to these AID advisers, even about our tasks of teaching English, was like talking to chrome bumpers in a parking lot or a pile of telephone books. Beneath all the phony-baloney blather about "nation-building," it was evident that our government overseers had no professions, no ideas, no views except a kind of vague Kiwanis boosterism. For them, Vietnam was just a well-paying job with perks in sex, booze, and power that they could never enjoy "back in the world." At one affair in an AID official's apartment, our host dramatized our absurd circumstances by simply forgoing all conversation and, while his maid served us gin-and-tonics, took photo after photo of us. Afterward, while we nibbled his Ritz crackers and Cheez-Wiz, he showed us photo books of other such cocktail parties. Then I think we each had to sign a chit so he could get reimbursed for the gin. Finally, we all left and went back to our miserable dorm, taking a squadron of little yellow-and-blue toy-car Citroën taxis through the diesel clouds of swarming Hondas, three-wheeled Lambretta vans, meandering pedicabs, trucks, jeeps, Ford Broncos.

Before we could go to our permanent stations, we were to learn to speak some Vietnamese. IVS broke us up into small groups to be tutored in the countryside where we could *really* see how Vietnamese lived, and where IVS could keep an eye on our progress as we continued our "orientation." So, just two months out of Harvard, only

a month after my declaration to my draft board, and after
a week in Saigon, I found myself jammed with three of
the girls inside a small, turbo-prop Air America Porter
Pilatus, bouncing through heat pockets over the cratered
Delta to Cao Lanh, a tiny provincial capital on a loop of
the Mekong just below the Viet Cong sanctuaries in Cambodia's Parrot's Beak.

The brick-and-stucco house that IVS rented for us in
Cao Lanh was sandwiched between the CIA station chief's
and that of the local USAID Public Safety Adviser, an ex-
cop from Los Angeles. The three-story row houses,
guarded by a Province Reconnaissance Unit employed by
the CIA agent, stood off from the town on a landfill surrounded by ponds, tombs, old paddy fields, and tidal lagoons that ran to the river. When our language teacher
finally came, he took a look at Cao Lanh, talked to some
of the local high-school teachers, and, after a day's wran-
gling over the phone with IVS in Saigon, flew home (the
roads had long been cut by the Viet Cong). He was a
married man, he said. He couldn't take risks; his wife was
pregnant with their first child. It wasn't altogether clear
whether he left because of the lack of security in Cao Lanh
or because at that moment, on the eve of the presidential
elections, bloody street demonstrations were taking place
throughout South Vietnamese cities. Whatever his fears,
his departure ended what was to have been a month of
language training. Now, although we had no good reason
to stay on in Cao Lanh because the street demonstrations
had shut down many of the schools where we were to
teach, IVS wanted us to stay put. We had little to do except
read and sunbathe during the day and trade language lessons with local schoolteachers by kerosene lamps in the
evenings.

So there I was, set down not far from a small Green
Beret camp in possibly the most insecure province in the
Delta, with an antiwar activist; a flyweight, bespectacled,
born-again Christian; and a rather attractive flirt, whose

polished nails and cruise clothing had caused smirks and even some anger from the more missionary-minded IVSers back in Saigon.

One morning I woke up to find the following glued to our door:

COMMUNIQUE

Kien Phong Province chief respectfully inform to the people the following:

Since the need for special security, I declare the curfew in Kien Phong province from 10 pm to 5 a. m that takes effect from the issued date to issuing new order.

Please, all the people, abide by this curfuw to avoid danger and disturbances from the security agencies.

In emergency case, the pasengers should use light and have I D card whenever security agents want to check.

CAO LANH, August 16th 1967

Province chief, Kien Phong.
L.T. Col. Doan van Guong

A few days later, at 11:45 P.M., Cao Lanh was mortared. When all the lights in the town blipped out and a siren whined and the whole dog population started howling, we scrambled out of our mosquito-netted bunkbeds and rushed downstairs to put the roof and two ceilings between us and the mortars—me in my shorts, the girls in their nighties, huddled with one of the CIA guards behind our accordion doorgate, watching as stray mortars kicked and splashed in the fields before our house. Fierce small-arms fire rattled all about. Around 2:00 A.M., a Dragonship was called in from Saigon, releasing its electric plasma of bullets at six hundred rounds per second, every fourth a tracer, in a deafening stream, a lightning arc of continuous fire that pulverized the flare-lit fields around the town.

By 6:30 A.M., it was all over. I went out with the CIA agent to survey the damage. Thirty-seven government troops and their families had been killed; another twenty-six wounded. When we arrived, their bodies were being stacked in trucks. Four Viet Cong lay sprawled where they had fallen, near the barbed-wire perimeter. One of them was just a boy in blue shorts. I couldn't see what had killed him. Lying face down in the mud, he seemed only to have some scratches on his legs. Fifty feet away, in the canal in front of the blasted barracks, a man and his family were happily bathing, all smiles.

What the hell was I doing here?

3

RIVER MARKET

It's odd, but one reason I stayed on instead of quitting was the trips I took with the CIA agent. (I'll call him Richard, for I so consciously blotted out his name, and so carefully refused to write it in my journal, that I actually finally forgot it.) At first, for want of anything better to do in Cao Lanh, I tagged along with him on runs to the airport to pick up the secrets pouch flown in to him each afternoon. I guess I fancied myself spying on the spy. Once, as we bumped along in his CIA Bronco, I got up enough nerve to square off and say what I thought: What right did we have invading this tiny country halfway around the world? Who were we to dictate its fate? Richard—fifty-five or so, tall, lanky, his sandy hair graying, quiet in a Gary Cooper way—looked away from the road and nodded. Greece, he said, where he had started his career by helping to put down the communist insurgency, was something he was still proud of, but this—he wasn't sure. I was stunned. Then I thought he was putting me on, but the more we talked the more I could see that his doubts were genuine. So was his pride in the Agency that he would never refer to by name. By the end of that first month of my stay, he was the only person I looked forward to talking to. At any rate, Richard could go anyplace, whereas I no longer dared to walk out of Cao Lanh. Tagging along with him, I saw the countryside.

One trip we took downriver led me into a Vietnam whose beauty was beyond the reach of the war, a beauty so captivating that I came to measure everything against it. Arguing politics as ever, we sped down the Mekong to the Army commissary at Sadec to buy pie-crust mixes and fillings for the girls, who were baking up a storm on the gas stove at the Green Beret camp. Richard's boatman kept the powerful CIA launch slapping along out in midriver for fear of ambushes from the banks, which were choked with head-high reeds or sugarcane, riverbanks that every now and then would break open into abandoned canals overarched in jungle, or where, when we turned a bend, a pyloned village would seem to scuttle at us right out of the trees.

Like the Mississippi, the Mekong runs flat and muddy. From its sources in the mountains of Yunnan, in the upland jungles of Laos, and in the great Cambodian lake, the Tonle Sap, near the ruins of Angkor Wat, the river twines and forks through three thousand miles of rich delta. In Vietnam, the Mekong's branches are called Cuu Long, The Nine Dragons. Like a dragon, the river is both ancient and ageless. Sunk in its mucky shallows above My Tho, about sixty miles southwest of Saigon, are the rib remnants of two huge ships that have been there since 1177 A.D., part of the great fleet the Hinduized kingdom of Champa launched into the South China Sea and then up the Mekong to attack the Khmer Buddhist kingdom at Angkor Wat. Nearby, deep in the middle of the Delta, below a little nodule of a mountain, the French excavated a site and found a cache of Roman coins.

Like a dragon, the Mekong has always given nurture and good fortune. In 1967, before the river's contamination by Agent Orange, you could hold a glass of river water up to the light, watch the silt specks tumble like motes in a sunbeam, and drink it. Even during the war, a cornucopia from those backwater villages filled the river markets with pungent heaps of jackfruit, melons, breadfruit, mango, papaya, stacks of sugarcane, dozens of kinds of banana— some as small as a finger—and a heavenly fruit called *mãng cầu* that has a sweet, chewy white flesh and a huge shiny black seed.

At the Sadec commissary, we got everything on our list to make apple pies except cinnamon. Richard's boatman said we could get cinnamon on the way back, at one of the villages that wasn't "too much VC," so, on the return trip, we pulled into a riverside market past a flotilla of peasant boats with spirit eyes painted on their prows, and docked. We left the boatman behind to guard the boat, its big Mercury engine, and the Sten gun stowed under Richard's windbreaker while we walked off the rickety jetty, armed with the boatman's carefully dictated *cây quê,* "cinnamon."

Under the shade of tattered umbrellas and tarpaulins, piles of live eels were sliding in flat tin pans. On benches next to the eels, in baskets bedded with banana leaves, catfish flipped for air as a young girl doused them with water from her hand.

"*Cây quê?*" I said.

She looked up, very startled, quickly shading her face from our smiles by lowering her conical hat off her silky hair and concealing her very pretty face. Sunlight filtered through the woven leaves of her hat, and I could see that four Chinese characters—a line of poetry—had been painted there, an elegant touch for a peasant girl who very likely could not read, whose other baskets on her little aluminum table brimmed with sunfish that she had gutted and gilled, whose cheekplates she had snipped off. "*Đó,*" she said through the leaf hat and its poem, pointing with her finger and extended arm. [Daw]: "Over there." Then I heard her mutter, more to the women laughing next to her than to us, "*Ghê quá,*" "Disgusting."

So we went on in the direction in which she had pointed,

two "disgusting" Big Noses with inhuman blue eyes, hairy ape arms, and preposterous, large, sweating bodies. Indeed, as we squeezed through the aisles of the arcade, Richard's head sometimes brushed the army ponchos and parachutes strung overhead while I, closer to the Vietnamese scale of things, led the way. Ducking as he shuffled behind me, Richard konked his head into a loudspeaker jerry-rigged to a bamboo pole and crackling out a scratchy radio broadcast of *cải lương,* the popular opera of kings, betrayed princesses, and young heroes. All about, as we passed through the fish stalls in search of the spice section, our shoes picking up glittery scales, blood-flecked leaves, and scraps of entrails, I could make out *Mỹ*—"Me"— "Americans" rising from the peasant hubbub above the racket of the amplified radio, the clacking sticks of soup vendors, the fruit sellers' chants, the whine of a knife sharpener's wheel, a lone flute song, and the cries of various monkeys, finches, canaries, lorikeets, and kingfishers caged for sale. We passed buckets of snakes, tubs of turtles; walked through the meat section where pig halves knotted with mushy fat and stringy haunches of beef hung from hooks in an orbit of green flies. I paused as a woman butcher raised her cleaver and brought it down, lopping off a piece of pork, then wrapped it up in some military newspaper with a fuzzy front-page photo showing Viet Cong bodies lying, disemboweled, on an empty roadway.

"Let's get out of here," said Richard, who saw the photo too. He waved his hand in the tropical air where the raw meat was starting to rot. "It stinks."

The smells of hacked, unrefrigerated flesh, dead fish, and caged creatures mingled in the heat with whiffs of marijuana, with acrid, woozy exhalations from bricks of opium and hashish, and with sharp scents from the spice tables just ahead. We pushed on.

An old man, enfeebled, nearly toothless, with a wispy white goatee, shuffled toward us—as the stall vendors burst into laughter—holding out a string of Cambodian cowbells fashioned entirely from bamboo. In his other hand, he offered a fistful of pipes and cigarette holders, carved from twisty roots that he had lacquered and fitted with brass tips. He shook the bells to show us how they clunked, then made puffing motions on a pipe. "Christ," Richard said, turning a cowbell in his hands, "they're beautiful." For a few dollars' worth of piasters, to the incredulity of onlookers, we bought him out.

We continued on, past palm readers, sorcerers, and apothecaries, past canisters stuffed with amulets or with religious papers stamped with the image of Quan Am, the goddess of mercy, protector of women in childbirth. On one table were packets of crude black-and-white woodblock sheets—favored by the Hoa Hao sect—portraying cattle and guns. Finally, we came to tables laid out with shallots, chives, and citrons, heaped with little volcanoes of saffron, mounds of coriander seeds, and overhung with strands of drying red peppers. There, at last, we found foot-long cinnamon sticks arrayed in big glass jars. We bought three of these veritable cinnamon batons, paying an outrageous price brokered by some of the people who had seen us buy out the old pipe-carver and who had shouted over to the spice seller to stiff us. They thought we were crazy; we thought we were lucky. We would have apple pie with lots of cinnamon. For us, it was all a kind of coup: like most Americans in Vietnam, we had never bought any food outside of the commissary or PX.

As we turned back toward the dock, Richard paused, scratched his scalp, and looked away hurriedly. When I looked over to where his gaze had been, I saw an elderly woman squatting near a soft-drink cart where a girl was cracking up ice and *mãng càu* in a blender into which she spooned brownish sugar crystals and then poured boiled water from an aluminum teapot. Between the big bicycle wheels of the cart and the old lady was a tin tub where a three-foot ice slab floated in water melt and chips of sawdust. What had he seen? I could see that the old lady was squatting by a little cement runnel choked with chewed-up stobs of spat-out sugarcane and bits of animal this and vegetable that. The old woman's silvery hair was tied up in a neat bun over which was perched a black silk cap. *She was taking a pee,* having squatted and pulled up one leg of her pantaloons, opening its wide cuff to relieve herself in the ditch.

"You wouldn't think it could be done," Richard said, motioning me to go, "a woman pissing through her pant leg."

Someone was laughing now. We had been Peeping Toms for only a second, but the whole jammed arcade must have been watching us, including another old lady with a crimson smile from lots of betel-nut slobber, who now leaned over, spat out a spurt of red juice, wiped her mouth with the back of one hand, and raised again her cackle of laughter as she pointed at us and caterwauled something that made her old friend jump up and disappear into the crowd, wearing a big, silly smile. When I looked back, the betel-nut chewer was gesturing for us to go after her friend, raising laughter all around by holding her hands over her heart and looking at us in a lovesick way.

We turned and took a shortcut back to the dock, dog-legging past the market television set, placed there by JUSPAO (Joint U.S. Public Affairs Office), to carry American propaganda to the people. There Richard paused again, his wreath of wooden cowbells making him sound like a whole herd coming to a halt. "You know," he said, "I'm supposed to be some kind of expert on Vietnam, but I don't speak a word of the language, and this here's the first time I ever was in a market." He was grinning as he continued along, tinkling his bells, while I walked beside him, clutching the pipes and the cinnamon. "It's funny, don't you think? I mean, I don't even know any reporters who speak the language. What the hell do we know about this place?"

"Well, we got the cinnamon."

"And *how*. But, seriously, the only guy I know who has ever been to a market is Bob, the JUSPAO guy, who was checking on one of his new TV sets when he heard some bad guys speaking in Vietnamese behind him saying something like 'Look at the stupid American. Let's shoot him on his way back to Cao Lanh.' "

"Christ, what happened?"

"Well, old Bob's got balls, so he just turned around and said in pretty good Vietnamese, 'You can try, but I'll get you first.' These two farmers just about fainted."

"Far out."

"Balaban?"

"Sir?"

"Let's hit some of these markets again. I haven't had such a good time since I got here."

4

THE END
OF ORIENTATION

Downstairs, there was a party; upstairs, up on the roof of our joined houses, the ash from burning documents tumbled up into the night sky like huge clumsy fireflies as Richard cranked a contraption that must have been government issue to all station chiefs. Over the ponds and rice fields, over the darkened town stippled by the dim dots of kerosene lamps and a few bare bulbs lit by puttering generators, the sky was strewn with huge stars. Below them, wisps of CIA secrets, whatever they were, winked bright, went out, and floated off. Above the frog croakings and cricket trills, the Milky Way—Silver River to Vietnamese—ran in two glittering streams over our little part of the world near the Cambodian border.

Downstairs, the girls were partying with some Green Berets, the civilian Public Safety Officer, a PSYOPS guy (Psychological Operations), and someone from CORDS (Combined Operations Revolutionary Development Services). It looked like an armory by the front door where they had left their Colt pistols and M-16s.

Or maybe like a skit from *M*A*S*H,* for I got it from both the girls and their guests, who looked on me as either the girls' chaperon or their pimp. Either way, I wasn't much wanted at these soirées. Just moments before I had gone up on the roof to escape the party, the antiwar activist girl (we'll call her Kate and change the other girls' names too) had lit into me for being polite to "these goddamn military." She was seated at our rickety dining-room table, alternately slugging gin from a Gilbey's bottle and dabbing her bleeding gums with a handkerchief while listening to our battery-driven record player drone out, at indeterminate speeds, the Mamas and the Papas' "California Dreamin'." This had been her routine for days. I looked over to see if the soldiers had heard her, but the music was so loud, and Kate's speech so slurred, that it appeared they only heard "military" and turned away.

"Kate, you guys invited them here. I didn't."

"I invited them for their goddamn booze. You don't have to be nice to them. You're supposed to be a goddamned CO."

"I *am* a goddamned CO, but I don't see what being opposed to war has to do with being rude to guests. If you don't want soldiers in our house, don't invite them to your party, for Christ's sake."

She was crying now, in deep, alcoholic, self-sorrowing jags. Her one cheek was smeared bloody from the handkerchief clenched in her fists. I looked over to see if Chrissy or Susan, our visiting IVS chaperon, would come over, but they were sitting with the soldiers, eating Planter's peanuts and cheese puffs out of pop-top cans. A pile of gifts was stacked beside them—beer, Jim Beam, Clearasil, Tampax, and packs of pantyhose. As the weeks had worn on aimlessly to the end of August, we all had learned to ignore Kate's rants against the Army, but this time I could see she was in real pain, whacked on her Darvon and gin, and feeling rotten. Like me, she had come to Vietnam on some vague mission and found her conditions absurd, but Kate also got bushwhacked by booze. Drunk, she shouted at soldiers who, of course, were uninsultable because they wanted to get laid. This only made her angrier. And now, after a pointless month in Cao Lanh, her sense of failure was so deep that there was little I could say to ease her hurt. Even so, I tried, saying lamely, "I'm sorry, Kate, but you know there's no point in your staying here. You're too torn up."

I left her at the table weeping into her hands. This party too I'd sit out on the roof.

It wasn't just any party. It was a goodbye party. IVS had decided to pull us out after the town was mortared. Chrissy was going to teach English in some province capital. Kate was being sent home to dry out. Kimberly, the pretty one, was already gone. She had simply up and left one day with a guy from CORDS who took her to Hong Kong on R&R. I missed her tanning herself up on the roof with one of those aluminum reflectors that appear in springtime on college campuses. I had never seen one before; I couldn't believe she had brought it (and her tennis racket) to Vietnam. One night, at her encouragement, I crept into the girls' room and lifted up the mosquito netting on her top bunk as Kate snored in the bunk below. Kimberly had a mud pack on her face. She reached out, pulled my head onto the edge of her mattress, and, with her face cold and slippery next to mine, gave me a kiss. Not much of a kiss, but a kiss bestowed on me for being nice to her, for chasing off the noncoms she wasn't interested in. It was a kiss that told me I wasn't a contender. I was, after all, a CO volunteer earning a few hundred dollars a month, and though my Harvard background made me a bit interesting, Kimberly was thinking ahead to the Cercle Sportif in Saigon, to gin fizzes on the veranda of the Continental Palace, to flights out when Saigon got dull, to an apartment in Tokyo or Taipei, to the Asian highlife, not to a romance with a penurious egghead. Now I missed her and wondered what she was up to in Hong Kong. In a couple of weeks, if the student strikes ended, I would be teaching linguistics at the new university in Can Tho.

Up on the roof, Richard looked ill at ease about my catching him at his spy stuff, but soon returned to squirting in lighter fluid and turning the crank of the revolving bin. In all things dealing with the CIA, neither of us acknowledged the fact. During our entire acquaintance, we never said "CIA." Instead, we used obvious euphemisms like "company," which allowed Richard to talk about his job without compromising, at least overtly, his obligations of silence and secrecy.

"Me, too," he said, as I walked over to the brick divider between our two houses.

"You, too, what?"

"I'm leaving, too."

I took a Camel from a pack I had bought on our last trip downriver to the commissary in Sadec. As I struck a match, an image from that trip sparked in my memory. I remembered the Navy Riverine Patrol boat that we had come alongside, burning in mid-river, its siren screaming as sailors scurried with fire extinguishers on the aft deck, which was boiling up black smoke and jetting flames.

"They fired me. The little carpetbagger won."

For months, before we all arrived, Richard had been locked in a battle with the Vietnamese Province Chief over who had what use of the men in the Province Reconnaissance Unit, some of whom were now picketed as house guards down below. The Chief, not unusually, regarded the province as his fiefdom; whatever law existed, existed at his whimsy. If he didn't like somebody, he had him shot. When Richard came in as CIA station chief, he said he found out that the PRU team was being used to assassinate noncommunist political enemies and even peasants who refused to sell the Province Chief their land. But if Cao Lanh was the Province Chief's fiefdom, Richard was its chamberlain. He controlled the purse strings, and one of the first things Richard had done after arriving was to remove the PRU from "field" work and consign them to guard duty around his house. The PRU, whose livelihood was murder, resented this intervention into their own avenues of extortion. They guarded our houses and drew their CIA pay, but sulkily.

"What are you going to do?"

"Reassigned. To Can Tho. A desk job. I can take it or quit." He pulled some more papers out of a valise and stuffed them in the burner, giving the machine another crank. He had a wife waiting at some resort town in Colorado where they had recently bought a home. They had a teenaged son. "I'll try it," he added. "I got a year and a half to retirement."

I nodded and sat down on the little rampart that rimmed our three houses.

"I'm not a murderer, John-boy. I told you that. When I was in Greece, we killed some bad guys, but usually they had guns in their hands. This little bastard's just popping off his enemies. Old ladies. Anybody."

I nodded again. I just wanted him to talk. On Bronco rides to the airport, on speedboat trips down the Mekong, or just sitting with our feet up on his glossy Filipino furniture and drinking San Miguel, we had argued long hours over the rightness of the war, the proper role of the CIA. For him, the Agency was a politically neutral tool necessary to defend the free world. This war, however, stunk. He hinted that other agents thought the same. Once, when we were debating the justifications for taking human life, he insisted that our government would not kill someone even if that person were on his way out of the country carrying military secrets to the Russians. He really said that.

"How can you talk to a pig like that!" Kate had once hissed. "You know what he does." But I didn't. I knew what he said, and that what he said had more ethical clarity in it than anything else I had yet heard in Vietnam. And now there wasn't any doubt that he drew the line at extortion and murder.

"Hey, don't get me wrong," he continued, slapping at a glowing cinder that floated by his shoulder. "I'm an anticommunist. I want to stop 'em wherever. But in Greece I could go home to our villa after a day's work.

My wife would have the drinks ready, and we'd set on the patio, pick oranges right off of our trees, and take in the sunset. It felt good, John-boy. It was *satisfying*. We beat those bastards. But this," he said, motioning to the burning bin, "stinks. You know what it would take to win this war?"

"An A-bomb?"

"Just about. We had a study that said we'd have to kill more VC than the male birthrate of the country. You get it? Just about every boy born will join the VC. And given creeps like this here Province Chief, we'd be killing the wrong ones."

After a month of orientation in Cao Lanh, everything seemed to me to fall into contradictions. Here, the only friend I had was a spy who refused to do what my generation assumed CIA agents like to do best: assassinate people. But Richard also had an associate, a young guy not much older than I, who lived in a fenced-in, isolated compound and who dropped by now and then for a beer, though he said very little. "Hotshot," Richard scoffed when the guy left one day, but from the JUSPAO officer I found out that this other agent had only one task: interrogation of prisoners and Viet Cong suspects. A Viet Cong suspect could be a ten-year-old girl. So there was my principled CIA friend, who wouldn't let his guards loose to murder for the Province Chief, and then there was his colleague with blood caked under his nails, whose eavesdropping on our debates could not have helped Richard's standing with any of the big boys in Can Tho.

So many contradictions. Next door, at the other adjoining house, the Public *Safety* Officer sometimes got drunk and shot rats scurrying in his kitchen. And if I thought of the Navy medic who had shown me the human ear in a jar of formaldehyde, I also remembered his Lieutenant, a quiet young naval officer who played chess and, the first time I saw him, had a book of Gerard Manley Hopkins' poetry in his hip pocket.

At the Green Beret camp, there was the foul-mouthed executive officer, a gung-ho major whom Kate especially hated, because he was the only happily self-confessed war monger she had yet found. To him all Vietnamese were "shifty-eyed slopes." His favorite troops were his Nung Chinese mercenaries, in whose trigger-happy viciousness he took great pride until the night they shot themselves up on patrol when one group opened up on some "ghosts" and the other contingent blasted the first because they thought they were VC. But, besides the Major, there was also his superior, a fiftyish, broad-shouldered, crewcut Lieutenant Colonel, who possessed more complicated military ethics. Once I heard him chew out the Public Safety Officer for hiring a Vietnamese known as Felix, a fast talker who bragged about killing VC, including some women in a Propaganda Team that Felix and his counterrevolutionary team had ambushed entering a village. ("I know your Mr. Felix from I Corps," the Colonel had told the red-faced cop who had just tried to introduce Felix. "He's a thief and a deserter. Get him the hell out of my province."). This same Colonel told us we could not invite our black benefactor, Sgt. James Johnson, to the goodbye party, but was shocked, and then relented, after Kate called him a racist. ("Good golly, Miss Jones. It's not because he's a Negro. He's not an *officer*.")

Getting burned at McNamara, then gambling my fate with the draft board, were rather simply arrived at compared to making heads or tails, let alone a moral testimony, out of this soup of personalities and events that engulfed me those first six weeks in Vietnam. Even Richard, churning his rotisserie of fiery secrets, was on clearer ground than I. He had made a decision, his own moral decision, and what he was burning in that rabbit-wire bin was not reports on VC plans and infrastructure, but his own career.

As we talked for perhaps the last time and Richard's files flew up in ash and smoke, crickets and peepers spun out their symphonics in the swamps, ponds, and flooded pad-

dies around Cao Lanh. As our humble Vietnamese neighbors stalked *cá lóc,* a kind of catfish, beneath torchlight, I
heard a thump and a muffled cry from the parking lot out
front where the partygoers' military vehicles were parked.
Richard heard it too and motioned me to keep down.
Creeping forward with knees bent, we shuffled to the little
wall at the front of the roof and peeked over. "Hung's
down there," Richard whispered, but nowhere could we
see the guard who usually sat, carbine across his knees,
tilted back in a chair beside Richard's front door. No Sgt.
Hung anywhere, just laughter, lamplight, and more
Mamas and Papas filtering out from the house, seeping
into the shadows of the mud-packed parking lot.

I held my breath the way you do when fear calls you to
stifle even the soft shuntings of respiration.

Again, I heard a muffled sound. It came from one of the
jeeps.

I pointed at the jeep. Richard nodded and squinted into
the dark. We could see something moving on the front
seats. Finally, we could make out two bodies struggling
against each other, and then Richard laughed softly and
slapped me on the arm. It was one of the girls fucking one
of the soldiers.

I watched until the couple came up for air. Then, as the
woman slid her legs out of the cramped jeep onto the
ground, I could see it was Kate. As she staggered her first
steps, I could see the man, who now grabbed her waist to
steady her. It was none other than the war-mongering
Major, the "pig of pigs," as she had called him, the guy
who said he liked to kill.

I looked at Richard and shook my head in wonderment.
He grinned and went back to burning his secrets.

5

DRAGONFLIES
IN AUTUMN

When dragonflies fly in the autumn wind, storms are coming. —*a proverb*

Can Tho, where I was sent in early September to teach rudimentary linguistics at the new university, was the regional capital of IVth Corps, the Mekong Delta. An ancient Khmer river market on the Bassac branch of the Mekong, it was in earlier times a Cambodian village that was seized by the Vietnamese in their historical, colonizing *nam tiến,* or "march south." In the eighteenth and nineteenth centuries, it fell to French colonials who made it the hub for their vast southern plantations, a *ville agraire* complete with botanical gardens, parks, airy villas, and broad boulevards lined with tamarind trees. Now, as a major airfield and river port for deep-water vessels, Can Tho was the southern headquarters for the U.S. Army, Air Force, and Navy, the CIA, and the Green Berets, as well as for their counterpart South Vietnamese units. As American troops flooded into the Delta, the town underwent a slow tropical collapse, its defoliated plantations swallowed by war zones, its paddies cratered into moon-scapes, and its nearby canal villages burned and abandoned. In the new economy fueled by war, where even the town's electricity ran on American diesel, Can Tho suffered a decay of falling porches, of rotted railings, of stucco flaking off walls in damp, gray-green blossoms of mildew. Now the immense tamarinds were almost all cut down or standing dead in the miasma of fumes churned up by convoys and motorcycle traffic. By 1967, the public fountains on the grand boulevards were dry, sandbagged, and fitted as machine-gun placements. Can Tho was a war camp.

Inevitably, as increasing swaths of land—mangrove forests, remote canals, plantations, whole districts, and the major portions of some provinces—were marked off on military maps as Free Strike Zones, and as death rained down on whatever moved there, peasant families from all across the Delta jammed into Can Tho's refugee ghettos, fashioning makeshift homes out of cardboard, tin, and plastic. These simple rice-farmers, whose men were dead, disabled, or off fighting either for the National Liberation Front or for the ARVN, now eked out lives in the service industries of the war. Mothers had become barracks maids; toddlers played and begged on the streets of the city; daughters whored in the massage parlors and bars that collected near the military camps, and sons wandered about as shoeshine boys or ran errands for pimps and black-marketeers. Often, as I rode my motorscooter home at night, one hand gripping a flashlight to shine back into my American face at roadblocks, my chubby front tire crunching palmetto bugs and bits of broken glass, watching out for patrols and for the strings of concertina wire strung across roads and sidewalks, I came across clusters of children wrapped in cocoons of mosquito netting, asleep in parks, in banyan nooks, on sidewalks, or in the doorways of shuttered shops. They had become *bụi đời,* "dust of life."

Home for me was the two-story IVS house not far from a roadside billboard that read:

WARNING
Attention all U.S. and free world personnel. It is recommended that no travel be done beyond this point

during the hours of darkness without contacting PHONG
DINH advisor team. Telephone CAN THO military 47.

Besides being home to the five of us volunteers stationed
in Can Tho, the IVS house was a kind of headquarters or
way station for the one hundred or so Delta volunteers
passing back and forth from Saigon to their posts as agrarian advisers and schoolteachers. My job was to teach pho-
nemics to Vietnamese students at the new university just
four miles up the road at Cai Rang. My tiny, dark room
in the IVS house had four bunk beds in it, and I never
knew who might be sleeping there, sometimes in my bed,
when I came back each day from teaching. It was hard on
my nerves. Can Tho and its ruined citizenry were difficult
enough to accept without the prospect of picking up mites,
lice, fungus, crabs, hepatitis, Asian flu, sprue, dengue
fever, TB, and God knows what other afflictions from
flopped-out colleagues who thought I was some sort of
weird grouch as I shook them out of my bed. I felt bad
about being cross with them—they were innocents, mostly
from small Midwestern colleges, really as unaware as most
of the GIs. Their beliefs were largely Farming and English;
their means, Starter Seeds and Pronunciation Drills. We
were all there to help ordinary Vietnamese improve their
lot somehow.

   I had no one to talk to. Richard never appeared in Can
Tho. One day when I was going into the CORDS building
to pick up my mail, I recognized his CIA boss and simply
asked him where Richard was. For a moment the guy just
looked at me. Then he said, "I don't know who you're
talking about." Failing Richard, my steadiest friend was a
big fat toad that wriggled forth each evening onto my tiled
floor from a hole in a wall, hunting for mosquitoes, hopping around the empty house as if it were the landlord. I
Magic Markered "Toad, of Toad Hall" onto the tiles over
his little door. I asked him about his ancestors. Often he
sat there while I lay on my bunk reading by dim bulb light

Meister Eckhardt, or John Hawkes' *The Lime Twig,* or Truman Capote's *The Grass Harp,* or while I fell asleep watching the upside-down geckos go after the bugs on the ceiling.

After a couple of months, this sense of isolation, and my corresponding vanity of being the lone moral watcher of the war, all but disappeared: I returned one day to my room to find a big hulking guy with a shaved head (for lice, he later explained) rummaging around in a burlap sack on one of the bunks. It was Dave Gitelson. I had heard about him and the nickname given him by peasants, "The Poor American," but I had never met Gitelson because, unlike the other volunteers who were always finding excuses to get to Saigon, Gitelson stayed put. Stayed put in the most remote station in all of IVS-dom, in Hue Duc, near Ba The Mountain, an area that had never been much in the control of the Saigon authorities, even when those authorities had been French.

"What are you looking for?" I asked.

He stood up from his crouching over the bed. He was easily over six feet tall, but seemed even bigger with his large shaved head. "The raffle tickets."

"Raffle tickets?"

Gitelson grinned sheepishly and pointed out the screened window at a piglet tethered to a bougainvillea branch. "For the farmers. I'm showing them how to run a raffle, 'cause they love to gamble, you know, and I want to introduce new livestock."

"They don't have *pigs?*"

"Not this kind." And then he went into the attributes of his young sow, her breed's fat-for-protein ratio, her dietary habits, her reproductive rate, her resistance to tropical diseases, even her companionability.

"Oh," I said.

"You're Balaban."

"Right."

"Roger said you might drive me to the bus station."

Roger Montgomery was our team leader who had a room
upstairs but who was usually out checking on the volunteers throughout the Delta. Since he was in Can Tho that
day, I wondered why he didn't drive Gitelson himself.

"With the pig?"

"Yeah, or I can walk."

"All I got is a Vespa. A scooter," I added, because Gitelson seemed a bit thick with his goofy grinning, his pig
facts, and the burlap bag that seemed to hold all his earthly
belongings.

"He said you could have the Landrover." Gitelson dug
into his cutoff blue jeans and gave me the key.

We had about forty-five minutes to kill, so I suggested
we go to my favorite hangout, the Ngoc Loi, the Golden
Pearl restaurant, where you could get iced coffee and papaya for about sixty cents. Gitelson was legendary among
us, living alone with farmers, roaming the Delta backwaters in blue jeans and flipflops, his voluminous sack filled
with seed samples and mimeographed tips for farmers that
he had painstakingly typed in Vietnamese on scraps of
notebook paper. A kind of Johnny Appleseed off by himself in Indian country. Montgomery hinted once that Gitelson even had some kind of safe pass to travel through
Viet Cong territory. I had heard that he had been a medic
in the Army. He was a strange combination of antiwar
vehemence and mumbly shyness. Once, when reporters
got wind of a young American living out in the middle of
nowhere and went to Hue Duc to interview him, Gitelson
hid out in the fields where they were afraid to follow.

The Ngoc Loi was like a big bird cage, with its entire
fifty-square-foot dining area enclosed in wire mesh to ward
off any grenades tossed in by terrorists zooming past on
motorcycles. I eased the heavy Landrover up on the sidewalk, careful to clear the capless sewer that ran along the
street. I had parked so close to the restaurant wall that
Gitelson had to slide out my side of the Landrover. When
his rubber-sandaled feet touched the ground, I was startled

by their deep mahogany tan. We left the pig, hog-tied and
happy, snoozing on the backbed, and went in through the
wire-mesh doorway. How many days, I wondered as I
followed Gitelson in, had he spent on dusty roads, his head
wrapped in that stained kerchief? How many days had he
spent threading the straggly green waterways in leaky taxi
boats or crossing the mud levees of flooded rice fields to
stand, in his fraying cutoff jeans and sun-bleached shirt,
confabbing with farmers about mixing insecticides and
raising pigs? He too had become *bụi đời*, dust of life.

Inside, it was always kind of shady and pleasant. A canopy of morning glory overspread the mesh roof. Sparrows
hopped about the metal chairs and cement floor, pecking
for bread crumbs. Irate mynahs, too fat to pass through
the mesh, clamored across the wire above our heads. A
breeze carried in a whiff from the sewer, and I remember
telling Dave that this side street off the market was a sleeping ground for homeless children. Some of them were still
there around 9:00 A.M., when I came for an oily *omelette
au jambon* and *café filtre*.

As usual, beyond the far side of the restaurant, some
paunchy government officials in tennis whites were lamely
slapping a ball across a sagging net. Their bodyguard, in
fatigues, sat slumped against a coil of banyan root, his M-
16 lying across his lap. Next to him squatted one of the
street kids who had been hired to fetch refreshments from
the restaurant.

"You know," Gitelson said, wiping his sweaty dome
with the soiled farmer's scarf he had wrapped around his
neck, "the Delta once fed the whole country. They could
even export rice to the rest of Asia." He knew the actual
export tonnage of the not-so-distant time when Vietnam
had been "the rice bowl of Asia." Now, he said, it had to
import rice from Louisiana. Thousands were starving. Although Gitelson had a quiet way of talking, he was full of
facts. But he didn't look at me much as he talked, the way
people usually do who want to drive their facts home.

Rather, he seemed shy, or even guilty. His recitation of
the wrongs done to the Vietnamese sounded as if he had
committed them himself.

Like conspirators, we pooled our litany of complaints.
I told him about one of my students, a girl at the high
school who had committed suicide out of simple, futureless
despair; about the old cyclo driver who had been killed by
GIs when one of them lobbed a sandbag at him from their
moving truck; about the bivouac of destitute soldiers living
under cotton blankets and ponchos down by the river;
about some of their wives' prostituting themselves; and
about my tenth-graders, so malnourished and weary I let
them sleep in class. Gitelson knew much more. He told
me about Hoa Hao farmers—resolutely anticommunist
since the Viet Minh had killed their patriarch—whose entire melon crop had been defoliated by American error.
He knew about military corruption, about a district chief
caught raping a schoolgirl, about American soldiers who
raped a district chief's wife in an armored personnel carrier,
about dead soldiers still kept on payrolls, about refugee
relief supplies resold by Vietnamese Province Chiefs, and
about the Tay Ninh Province Chief who offered an AID
official four million piasters to shut up about his graft. All
of these acts, he said, had gone unpunished. I realized that
he had memorized a long list of horrors and indecencies,
that he saw this as one of his tasks. Gitelson looked down
at his large hands, which were almost the color of the coffee
in his cup, and told me that each time he was in Saigon
he visited the place where the Buddhist nun Pham Thi
Trang had immolated herself. Gitelson seemed so obsessed
with injustice that I began to suspect he had done something bad, for he had the air of a man seeking repentance.
I didn't know then that he had an IQ of 175, that he had
been an Army medic in Germany before coming to Vietnam, that he had tried to bring a battalion of antiwar activists to work as medics in Vietnam, that he had tried to
get IVS to let him work for nothing or at least send his

measly eighty dollars a month home to his parents, who were comfortable real-estate agents in Los Angeles.

Finally that morning, as sparrows chirped about our chairs and tennis balls popped lazily outside, Gitelson said something that seemed perfectly practical. "You're a CO," he began.

"Yeah?"

"Don't you want to do anything about this?" He gestured to the street where I had told him the children slept, and then to the fat officials swatting at their tennis ball.

"Sure. You got a *plan?*" I was annoyed.

"Oh, lots of plans," he said, with that same proud, balmy grin that he had shown in introducing his pig.

He did indeed have a small, sane plan. There were, he said, some three hundred IVS volunteers in Vietnam. Each of us was paid eighty dollars a month to a bank account in the United States. We got another small amount in piasters for living expenses, and that, given our free housing, was meant to take care of our needs. Each of us also received ten dollars in military payment certificates (MPCs) to let us buy things in PXs and commissaries—shampoo, Band-Aids, toilet paper—products that were hard to get or exorbitant on the black market. "We don't need that stuff," Gitelson said. "All it does is separate us from the Vietnamese." He ticked off a list of such things that could be gotten on the Vietnamese market if you didn't have to have American brands: cruder products, sure, but by using them, he argued, one would come to know a little more clearly what it was to be Vietnamese. ("What about Kotex?" I asked. I knew I had him there, for Vietnamese women simply used wads of cotton. "They can get it from home," he finally decided. It was like dickering with Saint Francis or Gandhi.) Anyway, his idea was that we get each IVS volunteer to donate his or her MPCs to a refugee fund. "Ten bucks is nothing," he said, "but three thousand dollars per month is thirty-six thousand per year. We could do something. Start something."

"We'd be dirtier on the outside, but cleaner within."

"Right on," he said, grinning again.

I liked Gitelson immensely for that idea. It made things seem less helpless, more purposeful, less lonely. He knew what he wanted to do. He knew what he *could* do. He knew how to do it. Things were clear for him. He did indeed have lots of plans. From the middle of the Mekong Delta, from one of its least secure, least populated, most remote provinces, he was hatching schemes to stop the war.

Later, when I put him, pig under his arm, into a three-wheel Lambretta jitney bound for Long Xuyen (the nearest town to his lonely outpost), I wondered if I hadn't merely linked up with a loony with grandiose delusions. As he crammed his huge frame into the little tin can of a bus, scraping his kerchief off his head and revealing his shaved scalp, the pig started kicking and squealing. This delighted the farmers already jammed inside. Then Gitelson, his voice shaking because of the hooves raking his diaphragm, said something to the farmers in Vietnamese. They smiled and shouted advice on how to grip the pig. So, instead of dropping the creature, Gitelson just wrapped both arms around its back and, with his mouth next to one of its pink, bristly ears, started crooning "Un-uh. Un-uh."

"*Da*-a-ave," I said, for now the farmers were howling with laughter at my giant, bald-headed colleague and his pink, spasmodic friend. "What are you doing?"

"That's the way you quiet a pig," he said, and went back to his crooning. Gitelson's shirt was now sliced where the pig's hooves had stampeded on his stomach. Still he kept crooning, calm and happy.

Witnessing this, gripping his heavy sack with both fists, straddling it to swing it up to the kid on the Lambretta roof, I started laughing too. Now the farmers made a place for Gitelson on the aluminum benches inside, and the driver's kid pushed the sack farther onto the roof, where it was tied down among the empty duck-baskets, hardware, bolts of cloth, incense sticks, watermelons, straw hats, bamboo mats, and other whatnots bought at market.

"*Mỹ Nghèo,*" I heard one of the farmers say approvingly to another.

"*Mỹ Nghèo,*" repeated his friend, who hadn't recognized Gitelson but knew him by his nickname: *Mỹ Nghèo,* The Poor American. An oxymoron for them: no American could be poor, but there was *this one* who spoke their language, who understood the tribulations of farming, who lived like them in a dirt-floor thatched hut without electricity or running water, who walked the fields barefoot or in flipflops, and whose few belongings were carried in that sack. So it *wasn't,* I reflected, just an IVS romantic vanity, this Poor American stuff. Gitelson had really entered their world, maybe the only one of us who had. Now, in the laughter and mayhem, one of the farmers grabbed the pig's legs to stop it from hurting Gitelson. To my delight, the farmer also crooned something at the pig, which now worked its slobbery snout and considered this new development with dim, pale eyes. Then the Lambretta driver, gripping his hand throttle (the bus was little more than a big motorcycle with a tin camper), grinned back from his cab at all the commotion and revved the engine, which zoomed, crackled, and backfired as the Lambretta started out of the line of ancient buses amid the last calls from the soft-drink sellers and hawkers of sugarcane. In a flurry of horn honks, it edged off under the sizzling sun. As I waved goodbye to Gitelson, the farmers were chatting him up.

The encounter with Gitelson was a turning point for me. Perhaps, I now had reason to think, there was more to my associates than I had realized. I started to spend more time with them. I felt less alone. Montgomery, who had at first seemed a bit shallow, hadn't been too lazy to take Gitelson to the bus station; he wanted me to meet Gitelson because Montgomery too, despite his more official status, was opposed to the war. Similarly, Pham Van Chanh, our

notoriously taciturn fix-it man in Can Tho, who saw to
our vehicles, supplies, and rentals, startled me one evening
as we sat on parked scooters in front of our house, smoking
cigarettes and talking. Tall, round-shouldered, around
thirty-five, slumped and worn, Chanh told me that as a
young man, under Ngo Dinh Diem, he had been a minor
Treasury clerk, countersigning checks in a bank, and that
he had been arrested as a Viet Minh sympathizer.

"Were you?"

Chanh smiled a bright, toothy smile that was surprising
for one usually so melancholy. He said that he had been
imprisoned for eight years on Con Son Island.

"I'm sorry, Chanh."

He ignored me and went on talking as we watched some
water buffalo being scrubbed down in a mud wallow in
front of our house. "There are two kinds of courage: the
courage to fight and my kind," he said, finally looking
over at me, "the courage to suffer. I am often made
ashamed by it. I do not think that Ong Ro[ger Mont-
gomery] can picture in his mind the people struck by
bombs in the villages, but I see them all the time. People
think I am peaceful, but in my mind there is always war.
I am afraid that I will go crazy. If I die now, I will be a
terrible ghost who will come back to murder. If you come
back in five or ten years and find me alive, you will see
that I am exactly the same. I will not change."

Đứng giữa Trời anh nói không sai—"Standing before
Heaven, I cannot lie"—runs a line in a folk poem. Chanh's
words had that kind of testimony. I was so struck by what
he had said, by what really had been a speech that he must
have rehearsed with himself many times in English, that
when Chanh left on his motorscooter I went back in the
house and wrote it down.

By October, my circumstances had become more complex, and richer. As a university instructor, I was one of
four foreigners (including two Fulbrighters who were usu-

ally soused in PX gin and a Frenchman who did not deign to speak to Americans, even though I greeted him in French). I taught for about four hours a day. My students were mostly girls in fluttery *aó dàis* along with a handful of soldiers in uniform and some boys whose parents must have paid a lot of bribes to get them out of the Army. Each day, after teaching my students about allophones and phonemes, minimal pairs, and how to use the International Phonetic Alphabet, I was on my own time. Since I was as unofficial as one could get and still be sanctioned by the authorities, I met Vietnamese who would otherwise fear knowing an American. With some math teachers at Phan Thanh Gian High School, I played an Asian version of chess, *cờ tướng*. At the Catholic orphanage near my classrooms in Cai Rang, I helped a Vietnamese nun, Soeur Anicet, make contacts with GIs who might donate goods. I even brought her an Air Force pediatrician. With another Chanh, To Lai Chanh, a law instructor at the university, I traded English for Vietnamese lessons. Having his friendship gave me cachet with certain of my students, for To Lai Chanh was kept under fairly close watch by secret police. This Chanh—thirty years old, plump, given to laughter, half Cambodian, the very opposite in spirit from our melancholy IVS fix-it Chanh—had years before led Saigon students in a series of devastating marches against Diem that led to the dictator's fall. Indeed, To Lai Chanh had the kind of courage that Pham Van Chanh said he lacked: the courage to fight. But now he was lying low, especially since university students had marched in September with signs that demanded "Peace and Reunification" and "The End of the American Usurpation of Vietnamese Authority." These marches had resulted in the university's being cordoned off and shut down by police.

Chanh didn't participate in their demonstration, though one had the sense he was just biding his time. When his campus office became too risky a place for us to meet, we drove our bikes to a small house that he had bought by a

river outside of town. I remember his picking a plum from
a tree and saying that it was for his young wife, who was
still a student in Saigon. As children splashed in the muddy
river and cargo boats puttered by, we talked in English
about the political situation and, every now and then, he
remembered our agreement and taught me a few words
of Vietnamese. When the election was over and the Americans shuffled out Nguyen Cao Ky and put in Nguyen Van
Thieu, Chanh suspected that there'd be hard times for
dissidents, even silenced ones like himself. He showed me
a picture of his wife, serious in her big French-style eyeglasses. I felt sorry for him. His little home was simple,
poor, and pretty, but it seemed unlikely that he would ever
enjoy setting up house there or raising a family by the river
under the threshing palms, surrounded by the plum trees
and jasmine gardenias that thrived in the river breeze. "You
couldn't stay here at nigh', Mr. John. They snatch you
up," he said, repeating his plum-picking motion and
laughing. A memory of my experience in Cao Lanh rippled
through me. Chanh's house, only a few miles outside of
Can Tho, was just inside the territory held by the Viet
Cong at night.

At a much grander house nearby—two-storied, with
terra-cotta roof tiles, huge dark ceiling timbers carved in
animals and Chinese characters, and a front courtyard filled
with fantastic, miniature grottoes, potted bonsai, and magical topiary—Chanh and I drank parsley whisky, dashed
with ground-up deer antlers, with his notable neighbor, a
retired Colonel, who was now a Taoist patriarch selling
herbs, amulets, and love potions to the villagers. "Yes, the
communists will win," the neighbor declared out of nowhere as we took up our drinks. "I hope they let me stay
in business." He and Chanh laughed at this. I did too, but
since I really didn't see much of a joke in his comments,
I wondered if I wasn't talking in fact to the Viet Cong.
The Colonel held up a glass of his special whisky to the
sunlight shaking through the palms. "Distilled memories,"
he said.

A few weeks later, as students burned effigies of Ky and Thieu, To Lai Chanh disappeared altogether.

The war was changing week by week. American troops poured into the country by the hundreds of thousands, taking over the fighting from inept, disaffected ARVN units, even in the quieter Mekong Delta. The U.S. Ninth Division now left rumors of massacres in its wake, and the war started visiting Can Tho. My classroom windows rattled more frequently now as the air war heated up throughout Vietnam. Eventually, more bomb tonnage would fall on that tiny nation than had fallen in all of World War II. Cai Rang, the quiet, little river village a few miles above Can Tho where I taught in new USAID-built class-rooms, was shot up by the Ninth as the division floated past the village on barges. Some grunt in the lead barge fired at something in the river; an eighteen-year-old farther behind thought they were taking fire, and soon a fusillade of small-arms fire withered the sleepy village. Most of what the Ninth had done was known only to military intelli-gence, but somehow a version of this encounter reached the outside world. My parents, fortunately unaware that Cai Rang was where I taught, sent me a clipping from the Philadelphia *Bulletin:*

> Concern was heightened last month when units of the Ninth Infantry Division killed 72 civilians, wounded 204 and destroyed more than 400 homes in a single day. The Americans had been traveling in a 4-mile-long boat convoy on a river and had been attempting to defend themselves against Vietcong ambushes.
>
> In one of the incidents, the Vietcong attacked the end of the convoy. The boats at the head of the convoy joined in the shooting and shot up the town of Cairang, one of the most pacified towns in the delta.

One morning before dawn, while I huddled in my bunk, a siren droned and dogs barked as the Viet Cong tried to mortar the American MACV compound. But they were too far away. A breeze drifted some thirty mortars on high,

long, wobbly trajectories into the town itself, exploding
upon dozens of sleeping men, women, and children and
shredding them in a razory rain of ripped tin roofs, shrapnel, shattering glass, and flying splinters. A few days later,
the Viet Cong sent emissaries into Can Tho to apologize
for their error. When tigers and elephants fight, crickets
are crushed.

As the war intensified, sidling up even to big cities like
Can Tho, IVS changed too. The newest volunteers had
come from recently radicalized campuses. In Can Tho, I
suddenly had comrades in Roger Hintze, a tall, skinny farm
boy from Minnesota, and in Bill Seraile, a husky, soft-
spoken black from Seattle, and in a Princetonian volunteer
who spoke natively fluent Vietnamese, which he had
learned in the whorehouses. And, beyond Can Tho, in
Gitelson, in Don Ronk, an orphan himself who created a
home for the abandoned children of Danang, and, in Hue,
in the wily, poetical Clyde Coreil, stepson of the parish
sheriff in Ville Platte, Louisiana, and in his ironic, astute
colleague, Steve Erhart, who taught at the university there.
The month before, in September of 1967, Don Luce, our
Chief of Party, who had been in Vietnam since 1958, as
well as some of the other agrarian stalwarts, like Willie
Meyers and a barrel-chested Mennonite named Gene Stolz-
fus, had started to voice qualms about our organization's
being used by the war effort. Their concerns were well
founded. In fact, in the July issue of *The New Yorker*, Jon-
athan Schell's piece about the extermination of the village
of Ben Suc—which "we had to destroy . . . to save"—
mentioned the use of IVS volunteers to help with the forced
relocations of the villagers. Soon these complaints spread
from the IVS headquarters in Saigon to the volunteers in
the field. All of us were given a chance to help draft and
sign a windy, sincere, six-page condemnation of the war
in an open letter to Lyndon Johnson, a letter that Ellsworth
Bunker refused to accept and which then appeared on the
front page of *The New York Times*. "Perhaps if you accept

the war," our letter said along with snippets of Vietnamese poems and personal anecdotes, "all can be justified—the free strike zones, the refugees, the spraying of herbicide on crops, the napalm. But the Vietnam war is in itself an overwhelming atrocity." To everyone's surprise, the letter was a bombshell that exploded through the wire services at home. In Vietnam, it had an effect as well. Vietnamese with whom we worked suddenly warmed up. "Now we know who you are," To Lai Chanh told me before his disappearance. "We thought you were CIA." While the U.S. Embassy tried to downplay the forty-nine signers as a few malcontents who had broken their contractual obligations to the American government, the North Vietnamese were of course a bit warmer in their response (one of our recommendations was diplomatic recognition of the National Liberation Front, as the Viet Cong were more properly called). An IVS volunteer carried the letter to the North Vietnamese Embassy in Phnom Penh and brought back a response that was welcoming if also a bit chilling. They liked the letter but, as one NLF official said, "By doing good works, you are doing wrong, for you confuse the people about the aim of the American imperialists." He added that IVS volunteers would be safe where they were known, for local people would not harm us, but he advised us to leave Vietnam because soon "the people will rise up to struggle against you."

It was clear that to both American and Vietnamese authorities, the young, well-intentioned volunteers of IVS were more politically important that any of us had guessed. Though volunteers might effect good works in behalf of individual Vietnamese and their families, our real force was in propaganda. This assessment was a bit saddening. On the other hand, the North Vietnamese/NLF view largely coincided with our own, newly pragmatic sense of our usefulness in Vietnam. In fact, many of us, besides signing the letter, had offered our letters of resignation to A. Z.

Gardiner, the Director of IVS in Washington and a former
head of AID in Vietnam. Mine read, in part, as follows:

> If there is to be help for the Vietnamese it will come
> from political work, not social work; in America, not
> in Vietnam. I believe that IVS personnel can continue
> to do individual services for the Vietnamese, but I be-
> lieve that in doing so they are doing Vietnam a dis-
> service, for, willingly or not, IVS workers serve
> American propaganda and programs of "pacification."

At the same time I wrote that letter, I also wrote to the
Quakers and Mennonites who had programs in Vietnam,
as well as to a new organization, The Committee of Responsibility to Save War-Burned and War-Injured Children, a Boston-based group that offered hospital care to
children. After all, I couldn't just quit. I was under obligation to the Selective Service for two years; unless I found
another suitable job, my alternatives were carrying bedpans in a VA hospital, fleeing to Canada, or sitting out a
five-year sentence in a federal prison. Furthermore, the
response from A.Z., as Gardiner was known in IVS, was
surprising. Instead of firing me as I expected, he cabled
back asking me not to do anything until he flew in from
Washington to talk to me and all the other signers of the
letter to President Johnson.

Gardiner had headed USAID and now, in his retirement,
IVS, with General Bullmoose authority. When he arrived
in Can Tho, white-haired, portly, suffering intensely in
the heat, he was surprisingly gentle. He told me he shared
many of my hesitations about our role but that he thought
we could make a difference. "Without people like you,
John . . . and Roger and Bill," he added, sensing his appeal
a shade too patronizing and obvious, "who will the Vietnamese turn to? How will the world even know what is
happening to them? Please reconsider."

I said I would and went outside, leaving Gardiner to talk
to the others. Across the street, in the middle of the mucky

field between our house and Ap An Cu, one of the poor
suburbs that had sprung up in Can Tho, I saw Pham Van
Chanh and Lai, an IVS volunteer from Taiwan. They were
ankle-deep in the mud, the fungal, hepatital, polio-in-
fested, fecal mud of the field that had once been a rice
paddy, and was now a place to wash water buffalo and,
for many of the Ap An Cu villagers, a place to take a shit.
Often, from our house, we would watch schoolchildren
in white shirts and blue shorts navigate through the filth,
carrying their plastic satchels. Today, of all days, Chanh
and Lai had decided to build a dike for the villagers. I
joined them. Soon a bent, withered old man came out from
the village with a little boy and a shovel. "I was always
meaning to do this," he said, "but it's been too much for
me." We slogged away in the noonday sun like children
at a big mud pie. I was happy, even though fearful of
getting infected by the itchy yuck that coated my arms and
legs and splashed my face. Even before we had finished,
villagers were using the bridge—giggly girls in spotless,
fluttery aó dàis, young toughs cowboying their Hondas
across the remaining gap, a young mother holding her
conical hat with one hand and a chicken under an arm as
her plastic sandals slipped on the wet, new bridge. I was
feeling good until someone from the watching crowd said
something to the old man that made him stiffen and lose
his humor.

"What was that, Chanh?" I asked.

"They said the old man was just trying to flatter the
Americans."

"Fuck 'em," I said.

When I went in to tell Gardiner my decision, I told him
I'd stay.

A week or so later, I did get sick, fearfully sick. I remember voices penetrating the delirium of my fever and
then, out of that cloud of fuzzy words, our grandmotherly
cook, suddenly turned savage, appearing with a little knife,
leaning over my bed, pulling my shirt off my sunken belly,

and, despite my weak flailings, scratching multitudes of little cuts on my abdomen, then finishing off the job by pinching the skin between my eyebrows until the blood rose up in a therapeutic welt. Somebody gave me an Italian pharmaceutical, which I threw up. I remember the word "MEDEVAC" buzzing down in Montgomery's voice from that hover of voices in the doorway, and, when I lay alone for days, my own voice singing, balmily, deliriously, "All round my hat, I shall wear a green willow, All round my hat for twelve months and a day. . . ."

As soon as I was strong enough, during monsoon—or "rainy season," as it is more kindly called—I took a shower under icy water and sudsed up. My knees were shaky, but I was joyful at feeling clean, horrified at how skinny my body seemed to my hands.

With shampoo thick in my hair, I felt a tickling sensation all over my back. I figured it was some weakened, central-nervous reaction to the cold water. But it persisted. It seemed so real, as if something were *really* walking on my back, across my neck, and even down my legs. So I reached down and, JESUS CHRIST, THERE *WAS* SOMETHING on my back, and neck and head and legs. Through a film of soap, I saw roaches, hundreds of roaches, roaches as big as thumbs. They had been huddled in an air pocket under the drain when my shower water had flooded their sanc-tuary. Now I saw them—little matchstick babies and huge, fat granddads—pouring past my feet, scuttling up my legs and onto the slippery walls of the shower stall. I screamed probably the loudest scream of my life and ran out into the dining room.

Roger Montgomery, who had been napping in his bed-room upstairs, now ran down to me, holding a grenade in one hand, the pulled pin in the other. I never knew he had such a thing and, sudsed and roachy, I stared at him, open-mouthed, as he burst out laughing and reinserted the pin. "Christ, Balaban. I thought the VC were murdering you."

Then he went and got some Army bug spray and chased

after the roaches, which began flying about the dining room, splatting from wall to wall in a toxic ballet.

One night a week later, as I slept, some enterprising soul put a wire through my window screen to snag over my pants and take my wallet, all without waking me. I decided I had had enough of the IVS house and demanded they find me a place where I could live alone.

What I got was wonderful, the happiest place I lived in during all my stays in Vietnam. In an older part of town, near the river bend of islands known as Ninh Kieu, where there were no other Americans, I was rented one of three adjoining units in a long bungalow owned by a woman who had shaved her head and taken lay vows in Buddhism. Her twenty-two-year-old son, Luu Suong Hue, was a law student at the university. (Perhaps To Lai Chanh was looking after me from wherever he had gone into hiding.) Mrs. Luu and her large family (including her own mother, who was also a lay nun) lived two doors down; between us was a civil servant and his large family. On the other side of my apartment, in a kind of shed attached to our building, lived a poor soldier, his old mother, and his exquisitely beautiful young wife who had just given birth to twin sons.

In front of our house were three cement pillars for burning incense in the evening. Just around the corner was a small Buddhist temple where all night long a monk sat up chanting sadhanas and masses, jinging his altar bell and striking his fish-shaped wooden drum as he marked the intervals in his liturgy.

Inside, I had a front room with one window protected by an iron grate, a back room where I slept under mosquito netting, a little loft that I reached by ladder, and, farther back, in a tin-roofed shed, a kind of kitchen that consisted of a single-burner Hitachi kerosene stove, a solid stone sink, a shower head that drained right onto the cement floor, and an oil drum filled with water that I would dip into for washing and cooking. Behind the house there was an alleyway that led to a jakes that I shared with twenty-seven other people and which was set on poles above a

natural pond that had been turned into a ghastly toilet-
paper-floating septic tank ringed by similar outhouses from
the surrounding homes. I remember fondly my kindly
neighbors, their kids who fetched me small things from a
nearby mom-and-pop store, especially Hue's little brother,
Hoai, who gave me an iridescent blue butterfly with a four-
inch wing span, which I put under glass and hung on the
wall by my desk. I remember the evening incense wafting
toward my door, the rose light that came through the terra-
cotta roof tiles, the cool feel of the floor tiles on my bare
feet, the little mosquito larvae that wriggled up in my water
drum until my landlady showed me how a film of bleach
would eliminate them, and even the tiny fish that somehow
survived in the sewage pond and which I could watch
between my feet as they batted after whatever came their
way.

After Thieu won the elections without a majority of the
vote, he jailied Truong Dinh Dzu, the dark-horse candidate
who had run on a peace platform and had swept the Delta.
By a vote of sixteen to two, the Chamber of Deputies
invalidated the election results. It all meant nothing. Thieu
was the American choice. As the city seemed to brace for
worse times, I continued to roll up to the university on
my Vespa. The students were so polite, and still so filled
with the traditional reverence for teachers, that it made me
wince; they would rise when I entered the classroom and
stay standing until I asked them to sit down. If it was
raining, someone would come up as I struggled out of my
dripping Army poncho and fold it carefully while I rum-
maged in my briefcase for the chalk I had to bring. The
blackboard was more like a map, marred by continental
blotches and bleached-out oceans. Sometimes students
would arrive late, on motorcycles, in soaked uniforms,
stacking carbines or M-16s politely by the door. Then they
would quietly take their seats, open their books, and look
up with such reverential intentness that I was touched and
saddened. King. Scholar. Farmer. Worker. Merchant. Soldier. This was the traditional hierarchy of Vietnamese so-

ciety, and now the chubby King had been exiled to the French Riviera, the farmers were driven from their fields, and soldiers—illiterate nobodies like Thieu and Ky who were schooled only in Western uses of force—were on top. Even though the whole social order had been turned on its head, these students were still motivated by their Confucian esteem for knowledge. Sometimes the windows and doors shook with nearby air strikes; once we watched a ground sweep just beyond the thatched hut where we bought soft drinks. Still they came to classes.

It was bewildering to me how Vietnamese lives seemed to go on despite dangers and deprivations. Downtown, on my scooter one evening, I turned a corner and came upon a burned smell, smoke, then a gathering crowd; finally I saw a whole dead family, parents and children, twisted and stiff, charred and strewn about inside a jeep that had just been mined. A cop directing traffic, with gold front teeth like a bright brass whistle, smiled at me as I went by. In a *phở* noodle-and-soup shop nearby, diners were still chatting and lifting their chopsticks to their mouths. Life went on in an insane, threatening fashion, but no one seemed to notice.

Once, by the river, sitting with some fishermen as others, hip-deep in the brown shallows, were turning a large net with slow precision, I jumped when automatic fire burst out on the opposite bank. Startled, as I was, a flock of snowy egrets flapped off the bamboo islets near mid-river. None of the Vietnamese in the river even looked up, except to laugh at me. Another time, talking with Pham Van Chanh outside the IVS house, I was watching a teen-aged boy and a girl chatting in the doorway of a house. When a single shot went off, maybe seventy yards away, the kids hesitated just a bit, as did some old women who paused in washing clothes at the public faucet, but no one considered it a big deal. These were just the *noises* of war. Despite the recent mortaring and the incident at Cai Rang, the war was far off, in the countryside, where no one went anymore.

6

THE POOR AMERICAN

Sometime in November, Roger Montgomery and I were visited by a guy named Powers, an advance man for Edward Kennedy, who chaired the Senate's Judiciary Subcommittee on Refugees, Escapees, and Civilian Casualties. As Robert Kennedy was sweeping the polls on an end-the-war platform, his brother was coming to Vietnam to gather facts on the civilian casualties of the war. We were asked to help. IVS volunteers, whose closeness to the Vietnamese made them useful to those who wanted to win Vietnamese hearts and minds, were proving valuable, for the same reason, to those who wanted the war stopped. Roger, who knew that Gitelson had some information about an air strike on some farmers up in Hue Duc, arranged for Gitelson to come down to Can Tho to meet Kennedy in mid-January.

I did some snooping for Powers at the Can Tho Regional Hospital, speaking to the Vietnamese director, Le Van Khoa, who surprised me with his willingness to show me monthly admissions records indicating that 50 percent of the civilian men, women, and children admitted to the hospital were war casualties. Most of the war-related civilian casualties in Dr. Khoa's records were children. Vietnam had an unusually high birthrate, Dr. Khoa explained, smoking a cigarette as he stood in his office, wearing a surgical gown and cap. The war had largely become a village war, sparked in sudden crossfires. Where could the children run? Such a crossfire had recently happened near Can Tho when a Viet Cong sapper unit hijacked a military ambulance and, using stolen uniforms and fake IDs, drove past a parked tank manned by ARVN through the main gate of the Can Tho airfield, past armed Vietnamese and American guards, and onto the runway. Underneath twelve untended aircraft that sat on the sides of the runway, they placed coffee cans filled with gasoline. In each can they dropped a hand grenade, its pin pulled, its spoon held down by rubber bands. As the gas ate into the rubber bands, they had time to drive the ambulance to the end of the runway and hurry off even before the grenade spoons sprang and planes started blowing up behind them. A jet was sent in from Saigon to strafe the runway perimeter where the VC had disappeared. The only persons killed were some civilians tending gardens and fishing the looping channels.

When Kennedy came to Can Tho, I was stuck in Saigon renewing my visa. I didn't want to miss his meeting at our house, but I was bumped by some officer's Vietnamese mistress whose Air America flight orders had a higher cut than mine. I got the next plane. When I reached the IVS house, agitated at being late, I saw a crowd of neighbors and a few police milling around outside our gate. But I hadn't missed Kennedy. He hadn't come. Just before he was to arrive, both IVS vehicles parked in front of our house had been blown up by crude little bombs that sprayed pellets, blew out the windshields, and ripped up the seats. Only two children, who had been playing nearby when the bombs exploded, were injured when the pellets flew off and cut them. When I walked up with my suitcase, I could see Roger Hintze turning over some metal pieces in his hands. He said that the police in-

sisted that this was the work of the Viet Cong, but he
doubted it.

"I mean, why?" Hintze said. "Why would they threaten
a Kennedy? Bobby's going to stop this war."

I remembered the North Vietnamese and Front officials
had said in Phnom Penh, when we gave them the IVS
letter, that we would be safe wherever we were known.
Certainly we were known at this regional office. And,
certainly, if they knew that Kennedy was coming to see
us, they'd be daft to harm him. Furthermore, these fairly
piddling bombs had gone off well before his arrival. The
bombs were just a warning. To us.

"The South Vietnamese?" I said to Hintze.

"I'd guess."

"Did Gitelson get to talk to him?"

"He's over at CORDS talking to him right now."

A week or so later, on January 26, we heard the first
reports that an American, probably Dave Gitelson, had
been shot and was lying in a canal near Ba The Mountain.
Since no one could travel the roads at night, Roger Montgomery and I set off the next morning for Long Xuyen,
the capital of An Giang Province, thirty miles away. We
arrived around 9:30 and drove to the dock to wait for a
water taxi that would take us to Hue Duc. While we
waited, we ran into another IVSer, Phil Yang. Yang was
rattled. He had gone to find the reported body but had
turned back, scared that he too might end up dead in the
water. "C'mon," Roger said, "maybe it's just a rumor;
maybe it isn't Dave." It wasn't a rumor, Phil said. He said
an air strike had been called in and three companies of
ARVN sent out to retrieve the body.

"Wow," I said, "an air strike will help Dave a whole
lot."

By 10:00 A.M., we were all at the CORDS headquarters
talking to Lieutenant Colonel Edward Lane, the American
who was, more or less, in charge of the province. (A high-

ranking American, known as the Senior Adviser—à la the French "Protectors General"—was placed in charge of each province in South Vietnam.) Colonel Lane told us he had called in not one air strike but two—one the previous day, and the second, just that morning, before the ARVN units went out. He had also ordered the area pounded with 4.2 mortars. Yet all he could tell us for a fact was that Dave had not slept in his bed the previous night. The district militia had confirmed this by radio.

Colonel Lane said he had heard several rumors that made him conclude that Dave was dead. One was that Dave's body had been seen floating in a canal but tidal flux had carried it down into the adjoining province. Another rumor was that the Viet Cong had taken the body away in a sampan. Finally, he told us that a peasant who operated a water taxi on the river had seen Dave led off into a woods by four Viet Cong. Then he heard four shots. Instead of condolences, the Colonel expressed something like hatred for "that guy, who looks like a bum, who goes around like Santa Claus with a sack." He had been consulting his rule books all morning and couldn't find one allowing U.S. military to handle civilian bodies. As a result, he couldn't call in a mortuary team.

"I know you two have disagreed," Montgomery said, "but Dave is effective, and, for Christ's sake, he's an honorably discharged American soldier. Where's this water-taxi guy?"

Roger's use of the present tense gave me a little hope too. After all, he was missing from his bed; so what?

"He's disappeared."

Roger and I looked at each other.

"Well," the Colonel muttered, "some good may come of this." He gave Montgomery the name of an OSA Special Branch Adviser, a Mr. Lewallen, who had a possible lead, and then the Colonel left us with a propaganda leaflet that was already being dropped around Hue Duc. It read as follows:

CÁC BẠN CAN BINH MẶT TRẬN GIẢI
PHÓNG MIỀN NAM THAN MẾN!

Việt-Cộng xúi các bạn giết người Mỹ nghèo tại Huệ-
Đức.
Hành dộng ấy rất tàn bạo. Bạn đã giết người bạn
thân của các bạn và nông-dân vùng Huệ-Đúc.
Các bạn đã thấy Việt-Cộng tàn bạo chưa.
Vậy các bạn mau mau rời hâng ngũ sát nhơn đề về
vời Chánh-Phủ Qúoc-Gia xum hợp gia-đinh và hưởng
một mùa xuân đoàn tựu.

Dear friends and soldiers in the Liberation Front of
the South!
Viet Cong have incited friends to kill the poor Amer-
ican in Hue Duc.
This action was particularly cruel. These friends have
killed this close friend of the people and farmers of the
Hue Duc district.
Has anyone seen such VC cruelty?
Therefore all people should quickly depart from as-
sassination squads in order to return to the National
Government together with families and enjoy a pleasant
spring together.

We were stunned. The crude little leaflets in our hands
had been *printed* before anyone had proved that Gitelson
was dead. Equally odd, the leaflet did not accuse the Viet
Cong of killing Dave, but of inciting hypothetical
"friends" (*Việt-Cộng xúi các bạn giết người Mỹ nghèo . . .*)
to murder him. What friends? And how could Colonel
Lane and his PSYOPS people know so much about these
events when no body had yet been recovered and no wit-
nesses had come forward except an anonymous boatman
who had now disappeared?
It was hard for us to imagine the Viet Cong killing
Gitelson. Dave carried a safe pass from the Viet Cong in
his area; Roger had seen it. Furthermore, Gitelson was as
well known as any American in the province. The farmers

liked him. With his shaved head, huge frame, flipflops, jeans, and burlap sack, you couldn't mistake him. Finally, Gitelson had just spoken to Edward Kennedy. I couldn't imagine a political cadre existing in all of the Viet Cong so stupid as not to see the backfire that would result from killing Dave.

"It's a bit premature," said Montgomery, translating the parts that I couldn't make out and looking over at poor Phil Yang, who had been up all night and was nauseated with grief.

"We don't even know he's dead," I said.

Yang, a youngster to whom Gitelson must have seemed magical, just shook his head. He looked ill.

Around 11:15, we told Yang to go sleep, that we'd wake him if we heard anything. Then Montgomery went off to the province prison with the local CIA agent to talk to four Viet Cong who had been captured in the area the week before. Two were from the adjoining province, Kien Giang, and didn't know anything about Dave. A third said that he had been to Ba The Mountain and had heard people talk about Dave, but that he didn't know anything about him. The fourth said that he had met Dave many times and The Poor American was always helping destitute farmers, giving them insecticides and things from his big bag. None of them knew about any assassination.

The rest of the day was spent waiting or phoning Saigon to tell IVS what we knew, what they could tell Dave's parents. At 4:00 P.M., an American adviser with the ARVN operation radioed in that Gitelson's body had been positively identified by one of the Army medics. A chopper was sent out to bring it to Long Xuyen. All this we learned from a Major Black, the only official who had been the least bit helpful. Black also told Montgomery that an Otter was ordered from Saigon to get the body to a mortuary. "I don't give a goddamn about regulations," he said. "He's an American, right?"

We drove the Landrover, still listing out of alignment

from the bombing, out to the chopper pad to meet the body. It was nearly dusk and chilly after an early-evening rain. A small crowd of Americans were looking into the chopper. On its metal floor, in a huge puddle, Dave's body was shrouded in a sopping-wet light cotton blanket. He had been in the canal for almost a day. None of the military people who brought him in, or any of those who came from CORDS, would touch his body. Perhaps this was on the Colonel's orders; perhaps they just didn't want to touch anything so foul.

When Roger and I pulled the corpse out of the chopper and down onto the metal landing strip, Dave's large head—wrapped in the thin, seeping blanket—dropped backward against my knees, smearing watery blood and canal muck onto my pants. For a moment, parts of his chin, mouth, and neck were exposed. I saw the bleached, puckered flesh and covered his face again. Dead, he was very heavy, water-logged, and beginning to rot.

The Otter never came from Saigon, even though Mr. Elliot, the American in charge of the entire Delta, was supposed to be waiting at the Can Tho airfield with other officials to look at the corpse before sending it on to Saigon. Finally, Colonel Lane told us that the American authorities would not send the plane because of "security reasons," presumably darkness, though this made little sense since there was still enough daylight to make the small skip to Saigon. Despite all of Montgomery's protestations and begging, Colonel Lane would not authorize the chopper that had brought Gitelson in to carry him on. Then, as Roger and I stood there not knowing what to do, some soldier—a noncom medic, I think—muttered something like "Just get it out of here." I said "Fuck you" to him about an inch from his face; it seemed for a moment that all my grief, rage, failed hopes, and exhaustion could be erased in just one clear second of smashing the bastard's face, as if the awful memory tingling in my hands—of my friend's head like a broken, leaky melon—could be nulled by one good, nose-splattering punch. But the guy just shrugged and walked away. Then the Army and AID types left us with our friend's corpse, wrapped in a runny blanket, on a chopper pad, as evening fell.

There was no mortuary in Long Xuyen. We loaded Dave over the back gate of the Landrover and drove to the hospital, where Montgomery, with his expert Vietnamese, appealed to the human decency and bribability of a Vietnamese orderly who let us put the body on the floor of a storage room, although this was against hospital rules. Then, when we had shut the door and stood quietly for a minute by the tin-roofed shed in evening shadows thick with the smells of oleander and antiseptic, Montgomery noticed that there was a good two inches between the bottom of the door and the tile floor. He started to cry. "Christ," he said, tears streaming down his cheeks and his chest shaking, "the rats will get him." We stuffed the crack with rags from the Landrover. The strain and grief had been the worst for Montgomery. He had known Dave the longest, and all day long he had been obliged to argue, cajole, and haggle with the creeps who ran the show in An Giang, hoping against hope that it was all a mistake, that Dave was still alive, and that the meeting with Kennedy, which Montgomery had helped arrange, was not somehow the cause of Gitelson's assassination. In the scheme of things in Vietnam, Roger was just a nobody ranting at the big boys. As we all were. As Dave had been.

But Dave hadn't always been disliked by the authorities in Long Xuyen. The previous April, *Time* magazine reported that "U.S. officials consider him the most effective American of all the thousands involved in Delta pacification," further quoting one unidentified official (could it have been Colonel Lane?) as saying, "All he has is strength, stamina and awkwardness. I wish we had more like him." But crossed purposes were evident even in that article, which quoted Dave as saying: "We're nothing more than sugar-coating for the genocide that's going on here."

Indeed, throughout his two-year tour, Gitelson had nattered at American officials for abuses to civilians in An Giang, but he must have done this believing that Americans held common, basic moral assumptions, that the awful things wreaked upon Vietnamese civilians by American firepower were just mistakes. I think he thought he could change things. His agriculture report for October 1967 began:

> At least two varieties of fruit trees here suffer badly from disease. Infected custard apple trees, 'mang cau ta,' produce fruit that's hard, black and spore-filled. This is a very prevalent disease, so much so that people are discouraged from planting this tree, formerly a popular orchard variety. Another disease affects jackfruit trees, 'mit,' the fruit first develops brown patches then turns mushy. I'd appreciate advice on how to deal with these diseases. Dithane and other fungicides are available in Long Xuyen but they're expensive.

The report then continues with a long, detailed complaint:

> Previously I've had talks with the province and MACR on possible ways to reduce civilian war casualties, e.g. get the families of soldiers out of the remote outposts by providing them housing in more secure areas. Late last month, after one man was killed and another wounded by air-fire in a free fire zone west of Vong-The village, the local people made some suggestions. . . .

Dave's last report, for December 1967, which he wrote just before talking to Edward Kennedy, was the one which made it finally impossible for him to work amicably with American officials in his province. "3 weeks ago Tuesday morning," he wrote in his three-page, single-spaced, detailed inquiry into an incident that involved the very farmers that he had worked with for a year,

> there was an airstrike on the outskirts of Tan Tay Ham-
> let, Vong-The Village, which killed immediately 4 chil-
> dren, 2 women and 3 men and wounded 12 others. In
> two families both parents were killed. Later one of the
> wounded, a man, died. A community of 33 families
> was wiped off the map. Their homes were mostly de-
> stroyed along with their boats and livestock. The sur-
> vivors arrived in the market with nothing but the
> clothes they were wearing at the time of the attack,
> that is with no bedding or food.

In addition to this atrocity, which he had also described
to Kennedy, there was more that he never got to tell. Roger
Montgomery, in his report on Gitelson's death, wrote that
Dave "was onto something that was extremely sensitive,
which he had mentioned to Tom Fox [another IVSer] and
me just the previous Wednesday." Apparently, Gitelson,
in his meticulous, persistent way, had uncovered a program of corruption among the South Vietnamese officials
running the local refugee program. He was in the process
of getting that information to Kennedy when he was killed.
His report, in fact, only got as far as the CORDS building.
Montgomery believed it was read by some of the corrupt
officials Gitelson had intended to expose.

I never believed that the Viet Cong had killed him, although that became the official version. It was the version
put forth in Colonel Lane's strange leaflet. It was the IVS
version. It was the version reported in the February 9, 1968,
issue of *Time,* and, ironically, it was the version that appeared in Edward Kennedy's encomium in the *Congressional Record* of February 1: "Mr. President, during my
recent trip to Vietnam, I met and spent a great deal of time
with a brave and selfless young American, David Gitelson . . . taken prisoner by the Vietcong in the Mekong
Delta and brutally slain." Everything in the official version, when looked at closely, seemed faked or unlikely—
from the premature propaganda leaflet to the disappearing

witness and the bizarre air strikes that preceded the search operation. A more plausible explanation for his absence might have been that he had a girlfriend or was sleeping over at some farmer's house. Gitelson lived on his own terms in Vietnam. (Why was CORDS even aware that he had not come home that night?)

Despite these odd facts, I don't think any American in 1968 was prepared to believe that Gitelson had been murdered by his own countrymen. Even my own darkest assumption then was that the Vietnamese grafters whom Dave was about to expose either did it on their own or got a nod from CORDS officials who had grown weary of Gitelson. They were angry at him for making them look bad with the Senator, and they saw Gitelson as more useful to them dead than alive. But if one links Gitelson's murder with his meeting Kennedy and with the bombing of the IVS cars in Can Tho just two weeks before, then Gitelson's assassination was surely approved by higher authorities, authorities capable of coordinating intelligence and events beyond the province level. Authorities with that kind of power had to be American.

This saddest of conjectures is the one that seems likeliest more than twenty years later. Gitelson may have been an early victim of the CIA's Phoenix Program, which we now know was unleashed at that time to assassinate secretly anyone suspected of Viet Cong affiliation. Maybe *that* was the "extremely sensitive" thing that Gitelson had discovered. Perhaps Richard, my CIA friend in Cao Lanh, was balking at the start-up of the program, not just, as he told me, the depredations of an individually miscreant Vietnamese Province Chief.

In recent years, I have been interviewed by Lynn Kamm, once an undergraduate reporter at UCLA, where Gitelson was a student a few years ahead of her. As a college student, she wrote about his death, and was affected by it so much that for the past twenty years she's been tracking down the details of his assassination. Recently she spoke with Colonel Lane, now retired from the Army and a stockbroker in Georgia. She also spoke with the army medic who identified Dave's body and wrote the official "incident" report. According to Kamm, this former medic, who says he is afraid to have his name mentioned, was terrified when first contacted by Kamm. (Who was she? he wanted to know. How did she get his name?) During the war, he was stationed with a small unit on Ba The Mountain and often gave Dave medicines for the farmers. Twice the two of them went out on MEDCAPs, all-purpose medical missions that went into villages to, among other things, pull bad teeth, inoculate kids, lance boils, and hand out tetracycline. This former medic told Kamm two rather startling things. First, the incident report that now exists in Army files is not the one he wrote. The current report describes Dave as shot in the back while fleeing. The original report is very clear, he says, in describing Gitelson as shot at point-blank range from the front, suggesting that Gitelson was facing his murderers, that he may have even known them. The current report, he says, "is a pile of crap." The medic also described to Kamm several strange Americans who appeared in An Giang just before Gitelson's death. One of these was a GSO-14, a rather high-ranking U.S. government officer. They operated secretly, he claims, and very few Americans knew they were there.

When questioned about this by Kamm, Colonel Lane told her that this was all nonsense, that he would have known if a GSO-14 were in his province. Lane, who still expresses dislike for Gitelson although he admits he did respect Gitelson for holding to his views, also thinks his former medic is nutty. Indeed, the man himself told Kamm that he was scared out of his wits and had something like a nervous breakdown after Gitelson's death. Nonetheless, he believed then and still believes now that Gitelson was murdered by Americans.

All we know for certain is that the day he was shot Gitelson was trying to help a woman whose husband had

finally died from injuries in the air strike. The best guess
that his IVS friends have as to why Gitelson was out on
the canal that day is that he was bringing her some food
and clothing. It was a typical hot sunny day. One can
imagine the green water rolling past the bow, the putter
of the boat's engine turning its rotor at the end of the long-
poled rudder, the madcap cries of jungle birds chasing
about the coconut palms lining the canal, and the occasional
appearance of a thatched hut with its clothes-washing platform and earthen water jars down by the water's edge.
There would have been boys bathing in the water with
their buffalo; a man or a woman opening an irrigation ditch
into a household patch of potatoes or peppers. One can
imagine Dave's head wrapped in his farmer's kerchief, his
big knees sticking up as he moved along in the weathered
skiff, the bolt of black cotton across his knees, the bags of
rice set beside him on the wooden seat so they wouldn't
get wet. If he were facing forward, he could see the prow's
painted eyes reflected in the gliding water, the eyes that
boatmen paint there to ward off malevolent water spirits
under the command of Ba Thuy, the water goddess. Indeed, it was a day when Ba Thuy, the Water Lady, and
Ong Troi, Mr. Sky, must have reached some agreement
about Gitelson's fate. On that particular day, Gitelson must
have felt especially close to himself, to his fate, and to the
face of heaven, for at the very time he was carrying those
paltry relief supplies to the woman widowed by an American air strike, he was supposed to be in the United States,
at Macalester College in Saint Paul, receiving that college's
International Distinguished Service Award. But Gitelson,
in characteristic humility, had refused the award, suggesting to Macalester that they give it to another volunteer,
who Dave said had "come close to getting blown up a
couple of times, so you'd better grab him fast." Finally,
prevailed upon by his friends, he accepted the award but
refused to return to the States to receive it. Instead, an IVS
friend accepted it for him in a ceremony that took place

at about the same moment Gitelson may have been throwing up his hands to ward off the rip of automatic fire.

"Happiness or misfortune," we are told paradoxically
in *The Tale of Kieu,* "are prescribed by the law of Heaven,
but their source comes from ourselves." The sentiment is
a Buddhist, karmic version of Sartre's "man chooses himself." In Vietnam, under the prospect of Heaven, the scru-
tiny of Mr. Sky, Gitelson had achieved a life of fateful
clarity, redolent with moral choice, with risk, and with
humane purpose. It is hard to pity him for that, even if
the life he chose invited his murder. What wrenches my
heart, as I sit in my attic and sift through notebooks and
memories now twenty years old, is the thought of my
odd, brainy, compassionate friend's last seconds as the bullets sliced through his outstretched hands, and his eyes,
before closing, glimpsed an enormity of evil larger than
any of us imagined.

7

CAUGHT
IN THE CROSSFIRE

Around 3:00 A.M., collapsed in boozy sleep under the mosquito netting, snoring away in the slacks and white shirt I had worn for the first day of Tet, my sandals kicked off onto the floor, I heard a lot of thumping and muffled banging that echoed in my groggy brain like the fireworks that had gone off the previous evening, the eve of Tet Mau Than, the Year of the Monkey, not especially—I had been told again and again—a good year in the lunar astrology.

One of those bangings in dreamland seemed nearly as loud as the fat firecracker I had lobbed the night before, nearly blowing off my right index finger and tattooing a bruise on my stomach with bits of blue gunpowder, burned paper, and microscopic bits from my exploded shirt. The blast had rung my ears as I horsed around with my neighbors in our front yard. Tet is Christmas, Thanksgiving, and the Fourth of July all rolled up into one. At Tet, the spirits on each family's altar fly up to Heaven to report to the Jade Emperor. At Tet, all the family comes home. At Tet, the house is cleaned and whitewashed, readied for the return of spirits. Special foods are laid out for them as they are called home with incense and prayer. Then families "eat Tet." In prewar days, the celebrations went on for a month. The firecrackers for the 1968 Tet made up in bang the wartime shortening of the holiday. The gunpowder was very pure. (The rumor was that Chinese merchants had negotiated the purchase of five-hundred-pound bombs from GIs at Tan Son Nhut and had then removed the powder for their firecrackers.) The day before, I had joined my neighbors in the first ceremony of the New Year: driving off the bad spirits of the passing year with a mammoth barrage of fireworks that had left our alley ankle-deep in exploded firecracker paper.

My head ached something awful. All that day I had been with friends—students and teachers from the high school and university—who had poured Suntory whisky and 33 beer into me with a ceremonial gaiety that was hard to resist. That morning, with bandaged finger, I had lit a huge tail of firecrackers at the house of my friend and student, Lt. Trung, a Northern Catholic anticommunist whose father had died fighting the Viet Minh a decade before. Trung had invited me to be the first person to visit his house on the first day of Tet. Like all events and gestures on Tet, the invitation had significance, for the first person to enter a Vietnamese household on the first day of Tet is the person who brings his fortune to the house for the entire coming year.

In my drunken half-sleep that night, before the dawn of another day of Tet celebrations, thirsty, clammy in my clothes, I remembered that Trung had also given me some special rice paper on which I was to write a poem. Whatever is written on the first day of Tet comes true. I remember expressing regrets to Trung for writing a poem about warfare, and Trung—bespectacled, round-shouldered, studious, and kind—had replied that it mattered only that it was a good poem. Before our banquet ended, his teenaged daughter sang a poem for us, "Sitting Sadly by the Window." The beauty of her voice and the melancholy lyrics stilled our chatter and stray, drunken thoughts.

Now, the revelry over, I tried again to get back to sleep but my mind kept stumbling back and forth across the wavering line that separates dream from waking. The banging seemed loud. *Very* loud.

Finally, I was shaken awake by a series of mortars crashing through tin and terra-cotta roofs nearby. I bolted upright to listen in cold-sober fear as the cotton mosquito-netting near my cheek puffed with the explosions. It was the real thing. Every now and then, closer than I had ever heard one, a grenade launcher dropped a big whomp. Grenade launchers, I noted with further alarm, are fired at *close* range. Grenade launchers meant *they* were in the city.

From my bed, I could hear the pinging of a carbine; an assault rifle, maybe an AK-47, spat back a reply. A plane droned over our district, circling and dropping magnesium flares which hissed as they fell and then popped when their chutes bellied out and their flares caught. A weird, metallic, rosy light walked the walls as the flares floated overhead. I sat frozen in bed.

A siren was wailing from the guard tower of the province jail near the tennis-court restaurant. With the gathering siren came the dog chorus. A baby cried next door, and I was comforted to hear its parents hush it. As I strained to listen for footsteps or voices in the surrounding alleys, I could hear myself breathing, and, out there, in the muffled coughs and whispers that emerged between dog howls, the siren's cascades, and random explosions, I could tell that my neighbors were awake and listening too.

Keeping my head down below window level, I slid out of bed and crept to the front window only to stub my toe on a chair and trip forward, cursing the chair's loud, betraying scrape across the tiles. The window by the door was just a squarish hole with an iron grate that anybody could put his hand through to fire a gun or drop a grenade. I peeked out. The alley was empty. Even the local corner temple where the monk chanted softly through the nights, dinging a bell before his small altar lit by a kerosene lamp, was now dark and silent. Still listening intently, I tried to locate the direction of the fighting. I studied the lines on my hands as flare light drifted through the window. Then, as noiselessly as I could, I padlocked my front door, relieved that at least I had brought my scooter into the house despite my drunkenness. Then I turned and shuffled my bare feet quietly across the cool tiles to see that my flimsy back door was also locked. For the rest of the night, I lay in my bed listening to the awful havoc of American and ARVN troops responding to the siege.

At dawn, the sky above the city roared open as Cobra helicopter gunships dispatched from Saigon let off rockets over the town. Their racket shook my lungs. For most of the morning, the fighting continued but sounded localized in distant pockets. Through the bars of my front window, I could see some of the neighbors huddled out in the alley and looking worriedly at my door. Their stares made me decide to get out. Although no fighting had broken out yet in my part of Can Tho, it seemed from the volume of shooting and the unprecedented gunships that it was only a matter of time before our quiet corner would be hit by mortars or be used by the Viet Cong as a shortcut or as cover. Then, perhaps, some neighbor, jittery for his family, or simply out of hatred for Americans, or perhaps merely jealous of the rent I paid my Buddhist landlady, would turn me in. Some must even have believed I was a CIA agent.

"Go in. Go back in, Mr. John," called Luu Suong Hue, my landlady's son, as I wheeled my Vespa out the front door. My head and stomach slid around a bit in the hard sunlight. I was sweating and shaky and could not tell whether it was from the hangover or from fear. But instead of going back in, I pushed the Vespa over to their door, where, behind her son, my landlady was flapping her hand at me with that gesture that looks to Westerners like a wave of goodbye but means "Come here" to Vietnamese.

Inside their house, it was still Tet. Ong Tao, the Hearth

God, and the Luu family ancestors had flown off to Heaven
to make their annual report the night before, and now were
back at their respective altars which smoked with incense
and candles. Bright-yellow marigolds, a sign of the New
Year for ordinary people in the South, decorated the banquet table, but no one's attention was on the dishes my
landlady had been preparing for the last week. The Viet
Cong were *in the city*. For the first time, they were fighting
American and South Vietnamese units right in Can Tho.

"Where you go?" Hue's voice, always deferential, was
abrupt with fear. "VC in Cambodian temple," he told me.
A group of Viet Cong were surrounded in the temple
compound on Peace Boulevard. The government troops,
about a hundred soldiers who faced them with armored
personnel carriers and some Browning rifles, were afraid
to go in after them and had given them one hour to sur-
render. Meanwhile, the Viet Cong had allowed the temple's monks and its population of refugees to leave through
the cordon.

"Hue, I've got to get to the IVS house."

He was going to reply, but just then the elderly government worker from the middle house (where he grew
cascades of orchids on his tree in the front yard) came over
in his pajamas to say that American Armed Forces Radio
was reporting *"les VC attaquer toutes des villes."*

"You can't go on street, Mr. John," Hue said. "Police
and soldiers crazy now. They shoot anybody they see."

I shook my head as I took in what they were saying.
Hue's mother, with her wonderful gap-toothed smile and
shaved head, was offering me a plate of something
wrapped in rice paper. I took it, dipped it in sauce, and
swallowed. I asked her for aspirin. When she went back
into the kitchen to get it, the little nieces and nephews and
cousins who had been staring at me started to whisper.
Suddenly I felt like a convict on the lam. My presence, I
could see, as Hue's mother offered me four huge Vietnam-
ese-brand aspirin and a big glass of French-crock-filtered

water, was a liability to these decent people. They insisted I stay with them, but if things were as bad as they said, and if the Viet Cong actually took over our neighborhood, the VC might be hard on my friends. Even the children to whom I had given candy and little Tet money packets the day before, and who were now staring at me as my Adam's apple bobbed with drinking—even they knew it. Still, instead of letting me head out onto the uncertain streets nattering with gunfire, my neighbors were offering me their protection, which seemed neither decent nor wise for me to accept.

"Hue, I better get to the IVS house until this is over." I thanked his mother in Vietnamese and said goodbye to her, to Hue, and to the wide-eyed children. Then, with an *au revoir* to the old man, I got back on my Vespa and wheeled it through the yard gate and down the narrow cement walkway, noting a neighbor's house on my left where the yard and front door had been blasted by a mortar. I would never see any of those good people again.

Out on the main street, all the shops were shuttered. My Vespa puttered loudly in the deserted street. Now and then, I rode over glitters of bright brass shell casings from spent rounds. Almost all the upper stories of the shops and apartment buildings along the street had been peppered by small-arms fire. Shards of roof tiles littered house fronts where mortars or grenades had slammed through.

It was slow going. I had to brake every few hundred yards to get around ammo-box-barbed-wire-fruit-drink-cart barricades thrown up by the ARVN troops. I approached each roadblock slowly from the middle of the street so that the soldiers could see I was an American. When I got near, some skinny soldier with an oversize helmet would come out from behind a doorway to pull open the concertina wire and then wave me through with one hand, as his other clutched his M-16, its butt balanced in his belt webbing. Everyone looked scared. "VC! VC!"

one soldier warned, as I passed the last blockade and turned onto the main boulevard.

On that stretch—away from the river, jail, and Province Chief's villa—on the way to the main IVS house, there were two skirmishes going on. On my side of the street, some ARVN were huddled behind a couple of armored personnel carriers that were blasting into the Cambodian temple with its miniature Angkor Wat towers. On the opposite side, in the old part of Can Tho leading to the river, other ARVN hiding behind APCs were firing into the movie theater, withering the hand-painted *Gone with the Wind* marquee. I stopped, but then eased on, since hardly any fire seemed to be coming back from the temple and only a stray shot or two emerged from the movie house during the ARVN lulls.

When I finally arrived at the IVS house, set back behind its high stucco wall, I was relieved to find Pham Van Chanh, Bill Seraile, and Roger Hintze. Montgomery was out of the country. Chanh had spent Tet with his father, a bad-tempered but now frail old man who had beaten Chanh so badly as a child that Chanh had run away from home at eleven. Seraile and Hintze had waited out the night in the third IVS house on another edge of town, not far from the fighting. All of them had just gotten there. Hintze had tried to call IVS in Saigon. The phone was dead. We decided to go to the MACV compound to find out what was going on, leaving Chanh behind to protect our house from looters.

When we returned to the house from the army compound (which had been mortared the night before and now bustled like a battered hornets' nest), we brought sandwiches from the mess, and guns. Hintze had a carbine, Seraile, a .45 pistol, and I had a greasegun—a crude, slow-firing, M-3 .45-caliber machine gun whose ugly stamped-metal construction gave it its nickname. I wish I could remember more exactly how I got it, since taking arms was against my beliefs. We were issued these weapons from the MACV armory. No one made us take them. I remember we *lined up* for them with various other American civilians who had taken cover in MACV's walled Eakin compound. So it wasn't as if I forsook my testimony not to take up arms because anybody pressured me. Indeed, when I got to the IVS house, I went straight to Montgomery's room to find the grenade he had pulled to save me from the cockroaches. I found two—one a concussion grenade; the other, fragmentation—and put them both in a leather shaving kit that I tied to my belt. I am sure that at the time I was ashamed of having taken up a gun, but really what I remember most is the wonderful relief I felt at having one. *I think I just did not want to die like Dave Gitelson,* murdered at close range, unarmed, maybe even begging for life. Chanh said that ARVN troops were already taking advantage of the mayhem to loot shops and homes. I was as much afraid of them as I was of the Viet Cong.

The four of us sat out the rest of the day at the IVS house, following on the radio the fighting all across Vietnam, peeking through the grille of our big metal yard gate and trying to call Saigon on the dead phone. By evening, Chanh had brought in his old father and his aunt, who was also our cook, as well as some of his neighbors, a mother nursing a baby and her other children. Chanh was carrying Hintze's carbine by its sling. Somehow this was even more distressing to me than my own gun-toting. Chanh was carrying a gun—something he could be shot for out on the street—as if he too had concluded that the chaos was such that anything could happen. As evening fell and the town still crackled with gunfire, Roger and Bill walked down the street a few houses to the CARE representative's apartment, where they knew they could stay the night, rather than return to their house which they feared might be either looted by ARVN soldiers or taken by the Viet Cong or some awful combination of both. After they left, we chained and padlocked the gate, wind-

ing some barbed wire across the top. Then Chanh ran a
wire from the house electricity to the barbed wire strung
atop our stucco wall. One of the children, dressed only in
a shirt, wandered up to us in the yard, looked up at me,
and wailed.

That night, up on the second story, I sat with Chanh
watching the field in front of our house, the same field
where he and I had built the little dike to the poor hamlet
of Ap An Cu. Chanh pushed a bureau up against the window and we laid our guns on it and looked out, searching
for shadows moving our way, as the National Police dug
shallow trenches fifty yards from us facing Ap An Cu.

Soon the fighting started again. An APC barked a stream
of tracers across the field and into the village. With that,
a salvo of carbines, pistols, Browning Automatic Rifles,
greaseguns, and grenades opened up on the hapless slum.
Flare chutes popped open over its rooftops. A thatch roof
burst into crackling flames. Soon the whole village started
to burn, house by house. We could hear people screaming,
and saw—silhouetted against the angry glow—villagers
running out to crouch in the ditch along the road front as
tracers swam above them.

Neither Chanh nor I ever had cause to fire at anything;
we had agreed to fire only if armed soldiers tried to get
into our yard. We couldn't even tell where all the shots
were coming from, but when some splattered the second-
story wall just by our heads, we moved Chanh's entourage
into the kitchen, where they were safest from anything
that might plunge through the roof. For the rest of the
night, taking turns at the window, we watched the village
burn.

The next morning, Chanh gathered his family into our
Scout and took them to a relative's house. Hintze and
Seraile came back, and the three of us drove over to the
regional hospital to see if we could help out somehow. We
could see the survivors from Ap An Cu struggling along

the road, to God knows where, with their remaining possessions. A line of them walked by Saigon soldiers, still positioned behind APCs, still waiting for the Viet Cong to emerge. People were carrying chairs and wooden beds. Hintze stopped for a man and a woman toting all their possessions in bedspreads, begging a ride to the main road. Overhead, the Cobra gunships swarmed like wasps on the city outskirts just beyond our house and the new university buildings.

When we reached the sprawling regional hospital not far away, Roger, who spoke Vietnamese the best, got out to cajole the terrified gate guard to roll down the windlass that worked the heavy metal gates and let us in. Inside, the dusty yard with its sun-scorched hedges and topiary was jammed with wounded civilians, some standing only with the help of relatives, others lying on stretchers or on bamboo mats or simply on the ground. There was nobody to attend them, just swarms of flies, a drilling sun, and a blank, pitiless sky. As we stepped over them to get to the emergency room, people called out to us, *"Bác sĩ, bác sĩ,"* "Doctor, doctor." In front of the emergency room we found even more civilians lying about lacerated and bleeding, and, in the emergency room itself, still others sprawled on the tiled floor in puddles of blood and urine.

We hadn't seen any doctors, but when we approached the operating room, we literally ran into a MILPHAP team of Air Force surgeons. Their leader, Major Cruz Hernandez, told us they were pulling out. There were VC on the grounds.

"Where?" asked poor Seraile, who had only recently arrived in Vietnam.

Major Hernandez pointed his thumb over his shoulder, toward the warren of narrow walkways that led to the various Quonset wards of the hospital.

"What about them?" Hintze asked, nodding toward the injured.

We must have been an odd trio: Hintze, a skinny, utterly

mild-mannered farm boy, shouldering his carbine like a hoe; Seraile, a young, black *civilian* with a .45 tucked in the front of his belt; and me, a trifle long-haired, with my shaving kit of grenades, gripping my greasegun whose clip I had electrical-taped with another clip to add firepower.

"Who *are* you?" the Major asked.

Behind him, one of the surgeon-officers muttered, "Cruz, c'mon, let's get out of here." The Cobras had shifted their attack and now were over the hospital.

"IVS," I said.

"What's that?"

"Well, we're like volunteers with USAID."

The Major looked us over. "Look," he said, "you can't operate if you think someone's gonna stick a gun through the window. The Special Forces were supposed to be here an hour ago. None of the Vietnamese staff has showed. But if you guys are willing to guard the OR, we'll stay and operate at least until we're ordered out."

We looked at one another. Seraile and Hintze were just as much opposed to killing as I was. This would not be the same as carrying a gun to protect yourself. We looked around us. The Cobras had been using 2.75 rockets. Each rocket contained two thousand nail darts. Just two such rockets can fill a football field with darts. Moreover, the Air Force jets had been dropping cluster bombs that made the air on the outskirts of Can Tho dance with knives, for each of those cluster bombs contained four hundred bomblets filled with razor-sharp slivers. When planes swooped low and dropped them from formation, it was like a gang mower snipping off everything in its path. Whole families, reunited at Tet the night before, now lay about us shredded and bleeding to death in the dirt. It was evident that if we did not say yes, a lot more of the people lying in the courtyards would die. In the presence of that misery, our scruples seemed unimportant. So Seraile volunteered to carry patients in and out of the operating room while Hintze and I, who were better armed, became the guards.

According to the Vietnamese Catholic nuns who lived on the hospital grounds, four Viet Cong had come over the hospital's six-foot stucco wall, which was topped with jagged broken glass. No one knew where these intruders were at the moment, so Hintze and I began a slow circuit of the grounds, scared and also somewhat ashamed. Neither of us had any desire to kill anybody; however, I think neither of us doubted that we could. Hintze had grown up with guns on his family farm. Years before my conscientious objection, I had won an Expert Marksman rating with the NRA as well as a trap-shooting trophy at my dad's hunting club. Both Hintze and I, like a lot of American boys, had been schooled in guns from childhood.

After making our circuit and seeing no one, we each picked a spot and sat down as much out of sight as we could be and still watch the OR. The surgeons had worried that the VC seen by the nuns had been sent to kidnap a doctor or steal medical supplies.

By 10:00 in the morning, the battle outside the hospital walls was picking up and getting closer. For the next several hours, peering nervously at the Quonset huts and hedges, I sat on a rickety stool just outside the door of the generator shack. The inside of the shack was plastered with Japanese and *Playboy* pinups, which, like an attending troop of *apsara*s, the sexy Buddhist flying goddesses, further added to my confusion, especially since I realized that the footsteps shuffling toward me belonged to one of the hospital's Catholic nuns, who smiled, glanced at the pinups, and delicately shut the shack door as she held up a Red Cross arm band and sewed it to my sleeve. Above us, the water tower, riddled with bullets, spouted streams of water into the dust. Beyond the wall, a single-prop Vietnamese Skyraider was dropping bombs on the university where I taught and, after several bad misses, on our IVS house and the surrounding homes. As the nun stitched on the Red Cross patch and I clutched my submachine gun, I had never felt more morally bewildered.

The Viet Cong never showed up at the hospital, but the Special Forces did—big guys in jeeps with radios, packs, boots, and camouflage, who swept the grounds and then took over our guard duty. About the same time, some of the Vietnamese hospital staff returned, the X-ray technician and two nurses, one of whom took blood from us. Then we joined Seraile in moving patients into beds or onto stretchers, and in and out of surgery. A number of the patients were already dead. We hoisted them to the floor and put others in their beds. Bill had a strong stomach. ("How can you stand this?" I asked as he wheeled somebody out of the OR and I wheeled one in. "I like it," he said, as if surprised himself. "Maybe I'll become a doctor.") It was Civil War surgery. Men, women, and children were rolled out of the OR without legs and arms, only to be wheeled back to beds in the crammed wards, where two and three people lay together on thin, sheetless mattresses that dripped blood and urine, beds where they would wake up from their anesthesia with no one to give them a shot of morphine or Demerol or to refill the IV drips that the doctors had hastily rigged.

Hintze stayed in the wards, assisting a Vietnamese nurse. I continued to help Seraile but finally abandoned the OR after I nearly threw up when I hauled out a stainless-steel can that had a small, wobbly arm drooping from under the lid. I dumped the contents behind the building into a bin heaped with human debris, sucked in a lungful of air to stay my dizziness. When I returned to the ward, one of the Air Force doctors gave me a ten-minute course in sterile technique, which was what I settled into for the next several days, daubing and picking away debris, washing and bandaging wounds. At momentary lulls in the fighting, more and more wounded poured in, some of them with wounds several days old, some so hopelessly injured that after the triage evaluation they were just sent home to die: treating such cases was simply beyond the capacities of the hospital, or would take so much surgical time that two or three others could be saved instead.

I remember one nine-year-old boy, all alone, whom the surgeons wanted to know more about before they put him under. "You're okay here," I said in Vietnamese. "The doctors will help you." But the boy—naked, held down by our hands, thrashing in his pee on the steel table, eyes wild with fear—kept crying, *"Ðau! Ðau!"* ("Hurt! Hurt!"). His tiny hip had been slashed by shrapnel. He gripped my hand fiercely and kept screaming, no matter what I said. I continued to try and calm him until the anesthesiologist said, "Forget it. His ears are probably blown."

When the napalm cases started coming in, one of the surgeons—all of whom had labored for hours in the intense heat without a break—sat down for a minute as his knees went wobbly. I remember one napalmed woman wrapped mummylike in yellow gauze, her face swollen horribly, thrashing on the floor next to her beautiful, chubby, naked, tanned infant daughter with gold earrings who was perfectly whole except for one arm burned black. The child was lying quietly on an issue of the military's *Stars and Stripes* newspaper whose R&R ad said, under the ruined arm, "Expand your ego. Visit the exotic East."

There was a teenaged boy, a suspected Viet Cong, who gripped my forearm harder and harder as a nurse and I dressed his hopelessly gaping wounds and his burst bladder leaked through the fist-size hole in his right groin. There was the wife of Mr. Long, my village neighbor from three houses down, now deaf and crazy with slivers of shrapnel in her head; she had looked out during a lull in the mortar barrage just as one exploded in her front yard. Mr. Long, who had worked at the hospital years before, now begged me to get morphine and a catheter for his wife, saying he would apply them himself, just please help because I was an American and could. . . . There was an elderly couple—the man with a wispy white goatee; his wife with white, yellowing hair tied up in a neat bun—whom I wheeled up to the operating room together on one gurney. She went in first; he was next. Although he had a hole through his hand the size of a Ping-Pong ball, he asked for local anesthesia so he could tend his wife and guard their handkerchief stash of savings. There was a wounded mother and her two wounded children; despite her own pain, she comforted her children continually and told them not to cry as I dressed their ghastly wounds. The littler toddler couldn't help it and shrieked, *"Máy bay"* ("Airplane") again and again until I was ashamed to be alive, to be human, let alone to be an American, to be one of those who had brought the planes to this sad little country ten thousand miles away.

The burned families tried not to bump one another on their beds. Two pretty teenaged girls in thin pajamas tried to comfort their old father who had a plastic pipe of some kind stuck into his throat. I remember each girl climbing up on his bed and pressing against him, and one even throwing a leg over him to keep him warm, as he complained of being cold, as he slowly died, as they held him. Two shoeshine boys—twelve-year-old kids that I remembered from the bunch that slept out on the sidewalk near the Golden Pearl restaurant—both with lacerated legs, hobbled along, each trying to be brave and hold the other up.

I remember these few innocent souls out of that sea of misery, as well as the ceaseless calls to look after a brother, a son, a sister, a mother. These echoes and images will replay in my head forever: trying to shut the eyes of a man who died alone only to find the lids already stiff with rigor mortis; a calf severed to the bared bone; a dull needle bending as a surgeon drilled through a screaming man's shin; the blood spattering off the operating table onto the fouled, slippery floor; a monstrous glass tube shoved up into a man's thigh until the surgeon's hand and fist were buried in the flesh as he flushed out the cavernous hole with hydrogen peroxide; the hideous fizzing of peroxide as it was poured over a woman's back perforated like a cheese; the cries, the groans, the sudden sucking of air in startled pain as a wound was probed; and finally the blood leaking back up through a sodden mattress that I had set out with others in the sun to dry, as I pressed my palm to see if it could be used yet.

What collective karma, what shared fate, could Ong Troi have been weighing to have judged these innocent people so harshly? An elderly intellectual once told me that the war was the Vietnamese punishment for their destruction of the Khmer and Champa kingdoms centuries before. But for me, after Tet, no philosophy or ideology—least of all, crusading American democracy—could justify or even remotely explain the slaughter of those civilians. From that day on, I had no facts or beliefs except for what had been done to those people.

At evening when I had a break, I recorded these events in my notebook as if it were a duty, as if having an account of the horrors could somehow mitigate them, keep them from consuming me, and bear them witness. But for twenty years now, I have kept these notebooks sealed shut, and it is clear why: their contents are unbearable, and no testimony will ever help those victims. Now, forty-five years old, as maple seeds spiral past my attic window, I weep as I write this. Weep for Mr. Long, whose young wife went blind and crazy before she died a slow death with a head full of slivers, weep for the deafened boy who suffered alone without his parents, weep for the beautiful little girl who would lose her burned arm, weep for her napalmed mother, who would probably die or survive as a monster.

Twenty years ago, during Tet Mau Than, such tears would have seemed to me an obscene personal luxury in the presence of those wretched people. Tears would have rendered me useless: if I had begun weeping then, I could not have stopped.

But today is a sunny August afternoon in 1989. Later, when I have finished writing this part of my séance with

remembrance, I will go downstairs to help my wife organize our daughter's birthday party. Our daughter is four.
Hers is a world of play with screamy girlfriends under a
bright sky and sheltering elms strung with paper lanterns,
where locusts drone through the hot afternoon and katy-
dids and crickets will sing throughout the night. Today,
according to her usual whims, she will be Bambi, Thum-
belina, a "bad gorilla," or a wild puppy in the forest.
Physical tragedy for her and her little friends is a skinned
knee or a splinter in a thumb. When I watch her play, I
am constantly awed by her beauty and perfect health. She
has no idea how much the sight of her restores me, how
often her gay little voice summons me out of the murmurs
of the past into her happy world, how much rescue she
has in her little hand as she pulls me around town.

8

JOINING THE VICTIMS

*John Balaban, 24, . . . pointed out that there were
simply not enough beds in the hospital. "These mattresses," he said, "are like sponges. Literally like
sponges. You put your fist into them and they run
blood."* —Newsweek, February 19, 1968

The battle outside the hospital continued to
grow noisier and closer. At one point, there were so many
bullets zinging above the compound wall into the tops of
the Quonset wards that our Green Beret guardians called
a halt to operating and moved us all—that is, all the Americans—into the nunnery where up on the second floor we
watched the battle from the windows as the sisters with-
drew quietly together to the far side of their dormitory. I
remember nearly jumping out of my skin at the pop of a
C-ration can behind my back when the Cobras roared off
their rockets not more than a hundred feet above and the
gunships joined the Skyraiders walloping the university.
The nuns were making bandages; now one stopped to pray
with her rosary. Meanwhile, the Green Beret officer in
charge was on his radio with his home base at the airfield.
Finally, he put down his phone and said we were moving

out, that we were to line up our vehicles behind the main gate to make a six-car convoy dash to the airfield outside of town. Hintze, Seraile, and I—along with Mert Perry, the portly, genial *Newsweek* bureau chief who had somehow managed to get to Can Tho—all had no place to go, so we filed out behind the others toward the parked vehicles.

The Vietnamese gate guard, however, wouldn't open the gates for fear that the combatants outside might decide to rush in and take cover. So we sat there lined up and revving our engines while the sullen guard got yelled at by the soldiers. Then Hintze, who spoke Vietnamese well, tried to reason with the guard, calling to him from behind the steering wheel of our Landrover as Seraile sat squeezed into the small back seat next to Mert Perry and I clutched my greasegun on the passenger side. Finally, a Green Beret got out of his jeep and walked up to the guard, drew his .45 pistol, and put it to the man's head.

"Oh, shit," Roger said, but even before he could finish his sentence, the gate guard was cranking his windlass and rolling open the huge gates. As the first jeep shot forward, the noise of the street battle roared into the compound.

We were the last to get out, Seraile and I yelling, "Go! Go! Go!," as the ancient engine shuddered from the huge goose of gas that Hintze had given the carburetor, flooding it so that we were momentarily left behind until the engine finally coughed, and caught. Just as we rocked forward, chasing after the convoy amid a hail of fire, a pregnant wretch flailed and waddled toward the open gate, only to go down in the gunfire.

"Let's just pray she just stumbled," I said as we raced after the convoy heading to the airfield. We didn't have much choice. We couldn't stop and we had no place to go that night. The IVS houses were now in the war zone. The city was falling.

The main entrance to the airfield was blocked. A tank sat off to one side of the road, just at the edge of one of the mine fields that flanked the long entrance road behind strings of barbed wire. Signs painted with skull-and-cross-bones and "EXPLOSIVES" in Vietnamese and English stippled the fields. For the first time in days, I felt safe.

Mert Perry already had digs in the officers' quarters. The Officer of the Day put the three of us in with enlisted men, and we were given bunks, towels, soap, and shaving kits. We had hot-water showers. Then we had a hot meal of mashed potatoes and commissary beef; then beers at the noncom bar. Seraile joked that we should have been admitted to the officers' bar, like Mert Perry. We were giddy. We were safe. Safe. But in the mirror of the men's room, I looked strange to myself. It was more than the Vietnamese-tailored shirt or the funky, baggy blue trousers that Chanh had loaned me and which rode above my ankles; it was more than the three sleepless days. Back in the barracks, where I had just shaved off three days' growth of beard, I had found that *my eyes* looked strange. I suppose it was all the adrenalin and epinephrine that had pumped past them. I had an enormously *startled* look that was so strange that I found myself going back to the mirror to look at myself again and again.

When night fell, and the flares went up, Hintze and Seraile, who also hadn't slept in days, crawled into their bunks. I was too jittery, so I left them to sleep and went over to a sandbagged bunker where a black-and-white World War II film was being shown to about twenty soldiers in full battle gear. They sat crouched on board benches, their helmets capping their M-16s which they gripped upright between their hands and knees. Outside, beyond the air terminal, the base howitzers began pounding the darkness.

Down in the bunker, with the projector clackety-clacking through the frames of the film and with the small-arms fire picking up outside, the movie wasn't much of a success. It was one of those hard Iwo Jima–type films with Broderick Crawford as the platoon sergeant cradling one dying American youngster after another as the Japanese

advanced ruthlessly through the thickets on a Pacific island.
One by one, the soldiers sitting around me got up, scraped
their boots across the cement floor, gritty with sand from
leaky bags, and left without a word. Finally, it was just
me and the projectionist. "You want to see this?" he asked.
"Nah," I said, and got up to leave as he flicked off the
projection light and rewound. "Bad timing," I added,
looking back in before mounting the munition-box stairs.
"Christ," was all he said.

From the movie bunker, I wandered outside through a
light drizzle over to the radio room, not sure if I'd be let
into a military inner sanctum like that, but curious to get
the real lowdown, I poked my head in.

"C'mon in." A man in a green T-shirt, his leg in a huge
cast propped up on a desk, motioned me in.

"Hi," I said. Next to his leg, laid out on the desktop,
were two grenades, an M-16, and a .45 Colt pistol. "Expecting trouble?"

He laughed and pointed to a chair. All around his desk,
various radios squawked off and on as, the guy explained,
the radios all around the base perimeter called in every few
minutes to give their reports. "Listen to that," he said.

I tried to listen, but it was just a blur of static-roughened
voices and code words. "What's it mean?"

"You CIA or what?"

"Oh, no, I teach at the university."

He considered the complete unlikelihood of this, and
then, in the spirit of fuck-it-anything's-possible-in-
Vietnam-and-anyway-we're-all-Americans, he answered
my first question. "It means, professor, that they're coming in tonight," adding when I didn't seem to grasp this,
"the fucking *North Vietnamese,* the regular army; they're
going to overrun us."

"How do you know that?" I was aghast. I had come to
the place of last resort and it was under siege.

"Well, we *counted* them," he said. "Christ, they must
have a thousand troops out there. They can take us or the

town. Dealer's choice. Maybe take both. Damn!" He pulled out a desk drawer and then slammed it back in. "Why did that little dink have to break my leg?"

"How's that?" Whatever sense of security I had regained had now vanished. My last obstacle to reaching safety, I had thought, was getting *to* the Can Tho air base. Now it seemed that I had to figure out how to get off it.

"This dumb little slope ran a backhoe up onto my leg. Broke it. *Broke* it, and now we're gonna get VC coming through the windows. But let me tell you," he said, his voice becoming softer and even a bit sly as he pointed to his little armory laid out on the desktop by his broken leg, "I'm gonna take a few of them with me."

Just then one of the radios crackled with a message from the berm. I still couldn't make out what was said, but the radioman consulted a map and a sheet of numbers and told the guy to pull his squad back to another position. "See?" he said, turning back to me.

"Well, no, really. Can't the base defend itself? I mean, it's the biggest in the Delta."

He pointed up to the ceiling and looked at me knowingly. "No Spooky," he said. "No Spooky, no show."

He finally explained that because of the low cloud cover, the Air Force gunship currently circling the field—known variously as The Dragonship, or Puff the Magic Dragon, or simply as Spooky, and especially equipped with banks of automatic 7.62mm guns that each could fire 6000 rounds per minute—that this incredible death machine couldn't see the ground to fire. Without it, the sheer, surprising numbers of massed regular troops could not be stopped by the base defenses. Even the mortars and the howitzers, which were apparently now leveled to the ground and firing straight off the perimeters, could not stop them.

When I finally grasped what he was saying, I realized he wasn't talking melodramatically about taking a few of "them" with him. He expected to die.

"You got any paper?" I asked. He tore off a sheet from

his pad and shoved it across the desk. I picked up a pen
and wrote:

> TO WHOM IT MAY CONCERN:
> I, John Balaban, have no regrets for what I've done.
> I wish the world well. Stop the goddamn war.

I realized my message didn't make a lot of sense, but I
tried anyway to figure out someplace I could put it that
wouldn't be covered in blood. My recent hospital experience suggested the fatty tissue of the buttocks, so I shoved
it in my left back pocket, thinking that the North Vietnamese troops might likely take my wallet in the right and
the watch off my wrist but wouldn't bother about a piece
of paper.

"You take care," I told the radioman. "I'll go pray for
moonlight."

"Do that."

Outside the radio room, I ran into Michael Herr whom
Mert Perry had pointed out to me earlier and whose *Esquire*
pieces I had read and much admired. I introduced myself
and told him what I had just learned. Herr, overweight
and sweating, his glasses a bit steamed, dressed in fatigues
and carrying an M-16, said he knew. He had just come
from the berm and was going out again.

"What are you going to do?"

"Fight."

"But you're a reporter."

"When it comes down to it, you're an American."

I wished him good luck as he headed back out to the
perimeter, but wasn't certain what he meant by his ob-
servation: Stand and fight like an American; or, It couldn't
matter less to the North Vietnamese whether I'm a reporter
or a soldier. Either way, it wasn't my idea of how to handle
the situation. I intended to go wake Seraile and Hintze and
tell them what was happening. Then, figuring that those
who had to defend a perimeter, a tower, a piece of artillery,
a radio, or whatever, were the most likely to be killed, I

decided to wait until the attack came and in the mayhem
get off the base by squeezing along the watery ditch between the base road and the mine fields, like a muskrat
with a machine gun, until I got down to the entrance gate
which was in the opposite direction from the airfield and
the attack. Then I would somehow get across the road and
flee into the nearby village and gardens where I hoped to
find a place to hide out until dawn.

Hintze and Seraile didn't think much of my plan. I remember Roger sitting up sleepily in his bunk and saying,
"Well, good luck," and going back to sleep.

About an hour later, the attack came with a barrage of
mortars, the stutter and slap of small arms, and the boom-
ings of the howitzers. When it seemed clear from the noise
that one of the perimeters was falling, I edged through the
bunkers and Quonset huts toward the entrance road,
armed with my greasegun and shaving kit of grenades. I
waited there for about an hour, listening to the battle as
the base perimeters seemed to hold. Then the clouds broke
and, as the moon shone through, the Dragonship belched
off its banks of guns—sixty rounds a second, every fourth
a tracer—so that streams of wavy red lightning crackled
from the sky to the earth in a deafening growl. And then,
between the bursts of small arms, the popping of trip flares,
the crash of mortars, the slams of grenade launchers, and
the animal roaring of the gunship, I could hear the cheers
of soldiers who knew their lives were saved, heard them
hooting lusty rebel yells for the deathship sweeping the
battlefield with a slow, pulverizing plasma of bullets that
stopped the North Vietnamese advance, ending the battle
for the night.

In the morning, before heading back to the hospital, we
stopped for a moment to see the dead enemy soldiers being
pulled off the berm wires.

We got lunch that day at the MACV compound, which
had been shot up pretty badly the previous night when the
North Vietnamese, stopped by the Dragonship, simply

deflected their attack into the town. In the mess hall, we
wondered how Chanh had been doing since our last night
together at the IVS house. After lunch, Hintze and I
sneaked some food from the mess, dropped Bill off at the
hospital, and went back to the IVS house to find Chanh.
Chanh wasn't there. Indeed, the house itself wasn't all
there. The inside had been ransacked by Saigon troops.
Outside, the stucco wall, the roof, and the back side of
the building had been gouged, pocked, and sprayed with
a mulch of earth and shrapnel. The house, obviously, had
taken some close hits in the previous day's fight for the
now destroyed university buildings. One of our neighbors
told us that Chanh was holed up in the downtown garage
where he had taken our Scout. At that point in the fighting,
any Vietnamese adult male out on the street and not in
uniform was likely to get shot.

We drove over to the garage. Hintze kept the Landrover
running out on the main street while I got out with
some ham-and-cheese sandwiches. Things were quieter
throughout the city. The real fighting now raged in the
outskirts by Cai Rang, where the U.S. Air Force was
strafing the retreating Viet Cong and North Vietnamese.
In town, the Saigon troops, who had failed to engage the
attackers seriously except when directly assaulted, had
taken cover behind sandbagged gun placements in dead
public fountains or behind the ammo-box-and-barbed-
wire barricades they had thrown up along the streets. At
high noon, I was sure I could be recognized as an American, especially with the Landrover parked nearby, so I felt
safe and left my gun on the car seat while Roger watched
the street and remained ready to get us out of there in a
hurry.

As I stepped away from the Landrover, I saw Chanh
and his mechanic pals watching me through the accordion
metal grille that fronted the garage. In fact, it was their
faces suddenly flexed in a moment of shock that first told
me that *something was happening* as I pitched forward with

a wink of pain in my left shoulder. Suddenly and soundlessly something had hit me from behind, knocking me
down onto the dusty surface of the main boulevard.
Hintze, who must have been looking the other way when
it happened, now leaned over to call out to me through
the slide window of the passenger side, "You okay?"
He must have thought I had stumbled.
We were both perplexed. It seemed so stupid, my lying
there in the road.
"Yeah," I said, "stay with the car. I'm okay." But now
it felt as if I had an ice pick in my shoulder.
I had a hard time getting up. The men in the garage did
not come out but kept calling and waving in that hand-
flapping-down way. They called from the cool dark shade
and seemed very far away. I was now on my knees in the
glare of the noonday sun, feeling flushed and nauseated.
Then I reached behind and touched my shoulder. My fingers came back smeared with blood. I looked around for
whoever had shot me, but saw no one, just the crowd of
refugees milling before the gate of the Cambodian temple across the boulevard, a crowd that did not seem to
notice my mishap. There had been no report, no blast. I
struggled up and had gotten to the sharp edge of shadow
cast by the garage's tin roof when Chanh came out to pull
me in.
"What happen, John?"
"I don't know," I answered dizzily.
"You shot," Chanh said as he sat me down on an old
Citroën's running boad. I took off my shirt, and they all
looked at my shoulder. Outside, a mangy dog was lapping
up the sandwiches, meat and cheese first, then the white
bread, and, finally, nosing the wax-paper wrapper. For
some reason, this really distressed me. I couldn't sort out
what to worry about, and when Roger came in, forgetting
the guns in the car, I got upset about that.
I can't remember why Roger didn't drive me back to
the hospital. I guess because it was still lunch hour, as odd

as that sounds. Instead, I was treated at a U.S. Army post in town. "3 Feb. 68," my medical report says:

> 24 yr old civilian—teaches at Univ. here in Can Tho sustained frag wound L post shoulder at 1345 today. 1x1 cm entry wound L post shoulder—no exit wound. Wound opened—packed—tract ¾ inch deep—no frag found. We have no x ray—chest clear—no dispura—I don't think it penetrated.
> Pt. trying to get to Saigon.
> Rx 1 iodoform pack
>   2 0.5cc T.T.
>   3 May need chest x ray in Saigon
>   4 Darvon compd 65

Later, back in the civilian hospital's darkened X-ray room, against the ghost-light image aglow with my lungs and vertebrae, I saw a curved fleck, a sharp sliver, a tiny scimitar, something like a bitten-off fingernail, lodged against my shoulder bone. The best guess, given its shape and the silence that attended its flight to me, was that a snippet from a cluster bomb that had been dropped on the outskirts of town, almost spent, had nevertheless strayed my way, as if to remind me of the pure cheekiness of standing close to so much pain and death and expecting I would come out whole; as if to nudge me still closer to Gitelson and to the ordinary folk who suffered in the hospital or who died on the roads before they ever got there, the *bụi dời,* the dust of life blown about in the crossfire. It was as if Death had taken a step closer to whisper in my ear, to say: My young American friend, my little do-gooder, do you think you are less dear to me than the smallest child? This is what I have done to you. You know I could do more.

9

THE ARROW
THAT FLIETH BY DAY

*Thou shalt not be afraid for the terror by night; nor
for the arrow that flieth by day.* —*Psalm 91*

The next day, with the fighting well off in the
distance, my shoulder lumped with bandages under my
shirt, my one arm in a sling and the other toting a flight
bag sagging with my two grenades, the greasegun with
its wire stock folded down, the clips taken out but handy,
one round in the chamber, and the safety on, I was once
more trudging down a nearly empty Vietnamese road
under a heavy sun, feeling a bit nauseated by antibiotics,
tetanus shot, and Darvon. *Đi ra một ngày*—"Go out one
day"—and good luck, motherfucker. Again I was on my
way to the airport. This time I was going home. The
university was bombed, and I was out of a job. Even if
IVS reassigned me to teaching English in some high school
or helping refugees, I didn't want any part of it. All that,
I figured—now one radical step beyond Gitelson in my
sense of humane service—was just part of the war effort.
As I hiked down that road in the hot sun, my only goal
was to get to Saigon, get out of Vietnam, and go home
to join the antiwar effort. But I still had a Selective Service

obligation to complete. A few months earlier, I had ex-
changed letters with a private group calling itself the Committee of Responsibility, which had begún a relief program
for war-injured Vietnamese children who needed long-
term care in the United States. A first group of children
had already gone to the hospitals in Boston and Berkeley.
To continue, COR needed Vietnamese-speaking field representatives to assist their doctors in evacuations. If I could,
I'd return to Vietnam to work out the rest of my military
obligation for COR; if I couldn't, I'd work for the antiwar
movement until the FBI came to arrest me for dodging
the last year of my obligation. Then I would go to live in
Europe. Forget jail. Screw carrying bedpans in a VA hospital. To hell with Canada.

My shoulder wound, a fairly large hole packed with a
gauze wick that I was supposed to pull out a little each day
in order to keep the puncture from closing, now seemed
a lucky stab of fate from Mr. Sky. To my fellow Americans, the injury had changed my identity, as if I had earned
some merit badge. Automatically I was transformed from
an unobserved witness to the war to The Guy Who Got
It, a player. Now I hoped the wound was excuse enough
to send me home. It ached, but not badly. It looked worse
than it was, and I was happy for that. More than the nun's
Red Cross patch, which I still wore on my sleeve, it seemed
a right symbol of my state of spirit.

Despite my arm sling, none of the jeeps barreling up
the road stopped to give me a ride. I walked the whole
way, feeling a bit pukey, but determined to get out of Can
Tho. Down by the base's main gate, the ARVN were still
in their tank. Up ahead, I could hear backhoes and dump
trucks cleaning up the mortar debris. As I walked past
bunkers, ripped-up sheds, and the radio room, I wondered
about the radioman, but continued on into the deserted
civilian terminal, on top of which perched the control
tower. The door to the tower was locked from the inside,
and after banging on it for a while, I just sat on the steps

until someone came out; I brushed by him and headed up the stairs.

The two guys in charge told me that nothing had gone in or out the whole day. Their air conditioning was dead, and the glassed-in tower was as hot as a greenhouse even though one of the big windows had been blasted out. Out on a parapet beyond that window, I saw some Marine sharpshooters in olive-drab T-shirts and baggy o.d. trousers, taking turns at a big scope set on a tripod.

"What do you see?" I asked as I moved out into the sunlight and fresher air.

"VC, on that roof." He pointed far off to the edge of town. Another guy, his rifle resting on a sandbag set on the two-foot parapet, was now looking through his rifle scope.

"How can you tell it's VC?"

The first guy, maybe nineteen years old, looked at me as if I were stupid. "What would anybody be doing up on a roof during *this?*" He noted my arm in a sling and turned away.

"Washing clothes? Hanging them up?" I suggested. *This,* after all, was pretty much over. But who could say? Maybe it was a sniper looking at us through his scope. Anyway, the young Marines soon lost their target and started packing up their gear. Maybe I had ruined their fun. Anyway, now I was alone up there with the traffic controllers. I was nauseated and hungry. Hours passed. Nothing flew in that day and nothing flew out, so finally I went down and waited at the Air Force gate to hitch a ride back to town.

I did get out the next day on an Otter carrying some CIA agents and their manacled prisoner. I sat close to the guy, a man who was perhaps thirty-five or forty years old. He said nothing during the whole flight, did not look around or try to engage his captors in any way. His eyes were nearly sealed shut by puffy bruises.

Only when they were leading him off the tarmac in

Saigon did I have the nerve to say anything to him: *"Chúc
may mắn,"* "Good luck." Even then he did not look at
me, but one of the agents frowned as they hustled him
away.

After about a week in Saigon, IVS agreed to let me go
home and even wrote a letter to my draft board explaining
that I would be soon seeking other alternative service but
that I would need at least a month to recuperate. Yvonne
Whitfield, our new team leader's calm, sweet wife, was a
nurse; every couple of days—up on our compound's deck
where I slept a lot in a lawn chair and read Céline's *Journey
to the End of the Night,* whose first two parts on the
wretchedness of war and the tropics suited my mood while
I waited for commercial flights to resume—Yvonne pulled
out the wick and daubed the wound with antiseptic.

IVS had not fared too badly in the offensive, for a lot
of volunteers had taken their vacations at Tet and were in
Hong Kong, Bangkok, or Tokyo. Nobody was killed,
although several were missing in Hue, including some
friends, Sandra Johnson and Steve Erhart. Sandra, along
with her Quaker doctor friend, Marjorie Nelson, was taken
away during the fighting by the North Vietnamese troops.
Erhart had fled from house to house until his student
friends finally told him that they did not dare hide him
any longer. He spent the last few days of the battle for
Hue under constant siege in an old French fort held by the
ARVN. The USAID advisers had not been so lucky; almost all of them had been bound and shot in the overrun
MACV compound.

My parents, to my horror, had been sent a telegram
saying I was "wounded and missing." When I got to Saigon, I called them from the international phones over at
the downtown USO. My mother cried, "Oh, Johnny.
Johnny," before handing the phone over to my dad, to
whom I gave a lot of friends' home numbers so he could
relay to their parents the news that their children were safe.

Then, finally, Pan Am opened up a flight, and I was gone.

Psalm 91 was handed to us on a printed card, passed out by all-American stewardesses easing down the aisle like Cadillacs, as our plane leveled off from Tan Son Nhut on the way to Japan. Around me were a few lifers—rubbery, fat sergeants—but mostly the seats were filled with bony, uniformed boys whose big ears sprouted out from their shaved heads. Some were going home; some were going to R&R in Japan. You could tell the Saigon soldiers from the field troops. Support troops in Vietnam outnumbered combat soldiers by seven to one and the faces of these rear-echelon GIs, though pimply, were shiny and clean. They talked more. The field troops, by contrast, were fairly silent. They slumped deeper into their seats, and their flesh had a dirty hue that went deep into their pores, a jungle grime so sweated in that it would take more than a week of hot soapy water to soak it out. A lifetime, perhaps. Some of them were asleep. One guy just stared at the seat in front of him, not even acknowledging the Psalm in the perfumed hand of the girl in the aisle. Still others took the card, read it politely, then tucked it away. A few turned it over to read further about "a British regiment under the command of Col. Whitelesey, which served in the World War for more than four years without losing a man. This unparalleled record," continued the bizarre message, "was made possible by means of active cooperation of officers and men in memorizing and repeating regularly the words of the 91st Psalm which has been called the Psalm of Protection."

These poor guys, I thought—here in innocence, here out of ignorance, here out of patriotism or out of family honor—day after day, until their tours are up, they are sent off in tanks, in choppers, in boats, and on foot to kill people, mostly civilians, mostly children. All of them are asked to sanction such killing, to say it's all right. They

see their friends get killed or fall maimed and they finally
board a plane to Yokohama and a gorgeous American girl
hands them a card that suggests that, when they get back
to Vietnam, if they are Christian enough, they won't die
or be disfigured for life, but will be *delivered* by faith and
rote memorization from "the pestilence that walketh in
darkness . . . the destruction that wasteth at noonday." It
struck me that the powers waging this war could make
even the Bible obscene.

Covered with a wool blanket in the shock of air conditioning, I sat in my seat, drinking a glass of red wine,
watching Elvis Presley on the screen as a happy-go-lucky
frogman diving for treasure in *Easy Come, Easy Go.* My
horoscope, divined by Stella in the Saigon *Post,* said, "You
know how to pick yourself up from disaster and carry
on." I preferred it to the Psalm.

Above: The ferry at Long Xuyen where David Gitelson was last seen alive.
Below: The university at Can Tho after the Tet Offensive, February 1968.

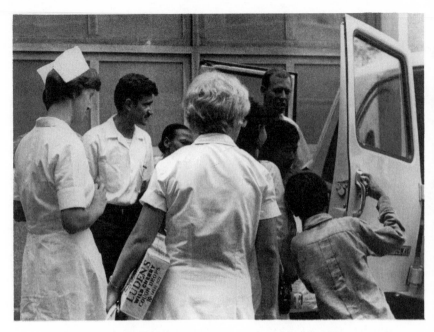

Above: Dick Berliner and I with British nurses preparing an evacuation from Nhi Dong Children's Hospital, 1969. *Below:* At Nhi Dong Children's Hospital with Nguyen Thi Bong.

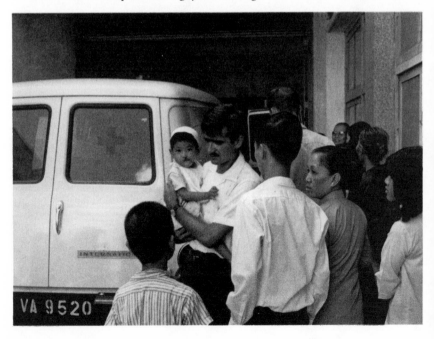

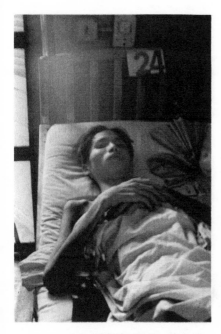
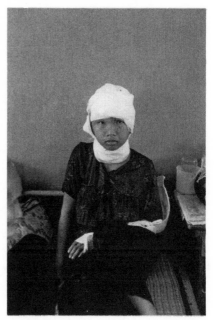

Above left: Huynh Van Tien, the Viet Cong boy who never made it to the United States, a month before his death in 1968. *Above right:* Dao Thi Thai waiting in the Can Tho hospital for evacuation to Boston, 1968. *Below:* Dao Thi Thai, twenty years after her stay in Boston.

Right: Mary Bui Thi Khuy in 1969,
holding a friend's baby. *Below left:*
Pham Thi Huong and her mother
in the Danang Regional Hospital,
June 1969. *Below right:* Pham Thi
Huong in 1989.

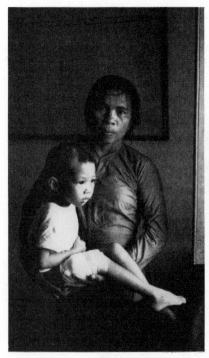

Above: Lonnie Balaban and Twiggy on the Mekong, October 1971.
Below: Twiggy and Steve Erhart waiting for the Mekong ferry.

Above left: Jerry Liles on Phoenix Island, October 1971. *Above right:* Steve Erhart and I on the Phoenix Island dock. *Below:* Prayer circle at Phoenix Island, 1971.

Above: The Coconut Monk in 1968. *Left:* An invitation to the Coconut Monk's Peace Talks Conference Table at Phoenix Island, Nine Dragons River.

Above left: Sister Lien-Huong preparing to sing *ca dao*. *Above right:* On the way to meeting Dao Thi Thai, Mekong Delta, 1989. *Below:* At Tran Hung Dao's temple in Hanoi, 1989.

PART TWO

CALLING
THE WANDERING
SOULS

THE COMMITTEE
OF RESPONSIBILITY
TO SAVE WAR-BURNED
AND WAR-INJURED CHILDREN

10

DOING GOOD

I flew on to San Francisco where I was met
at the airport by Madeline Duckles, a tall, middle-aged
woman who was one of the West Coast organizers of the
Committee of Responsibility ("to Save War-Burned and
War-Injured Children" completed its rather extraordinary
name), which, she said as we walked to her car, had agreed
to interview me later in Boston for their field representative's job. This was a special day, Mrs. Duckles said, both
for her and for her husband, Vincent, a Berkeley musi-
cologist. Their five sons, some with their wives and babies,
were home for the first time in years, and they were having
a celebration that evening. In fact, she added, as she gunned
the engine of her Karman Ghia convertible and her long
gray-streaked auburn hair unwound in the wind, we had
to get home right away so she could bake the huge sea
bass that stared up with a cold walleye from a tray that
filled most of the back seat. As we barreled down the
freeway, zoomed across the Bay Bridge, and then maneuvered through Berkeley streets into the surrounding hills,
I was stunned by a realization: *not everyone was preoccupied
with the war*. All about, leggy girls and boys in tennis whites
were dallying at sports and hanging out. In the offices,
people were at work as usual. Others were getting their

hair done, their cars washed, their kids' teeth braced. Multitudes, I imagined, were calling their boyfriends, their girlfriends, their ex-wives. Many were probably bored and thinking about vacations. In other words, I realized that life was going on as usual in the United States. Indeed, the person I was riding with was likely one of few individuals willing to interrupt her routine to acknowledge the war. Since life-as-usual had ended for me in the Can Tho hospital, these routine pursuits unfolding in the cool, fresh, eucalyptus-scented splendor of West Coast sunlight were a disorienting fiction that made me angry. The ordinary pleasures of Americans now seemed to me improper.

I felt no less disoriented at meeting the Duckles boys, the shortest of whom was six feet five and still growing. Over the past seven months, I had grown used to standing a bit taller than the Vietnamese; now, as I reached up to shake hands with these behemoths, I felt like Gulliver among the Brobdingnagians. It was all so odd. The sense of estrangement I'd felt in Vietnam was beginning to intensify in my native land.

But that evening after dinner, when we went downstairs to the Duckleses' music room and the boys took their violins, viola, and cello out of their cases to join their gentle (albeit huge) father at the piano in Schubert and Brahms, I was overwhelmed by an utterly contrary sense of finally having found friends as the matchstick instruments sang in their giant hands and they accompanied their father at the piano. Even if I were never to see these people again, I reckoned, their talents and their upbringing seemed to hold an energy—a civilized American energy—that was sane, whole, and generative, and not only contrary to the American-made horror I had traveled from, but indeed curative to that horror, at least curative to me.

Soon I was to encounter numbers of such people and my initial culture shock, my weird lonesomeness, my damaged sense of other Americans began to ease. In the next few weeks, as I traveled home to Philadelphia and

then to Boston to meet the COR Board of Directors, I
was fortified in this sense of no longer being alone, of no
longer being the odd man out, or of feeling like some kind
of accusing, moral spy, an outcast to my own countrymen. "Balaban," I had been recently told by a CORDS
official as he tried to decide what was wrong with me,
"you're not a team player." Well, not on *his* team. Instead,
I found other Americans I could admire. Herbert Needleman, the child psychiatrist who presided over COR, put
me up at his home and we went to work together
at Temple University Hospital, where I typed up a description of the civilian scene at the Can Tho hospital. I
was dead broke and think I would have cracked up if,
at twenty-four, I had gone home to live with my parents after what I had just gone through, so I ended up
living and eating with the Needlemans. Needleman's colleague John Hall, the Chief of Orthopedic Surgery at
Temple, looked at my shoulder wound for free, and a
cardiologist, another COR doctor, Harold Rutenberg, sent
me in for lab tests which indicated that my skinniness
and exhaustion were at least partially due to amoebic
parasites.

Two weeks later, up in Boston before the COR Board
meeting, I wandered old Harvard haunts with Vida Ches-
nulis, my brainy, good-looking former classmate. We visited the Fogg and Gardner museums; looked in on
Professor Whiting, our crusty, wonderful Chaucerian; and
went to a reading by another former teacher, John Barth,
who afterward invited us along to a party. Finally, before
saying goodbye, we drove to Walden Pond and Crane's
Beach, where the woods and the dunes were steeped in
snow. As we talked, and I tried to explain what I had seen,
all the words that had been choked inside me began to
pour out. "Only I am come back to tell you all," says the
proverbial returner in our literature, and I think that at
that moment in my life, as I met these new and old friends,
I was never more filled with the power of the books I had

once studied, never more filled with the value of friends. Instead of feeling mute and locked up in a ward in Can Tho, I felt rescued.

COR was my means of extending that rescue to others. Its Board of Directors, consisting mostly of professors of medicine, men and women distinguished for their advancement of humane science, included Albert Sabin, Benjamin Spock, Helen Brooks-Taussig, and Albert Szent-Györgyi, among others. They had an interesting plan: to bring to the United States those children whose war injuries were so extensive that they could not be treated in the abattoir wards of Vietnam. The very presence of these injured children, the Board believed, would be so upsetting to Americans that a grass-roots antiwar effort would spring up in the cities where these children were to be treated. Naïve as this now sounds, the plan reflected an implicit faith in the goodness of Americans.

I agreed to return to Vietnam as soon as my shoulder healed. Since the street fighting continued to flare, I was a bit nervous. In late February, I learned from Clyde Coreil—still marooned in Saigon, because Hue was being retaken, house by house, by the U.S. Marines—that all the province capitals in the Mekong Delta, as well as Tan Son Nhut air base in Saigon, had been hit again. Nonetheless, on March 25, six weeks after I had left Vietnam forever, buoyed by a sense of purpose, I flew into Tan Son Nhut. Earlier events had been thrust on me, but whatever was now heading my way was of my own choosing. I was reminded once again by *The Tale of Kieu* that "happiness or misfortune are prescribed by the law of Heaven, but their source comes from ourselves." I was choosing my fate. It was a powerful feeling.

COR, I quickly found, was one of the smallest of the hundreds of foreign voluntary agencies operating in Vietnam. There were medical teams of French, English, Swiss, Germans, Japanese, Iranians, Spanish, Filipinos,

Koreans, and a group from UNESCO. There were also Quakers, Baptists, Seventh-Day Adventists, Mennonites, Brethren, and all kinds of Catholics, all purportedly doing good in some direct way by building hospitals and clinics, training nurses and doctors, doing specialized surgeries on brains, bones, eyes, and skins, making prosthetic limbs, and giving away blankets, foods, vitamins, maternity kits, surgical equipment, clothing, vaccines, and medicines. Some, like the Quakers, Mennonites, and Seventh-Day Adventists, had come to stay in substantial, long-term programs; most, however, came for a short look and a charitable gesture. Many of these organizations, in fact, did nothing. Some perhaps even did some harm. There were AMA volunteers who had come to experiment at surgical procedures they wouldn't dare perform on Americans; USAID boozers who came to escape rotten marriages; a French priest who finagled a law (in this country of Buddhists) that would allow relief supplies to be handled only by Catholics. Among the do-gooders I encountered were a sad, heat-bedraggled Englishwoman who hung around orphanages to cradle dying children; a Quaker who had come to adopt orphans for American families but who spent himself tongue-lashing sullen bureaucrats until they froze him out of the country; and a Baptist missionary who preached relentless anticommunism to his captive leper fiefdom near Danang. And, of course, there were also the campaigning hawks and doves who spent their obligatory week in Saigon so they could summon the cameras when they arrived back home. For the South Vietnamese population of some sixteen million, there were two hundred Vietnamese doctors, most of them either in the military or in exorbitantly priced private practices—in other words, nearly all of them out of reach of the thousands of civilian casualties that were occurring each month. Doing good in this morass was not going to be easy.

The previous COR visits to Vietnam had been explor-

atory, and only a half-dozen or so children were now waiting in Saigon hospitals on their way to the States. For my
first few weeks, I began each day by hopping on my Lambretta and taking a couple of raw eggs across town to Nhi
Dong Children's Hospital where one of our boys was so
shot full of holes that his doctors feared he'd die of protein
loss before his evacuation. While waiting for our first COR
doctor to arrive from Boston, I began setting up some
semblance of an office with Dick Berliner, the other new
field representative, who had also come from IVS and
knew his way around Saigon and the government bureaus.
With his sandy hair already thinning, his slow, deep voice,
and his fairly fluent Vietnamese, Berliner had a positive
effect on the families and bureaucrats that we dealt with.
I was far more on edge, far angrier, and not nearly as good
with the language, yet somehow we were complementary
and effective, although once I ragged him so bad he
punched me. (Even at that moment, we both knew our
work was more important than our feelings. His punch,
my holding back my punch, his apology, my acceptance,
and, finally, my apology for my words all transpired in
about sixty seconds.)

We lived and worked out of a warren of rented rooms
in a house down the end of a tiny street in an obscure part
of Saigon, in the same household as eighteen members of
the extended family of Tran Quoc Buu. Mr. Buu was the
head of the trade unions in the South; I could never figure
out if Madame Buu, middle-aged, gold-toothed, and pin-
curlered, was really married to him or if she was his second
wife, his *vợ lẽ*. Anyway, Mr. Buu—either for marital or
security reasons—seemed to live at the trade-union offices
and visited us, or, rather, Madame Buu, sporadically, always arriving in an ancient black chauffeur-driven Citroën
with two bodyguards standing on the running boards,
pistols drawn.

The impending task for Berliner and me was to accompany a COR doctor, who had left his own practice for a

month or more, on visits to province hospitals where we would take case referrals from Vietnamese and foreign physicians. In Boston, Dr. Needleman would then try to find a hospital in the U.S. where specialists could handle the particular problems of each case. When a hospital had been found, we would talk to the children's parents and explain realistically what we could do. Some parents thought, for example, that we could actually grow new legs for their sons and daughters in the United States.

Berliner and I had to explain to them things we ourselves scarcely understood: artificial limbs, tube grafts, pedicle flaps, bone transplants, keloidal scarring, maxillary reconstruction. Neither I nor Dick Berliner ever had much hope that we were realistically understood by these families, who wanted to believe in miracles. Furthermore, for Vietnamese farmers who had glimpsed our electronic armadas and our vast spilling of wealth in Vietnam, Americans were *tài kỹ* and *tài phú,* capable and rich. They thought we could do anything. Their children, however, represented the worst cases—children so badly burned, so ripped up by gunshot and shrapnel, their bones so badly fractured, that no one could pretend they could be treated in South Vietnam. Often our doctors, some of them specialists in surgery, were unable to say for sure if these children could be saved anywhere in the world.

At this point, Berliner and I would write up with the COR physician a description of each child's injuries to present, along with the child, at a special medical examining commission, the Hoi-Dong Giam-Dinh Y-Khoa (HDGDYK), established by the Ministry of Health. After that, we had to complete each dossier with twelve separate forms—some not in duplicate or triplicate but in *nine* copies, each of which we would then have to hand-carry through the various South Vietnamese ministries (or else the papers would never move from one desk to another). Each child's dossier had to include:

one copy of a request for a passport
two copies of a request to leave the country
nine copies of the father's information sheet
nine copies of the mother's information sheet
nine copies of the child's information sheet
two copies of the parental permission form
two copies of the child's birth certificate
six frontal photos
two side photos
two copies of the Ministry of Health's certification

In addition, each child had to have a tax clearance and an exit-tax waiver from the Ministry of Finance. From the Ministry of Defense, if the child was over sixteen years of age, we had to have a security clearance and exit permission.

Then, when all of these forms had been completed and stamped with seals of approval at each ministry, I had to request from the Joint Chiefs of Staff in Washington, D.C., through a Mr. Faircloth at USAID Public Health in Saigon, individual permissions to fly these children out of Vietnam on the special hospital planes that the Air Force used for wounded American soldiers. Our children, Mr. Faircloth often reminded us, flew on "a space-available basis."

To accomplish all the above was next to impossible. American and South Vietnamese authorities were obliged to let COR into Vietnam but had no serious interest in letting us take these rather bad advertisements for the war out of the country.

Each of the forms held an obstacle in it. Many rural Vietnamese, for instance, simply didn't have birth certificates; indeed, most rural people wouldn't have a clue as to their birth dates, let alone their grandparents', which were also required. Sometimes, instead of asking for waivers for these missing details (which of course required other forms and approvals), I just made up the facts. Often I listed the grandparents as dead, so we wouldn't have to try to get biographical data on people no one knew how to reach. About a dozen children magically acquired my own birth date, December 2. Similarly, a general surgeon in Danang, Dr. Phung Tuan Hanh, frustrated by red tape after urging us to take a boy with a severed sciatic nerve, signed as the boy's legal guardian. "It's legal and it's right," Dr. Hanh said, flourishing my pen over the documents; "they are all my children." For every Dr. Hanh, there were ten obstructors. Soon I realized you could go a little nuts in this job.

One oppressively hot afternoon in the Ministry of Interior, as the hair and skin on my arms shone with sweat, my white shirt spattered with tar from the scooter ride through town, my eyes rimmed with exhaust soot, my hair matted to my forehead, I remember thinking I would strangle the next bureaucrat, man or woman, who looked at some child's papers, sucked their teeth, and said, *"Không được,* "No good," without even looking up from the desk. My particular problem that day was a bespectacled little man who had been trained, like most South Vietnamese officials, in the French civil service. I really thought of hitting him, if not strangling him, but of course that was a luxury I couldn't afford. The child whose papers he wouldn't accept had been burned by a white phosphorus artillery shell. Her scalp was bare and burned in patches, her eyelids were partially burned off, and her chin was glued to her neck, permanently yanking down her lower lip and exposing her teeth.

Suddenly I had a bright idea. I reached into my briefcase, took out the girl's photos, and, without saying a word, put them on the desk in front of the man, who had continued to look down at his other papers in the hope that I would go away. For a moment, the man looked at the two photos, front and side. Then he gathered them back up, handed them to me, and, perhaps for the first time in our dealings, really looked at me. His face was a mixture of grief, shame, and nausea. "It's awful," I said, almost feeling guilty for what I had done to him.

"Moment," he said in French, taking back my papers and stamping them approved.

Since I knew the Can Tho hospital and reckoned I was on good terms with the staff there for having volunteered during the Tet Offensive, I convinced the newly arrived COR doctor, Peter Wolff, a child psychiatrist from the Judge Baker Guidance Center in Boston, to take our first referral trip there. Can Tho was the only place outside of Saigon where the Ministry of Health had authorized a medical examining commission and so, I argued, we could cut through at least some of the red tape right at the start of the evacuation process. The Vietnamese hospital director who ran the HDGDYK, Dr. Le Van Khoa, was friendly and invited us to search the wards; the American surgical team, still headed by Major Cruz Hernandez, and now including some civilian volunteers from the AMA's Volunteer Physicians for Vietnam (VPVN) program, was somewhat cool: I was okay with the Air Force surgeons who remembered me from Tet, but it was clear the Americans had already been given a negative fix on COR. Regardless, we toured the wards and considered some eighteen cases ranging in age from three to eighteen, the maximum age for a child under Vietnamese law. These eighteen were children who could not be treated adequately in Vietnam, children whose gunshot and shrapnel wounds had left them with perforated colons, cut Achilles tendons, gaping holes in their buttocks, lacerated arteries and nerves, chunks of missing bone, and pierced eyes. In addition to these cases, we were referred three others by the American surgeons:

• Dao Thi Thai, a fifteen-year-old girl, scalped by boat propeller blades after tumbling into the water during a mortar attack. The incident left her with an exposed skull cap, as well as a fractured humerus in her left arm.
• Ngo Thanh Viet, a fourteen-year-old boy, wounded

by a grenade that left him blind in his left eye and with his retina three-quarters detached in his right. His American ophthalmologist, a Dr. Monohan, warned us that we had only two weeks to save his right eye.

• Chau Quynh, a fifteen-year-old girl of Cambodian ethnic origin who suffered a single gunshot wound to her upper chest that left her paralyzed and without bladder function.

Of the eighteen cases like these, there were only six that Dr. Khoa's HDGDYK permitted us to help. It was as if Dr. Khoa had been given a quota from the Ministry of Health, but since the Vietnamese HDGDYK had the first and final say, if a child was turned down by the medical examining commission, there was nothing COR could do about it. So, for some of those denied evacuation, we arranged referrals to the Cho Ray and Nhi Dong hospitals, where Japanese and British surgical teams were prepared to take on certain kinds of cases—hand surgeries, for instance—too complex for the province hospitals. Of the six children we were finally authorized to evacuate—three girls and three boys—only four made it to the United States.

What happened to these six is a story by itself.

11

LIVES LIKE DUST

In war, human lives are like dust
as bullets and arrows fly with death.
The wandering ghosts, the lost souls,
make the scene still more mournful.

There were children, just tiny things,
born in a bad time, separated from their parents.
No one was there to hold them close.
Heart-rending were their infant cries.

—"Calling the Wandering Souls"
Nguyen Du (1765–1820)

The six children we were permitted to take
were Chau Quynh, the paralyzed Cambodian girl; Bui Thi
Kha, an older girl with numerous severe fractures and
infected fragment wounds; Dao Thi Thai, the scalped girl;
Huynh Van Tien, a teenaged boy with multiple gunshot
wounds; Nguyen Van O, whose left arm—now in a cast—
was hanging on by some strands of muscle that luckily
had kept his nerves and arteries intact (his parents, Hoa
Hao Buddhist farmers, had twice refused to let his arm be
amputated); and, finally, Ngo Thanh Viet, the boy who
would lose all his eyesight within two weeks unless we

moved his papers through the ministries at unprecedented speed.

After our visit to Can Tho, Berliner and Wolff went north to Danang to take new cases, while I pursued the paperwork. Viet's case was especially urgent since there was little reason to doubt Dr. Monohan's assessment that the disease in Viet's already destroyed eye would, in two weeks, overtake the other where the retina was mostly detached. Viet, although fourteen now, had been wounded by ARVN troops when he was nine, attending a party at his grandmother's, near my old haunts in Cao Lanh. He was referred to us on April 18, 1968; the next day, having stayed up most of the night, I completed and submitted all his paperwork. On April 23, I had his photos and his HDGDYK approval and went to USAID to ask Mr. Faircloth—who I learned was actually Captain Faircloth, USAF, despite his civilian duds—to request a berth on an Air Force hospital plane. Faircloth, in his consistently pissy way, reminded me that he had to have a minimum of thirty-six hours' lead time and that it might take much longer. In any case, on May 4, sixteen days after taking Viet's case, I was back in Can Tho to check on our other cases and to tell the hospital authorities that Viet would be leaving in a day or two for an eye clinic in Boston. I had done the impossible, and was exuberantly relieved.

But in the tiny doctors' office just outside the operating room at the Can Tho hospital, where I waited to give Dr. Monohan the good news, he told me it was too late. Viet had gone completely blind and had been sent home to Cao Lanh, the backwater town where for the rest of his life he would wander the dirt roads in darkness, perhaps remembering on some mental screen the bright images of his boyhood that ended in an explosion at his grandmother's house and in an ever-dimming hospital ward in Can Tho.

As if this weren't awful enough, Dr. I. Richard Bowers, the AMA physician who had drafted our initial referral recommendation on Huynh Van Tien, now told me that he had taken back his recommendation, that in fact he had sent a letter to the Province Chief demanding that the boy not be allowed to leave.

"Why?" I asked, as I looked up at the face of this tall, thin, sweating, agitated man.

"Because," he said, "he is a political bum, a crumb, a vicious killer, a Viet Cong." He added that Tien had threatened an American nurse, a Miss Melva Amacher, and that Tien had admitted to being a Viet Cong.

"And these are your medical considerations?"

"No, medically he's improved. He doesn't need to go to the U.S. He needs to go to jail."

As I left, he called after me, "The Cambodian girl doesn't need to go either."

I walked across the littered grounds, where flies were feasting on bloody bandages tossed off into the knee-high hedges and raggedy topiary that some poor soul of a groundskeeper continued to keep up, past boys chasing one another with used hypodermics they were squirting like water pistols, and strode down the crunching gravel path to Dr. Khoa's office. Dr. Khoa was not only the director of the hospital, the *médecin chef,* but he was also the chief medical officer for the entire region. It was his hospital; it was by the authority of his medical commission that Tien had been approved for evacuation; so I figured I'd better find out what he had to say before I did or said anything further.

Dr. Khoa was a small middle-aged man always dressed in a white cotton hospital gown and surgical cap. He was a bit round, but the most striking thing about him were his black, twinkly eyes. In my previous dealings with him, in the company of a COR doctor who had done the talking, Khoa had shown little excitement for our concerns. He was always polite. His French-accented English was always correct and charming. But he was distant.

This time, as a woman in a nurse's uniform brought us

tea and I told him what had just happened, he was so angry that he got up and looked out the window for a few minutes before he began talking. Then he showed me the dossier on Huynh Van Tien, from which Bowers had actually torn out his original recommendation.

"These guests of ours," he began, "of course have no authority to do such things, yet they do them. They have asked me to keep you out of the hospital. I told them I had no reason to do like that. You must help me now, Mr. Balaban."

"How, Dr. Khoa?"

He wrote down the name of a Mr. Khanh, an official at the Province Chief's headquarters. "Take all your papers—Ministry of Health, Interior, et cetera—and show them. *Demand* the Province Chief," he continued, his diction lapsing toward French, "permit the boy to go, and promise that you will return him here when he is well. He *is* better, you know. Since they decided to do this, he has become their privileged patient. But, Viet Cong or *non*, the boy will die in Vietnam."

Huynh Van Tien probably *was* a Viet Cong. He had been wounded, most likely by an M-16, on January 31, the first day of fighting in his home province of Chuong Tien, in an attack on an ARVN compound. Lots of village boys his age had been pressed by the Viet Cong into service for the first time at Tet. Tet was to have been a "national uprising." These peasants—young, patriotic, and untrained—suffered huge losses. Though no weapon had been found on Tien, this proved nothing: it would have been grabbed by his retreating cohorts. When we found him on April 8, he had been lying in the Can Tho hospital for nearly two and a half months. He was actually one of those whose wounds I had cleaned during Tet. When I saw him again in April, he was not the husky young farm boy that had clenched my arm in pain, but a skeleton with a shimmer of death in his eyes, a voice now so frail it was pitched like a child's, and hair grown to his shoulders and visibly weaving with lice. The idea that he was a danger to anybody—or that he had actually threatened an American nurse—was ludicrous. The following is part of Dr. Bowers' earlier description of Tien, written and signed by the doctor on April 8, 1968:

> Source of gun shot wounds is not clear. He had wounds of both knees, a fracture of the right knee, and right flank and buttock wounds. . . . On the 4th of February his abdomen was explored and he was found to have a large retroperitoneal hematoma. . . .
>
> On February 10, he was discovered to have leakage of urine through his flank wound, as well as a cutaneous vesicle fistula through the abdominal incision. Because of the suspected bilateral urinary fistulas, both ureters were catheterized for external drainage of urine. Fracture of the right knee was closed secondarily on February 15.
>
> He has had four exploratory laparotomies, and appears to have an enteric fistula and an extensive introperitoneal infection, and has steadily lost weight. On April 8, he received a blood transfusion, one unit.
>
> In view of his progressive downhill course, it is believed that this patient will require extensive abdominal, urological, and orthopedic surgery under more favorable conditions, if he is to survive. Although he was initially suspected of cooperating with the Viet Cong, he has apparently been cleared in the meanwhile, of suspicion.
>
> RECOMMENDATION: Because of his serious condition, it is recommended that this patient be evacuated to the United States for definitive surgery and repair after proper stabilization of his current condition.
>
> [signed]
> Dr. I. Richard Bowers, M.D.
> Member, surgical AMA team,
> with the approval of Maj. Cruz
> Hernandez, US. MC., MOC

Bowers may have torn out his original, but I had kept copies, and now handed one to Khoa.

Before I left to see the Province Chief, Dr. Khoa insisted I smoke a cigarette with him while he told me a story. "You know, Mr. Bala*ban*"—accenting my name on its last syllable—"these doctors of yours have some curious ideas."

The "of yours" told me to keep silent.

"One of them was in here the other day complaining about Negro situation in your country. I will not say what doctor was this, but he told me that 'niggers,' as he called them, are really not like human beings, that we should not treat them like such. Do you think zis is true?"

"That he said that or that they're really not human beings?"

"Not human beings." His small hands were folded before his face and he was looking over them with his sharp eyes.

"Of course they are human beings." I didn't see why Khoa was talking like this, and I was getting nervous.

"*Vraiment*. Well, I was thinking, Mr. Balaban, as this doctor shared his ideas with me . . . that it is not a big jump from a Negro to a Vietnamese, is it?"

Later that afternoon, before returning to Saigon, I delivered to Dr. Khoa (whose smile and handshake told me I now had a crucial ally at the hospital) a special waiver from the Phong Dinh province chief, Lieutenant Colonel Nguyen Van Khuong, permitting Huynh Van Tien to leave the province to travel to the United States. The Colonel's okay was one of the fastest I ever got in Vietnam. I had waited for him for about an hour in a peeling, pastel-yellow, heavily guarded French villa where slow fans stirred the dense air trapped in the high ceilings and the breeze from the river carried in a scent of gardenias. Followed by bodyguards and advisers, the Colonel arrived— about thirty-five, trig in his pressed, decorated uniform— and I could see immediately in his brisk stride why he was admired as a "go-getter" by his American advisers. After ten minutes of listening to me describe the situation and looking at our documents, which included Tien's acceptance by the National Police in Saigon, he agreed to authorize the extraordinary waiver. "How stupid," he said to me, as he signed the letter his secretary had just typed, "if he is a Viet Cong, we can only look good by letting him go. And when he comes back, all the better. Take good care of him, Mr. Balaban."

And so, having lost Viet but having rescued Tien, I went back to Saigon, where another flood of problems rushed down on Berliner and me. Dr. Wolff, who had made only two trips with us in his one-month stay, had left on April 27. He had actually accomplished quite a lot in that time, but it had taken a toll on his marriage and aggravated his ulcer. His wife would call him from Boston almost every other day, begging him to come home, and the next morning a sleepless Wolff would come down to breakfast with his lips chalked white by Maalox. His departure left Berliner and me to sort out an awful mess with the children who had been brought down on an Air Force flight from Danang six days earlier. They had arrived on a Sunday and we had no beds for them. Two of them who were in particularly bad shape were headed for Montefiore Hospital in the Bronx. One was Bien, a ten-year-old boy whose wounds stank so badly that when we laid him on a cot on the floor in Nhi Dong Children's Hospital, the other patients and their parents demanded we take him away. The other, Le Thi Thom, an eight-year-old girl with major destruction of her chest, right forearm, and face, now also had chicken pox and was crying that she wanted to go home. Imagine being eight years old, maimed, and taken from your parents by foreigners, and then put in a hospital in a strange city. The best Berliner and I could do for her was to take her home with us to the Buu family, who were so shocked by her disfigurement that they didn't question the chicken pox, which had already gone through the household enough times to be boring.

To make this all the more chaotic, on May 5, when I got back to Saigon, the Viet Cong attacked again. I remember sitting in the parlor of a barber shop after a harrowing day at the ministries. An evening rain had flooded the city streets. My shoes, socks, and pant cuffs were soaked with the filthy rainwater that had surged up over the footboard of my Lambretta. Outside the barber shop, the usual street racket was so hushed by the rain that I could hear the barber's straight razor as he scraped the fat, wrinkly pate of the bald man in his chair. I waited my turn and flipped through a dog-eared *Playboy*. Then small-arms fire and grenade bursts echoed in the outskirts. It was getting dark, and I was getting nervous. The barber was now twirling a little wire brush in the fat man's ears. Then an incoming mortar started popping off from across the river. I got up to leave.

"*Mot phút!*" the barber said—"One minute!"—as he struggled not to offend his old customer and yet accommodate an American, whom he could charge more.

"*Ngày mai,*" I answered—"Tomorrow"—and got on my scooter and steered home in the drizzle. When I got back to the Buu house, one of the kids told me that three unspecified Americans had been wounded in the alley behind our house.

The fighting continued for the next few weeks as the Viet Cong, on the eve of the Paris peace talks, tried to show the world that they hadn't been whipped at Tet but could mount similar offensives whenever they chose. On May 10, the fighting was just across the river, maybe a mile south. To the southwest, toward Cho Lon, the Chinese district, jets were dive-bombing and a pack of Cobra choppers were swarming on their targets. I remember looking out my balcony window to see the jets dropping.

I ran upstairs to warn the Buus, clustered as usual around their television set. Everyone from little Muoi, Mosquito, the happy three-year-old daughter of one of Madame Buu's daughters, to Muoi's great-grandmother was lying on

the beds or the floor watching television. Even Quang
and Kiet, the Buus' draft-dodging sons, were there. Kiet
—a good-natured, dope-smoking, long-haired wastrel—
shushed me with great annoyance as I tried to tell them
how close the fighting was. "Ssssh, Ba Lang Nhang!" he
said, using my household nickname, Scatterbrain, which
was easier to say than my real name and sounded like it.
"Look!"

What they were all watching on television was the
nearby fighting I had come to warn them about. In fact,
framed on their television screen, exactly as it was now
being framed in the window behind them, was a jet making
its dive.

"Kiet," I called, "it's right outside."

He looked at the jet looming briefly in the window and
turned back to the one he preferred on television.

It's still hard for me to understand the Buus, so representative of a class of Saigonese who profited from the
war. They seemed oblivious of the war. Yet the Buus were
funny and warm, not predatory or cold-blooded. On a
few occasions when I had absolutely no hospital bed for a
child—kids with no noses or legs, who were just oozy
masses of burns—I took them home to the Buus, who
clucked their tongues in pity and always took them in,
going to great lengths, as they had for Le Thi Thom, to
see them fed and comfortable. The Buus *knew,* but didn't
want to know. They just didn't want the war to get personal.

As we watched the fighting, Berliner stomped up the
cement stairs in his big wing-tip shoes, clutching some
safe-conduct passes that a Huey had just dropped over the
neighborhood. The Buus had no interest in these either,
but Berliner and I grabbed the flight bags we always kept
packed, hopped on our scooters, and left the neighborhood
to stay with friends.

Through all the chaos that month, the two of us maneuvered our ways through the thickets and backwaters

of the ministries; briefed the COR New York office with almost daily reports; answered letters from all sorts of people at home, even arranging two adoptions through Soeur Anicet and her orphanage in Can Tho. We wrote to our friends and families; and we referred in-country cases to the British surgeons at Nhi Dong or the Japanese at Cho Ray. Occasionally we joined other ex-IVSers for drinks or dinner and fended off the lunacy of the city— the shakedowns from traffic cops, the clamor of whores and shoeshine boys, the temptation to sink into the easeful reveries of the Marlboros laced with heroin that one could buy for a buck at the street corners downtown, and, of course, the political ferment. Both Berliner and I assisted the family of Truong Dinh Dzu, then in jail for having had the temerity to run for President on a peace platform and winning more of the popular vote than either Thieu or Ky. A couple of times, we helped some AWOL GIs trying to get to Sweden; once I arranged a secret meeting between a group of antiwar students and Donald Duncan, an ex–Green Beret, now a reporter for the left-wing magazine *Ramparts*. We interviewed and hired Vietnamese women—usually social workers—to look after the children and eventually accompany them to their destinations in the United States. I remember one pretty woman, with no qualifications, who came to the interview in a see-through *aó dài* and see-through panties. When that got her nowhere, she came back with a brass-and-teak plaque inscribed with thanks for my compassion from the Vietnamese people. In the savage barter of Saigon, it never occurred to her that no one honestly engaged in our work would even dream of sending her anywhere with these children.

During this period, I received a letter from MACV Headquarters in Can Tho: "SUBJECT: Request for Return of Weapon. Request that you return the M-3 Submachine Gun, SW 734208, hand receipted from this Headquarters at Eakin Compound during the TET Offensive." I had left the gun at IVS months before and had forgotten about it.

I don't even remember what I did with the two grenades. Currently, although no one (not even Berliner) knew it, I kept a standard .38 Smith & Wesson hidden in a pouch inside my elephant-hide briefcase. Saigon was starting to sour on Americans. Americans had always thumped on Vietnamese with colonialist *noblesse oblige,* but now one heard of muggings, drunken shootouts, and knifings directed against Americans. Recently, the National Police had shot to death an unarmed USAID official as he trundled home in his VW, ignoring the curfew and a roadblock; he got drilled in a fusillade that ripped his car open like a tin can. Throughout the districts where Americans lived or played, gangs of draft-dodging young toughs, raised on the streets and loony with reckless, nihilistic fatalism, preyed on the unwary. Downtown, and around GI billets, huge amounts of drugs were hawked by children and old women who also sold tobacco, peanuts, and tangerines from bamboo trays or little corner stalls.

Yet, even as the streets grew meaner, Saigon was still a big party, flooded with American cash. Restaurant façades were covered with rabbit wire; their metal gates were bolted and fitted with sliding peepholes. One, featuring "soul food" and run illegally by a black GI and his Vietnamese wife, had a room for whoring right off the dining area. The soldier bars were filled with country girls whose lives were now "like dust"; indeed, Saigon was so corrupt and accommodating that at one point that spring, Vietnamese boys in *aó dài*s and makeup started gracing the tables at the famous Continental Palace. In this preposterous landscape, Buddhist monks and nuns immolated themselves in protest of the war, and the monks of the An Quang Pagoda defied government bans and led street demonstrations.

Sometimes all this chaos seemed to merge into one telling event, as it did one night for an ex-IVS friend, then a stringer for the wire services. That night, after getting roughed up by Saigon cops and hit over the head with his own camera while covering a demonstration, he found himself in an opium den, lying on his side, inhaling huge soporific streams of smoke from a pipe, and thinking that he somehow *knew* the man who lay facing him through the smoky, narcotic haze, and who shared the pipe . . . and, indeed, it was the cop who, hours earlier, had busted him over the head with his Pentax. The cop recognized him too, but just slowly closed and calmly opened his murky eyes, as if to say, "Oh, forget it. This is what counts."

It was in this world that I began each day by visiting the children in our care, who had now grown to thirteen in number and who seemed to be going nowhere. Some of them, like Bien, the boy with the foul-smelling wounds, were close to death. All were burdens to the hospital they were in, since they took up beds that other children needed, and since some of them demanded intensive medical attention. Moreover, all of them had stayed beyond the temporary welcomes we had gotten from hospital officials. Back in the United States, COR—which had been trying to establish a large-scale evacuation program for nearly two years without much success—decided to press publicly for the immediate relief of these thirteen children and for the thousands of others dying each month. A cable was sent to President Thieu, to Vice-President Ky, and to Ambassador Ellsworth Bunker. A separate plea had already been delivered to President Thieu in March. In addition, a COR five-point "letter" to the "people and the President of the United States," calling for a cease-fire and describing the civilian toll, appeared as a full-page ad in *The New York Times*. Dr. Needleman also contacted Neil Sheehan, the *Times* reporter respected for his dispatches from Vietnam, and asked him to investigate the bureaucratic delays in Saigon that were threatening the lives of our children.

Before letting loose this media barrage, Needleman asked us how it would play in Saigon. Berliner and I cabled back our consent to his new tactics, but braced ourselves

for the backlash. It was possible we would be expelled
from Vietnam. *Then* what would become of these thirteen
children? For the time being, most of them were in good
hands at Nhi Dong and Cho Ray, but even the Nhi Dong
and Cho Ray hospitals were not equipped for their long-
term reconstructive surgeries and rehabilitations.

COR's May 9 cable, which held the substance of our
pleas to the South Vietnamese since Tet, read as follows:

13 WAR-INJURED CHILDREN SELECTED BY THE COMMITTEE
OF RESPONSIBILITY, INC. AND CLEARED BY MINISTRY OF
HEALTH FOR TREATMENT IN U.S. ARE HELD UP IN SAIGON
AWAITING PASSPORTS. BUREAU OF POLICE HAS THEIR DOS-
SIERS BUT HAS NOT SIGNED THEM. CHILDREN IN GREAT
NEED AND MORE DELAYS WILL HAVE SERIOUS MEDICAL
CONSEQUENCES. BEDS WAITING FOR THEM HERE. HUMAN-
ITY DEMANDS THEY AND MANY OTHERS RECEIVE CARE THEY
NEED NOW. C.O.R. URGES YOU INSTRUCT AUTHORITIES IN
YOUR GOVERNMENT TO ACT IMMEDIATELY AND LET THESE
CHILDREN COME TO THE HELP THEY NEED. WE FURTHER
URGE YOU ACT ON OUR PREVIOUS REQUEST FOR RADICAL
SIMPLIFICATION OF THE PROCEDURES SO THAT FUTURE CHIL-
DREN CAN BE TREATED WITHOUT CRUEL DELAYS. THE NEW
CIVILIAN CASUALTIES IN THE CITIES MAKE THIS STEP MORE
IMPERATIVE. WE STAND READY TO HELP NOW. WE AWAIT
YOUR EARLY RESPONSE WITH DEEP CONCERN.

The current evacuation procedure placed the children in
the same legal status as that of ordinary Vietnamese citizens
applying for passports for tourist trips abroad. In a letter
to Thieu two months earlier, on March 12, COR had asked
that this procedure be changed:

Specifically, we request that once parental permission
has been obtained, medical ratification by the Vietnamese physician in charge be entirely sufficient for evacuation. Secondly, we request that Temporary Group
Exit Documents be promptly issued permitting the
children to leave and return *en masse*.

All of these past and current pleas were officially ignored. The fighting continued in Saigon and in other Southern cities, increasing the flow of casualties. The Viet Cong were now rocketing the urban centers. Sometimes in the predawn, lying in bed, I could hear the rockets whooshing overhead from out of the defoliated swamps across the river, wobbling their clumsy ways toward whatever tall building the Viet Cong gunners were attempting to sight upon. Unfortunately for our children, one of the tall buildings that got hit was the Mondial, where USAID Public Health and the inimitable Captain Faircloth had offices. No one was hurt in the blast and fire, but more delays ensued.

The children continued to lie in their temporary beds in Saigon. For some, it meant that certain surgical repairs could be started or that the children could simply be strengthened before their trips to the U.S. For others, like Bien, there was a real chance that he would die in the delay. Another, a boy who had lost his lower jaw from a mine explosion and who was supposed to go to University Hospital in Madison, Wisconsin, had been delayed so long that his American entrance visa had expired. Indeed, his Vietnamese exit visa had expired two weeks earlier. Now we had to ask for extensions from the National Police and the U.S. Consulate.

Berliner knew Bernard Weinraub, *The New York Times'* current reporter, and convinced him to do a story on the children waiting to go. Mert Perry, the *Newsweek* bureau chief I had met in Can Tho, wrote a short complaint for the Periscope section. But the luckiest thing that happened for these cases was a phone call from Nguyen Trong Nho, a Saigon member of the National Assembly. Mr. Nho said he had heard about our work and the delays in helping these children and was ready to help. Naturally, we were suspicious. Whoever heard of a Vietnamese politician actually volunteering help for ordinary civilians? Moreover, Mr. Nho ran an opposition newspaper. *How* could he help? An editorial politicizing the issue in Vietnam might only reduce the chances these kids would ever leave the country.

"Mr. Nho," I said, "thank you very much for your interest. How do you think you could help?"

"We must go to the top. To Minister Khiem."

General Tran Thien Khiem was the current Minister of Interior, which, after the Presidency, was the most powerful post in Vietnam. One of his brothers was the general in charge of the Saigon region. Khiem himself had been the Vietnamese Ambassador to Washington. Through his underling, General Nguyen Ngoc Loan (who had just made himself famous by shooting a captured Viet Cong in the head as an American photographer stood by), Khiem controlled the National Police. He controlled the customs officials and all ports of entry. He controlled the issuance of all passports. For our purposes, he *was* the top, and so we could scarcely believe it when Mr. Nho called back to say that he had made an appointment for us with Khiem and that, if we were prepared, he would take us to see him.

We drove into the cobblestoned central square of the heavily guarded precincts of the Ministry of Interior in Mr. Nho's little white Simca, driven by a young woman who Nho said had first brought our problem to his attention. A guard escorted us to Khiem's office. Just outside the office, another guard motioned to Nho and, without a word, Nho bent forward a bit, reached into his suit jacket, and handed over to the guard a Colt .45 which loomed so large at that moment I wondered how I hadn't noticed it under his coat. I considered opening my briefcase and handing over my .38, but thought otherwise.

Inside the paneled office, General Khiem, a large man wearing a light-green safari suit and the latest, French-style eyeglasses, got up from his desk and shook hands with us. In utterly natural English, he said he had heard about our

Committee and was glad Americans were helping the "unfortunate ones caught in the war." He asked us to sit down. He asked us what our problem was. Berliner explained the difficulties of the evacuation procedure, and I handed the General a copy of COR's letter of appeal to President Thieu. Then Mr. Nho made a short speech in which he said that the Vietnamese government should do everything it could to assist these humane Americans who had come to help the Vietnamese people. The General shook his head in agreement. Amen.

Mr. Nho smiled at us and sipped the tea that had been brought in. I think he was relieved that the meeting had started well and that the two young Americans he had befriended did not appear likely to embarrass him.

Khiem read our letter and then made us very nervous by running his finger down the left margin, where our Board of Directors and Honorary Chairmen were listed. "Oh, Dr. Spock," he said, "I hope *he* isn't very active in your Committee, gentlemen."

I smiled and said, "Minister Khiem, please let me tell you about some of the others who aren't so famous."

"Sabin, I know. The polio vaccine."

"Yes, and Helen Brooks-Taussig is a pre-eminent pediatrician. . . ."

He nodded for me to go on.

". . . Dr. Lown invented the pacemaker. Reverend Moore is Bishop of the Episcopalian church in Washington. Our Board Chairman, Dr. Needleman, is both a pediatrician and a psychiatrist."

General Khiem shook his head as if to say "Enough." I don't think he really wanted a rundown. He just wanted us to know that he had our number with Spock and that he didn't owe much of a bend in the passport procedure to any organization that included antiwar activists.

I told him about the boy who had gone blind because of delay. This he commiserated over briefly by sucking his teeth once. I had the feeling it was a loss he could bear.

Then I mentioned the American hospitals that had already taken our cases and those that had agreed to take the children currently delayed: Mt. Zion in San Francisco; UCLA Medical Center; Beth Israel Hospital in Boston; Albert Einstein Medical Center in Philadelphia; Children's Hospital in Washington, D.C.; University Hospital in Madison, Wisconsin; Montefiore Hospital in the Bronx; Good Samaritan Hospital in Portland, Oregon; Nyack Hospital in New York; University Hospital in Iowa City; and Campbell Community Hospital in San Jose. This list seemed to have an effect on him. He was, after all, a diplomat who had served in the United States long enough to understand the PR aspects implicit in this across-the-country list.

"Gentlemen, please tell your Committee of Responsibility that we are grateful for its work and will do what we can to make the evacuations go faster. Ask them also to please understand the particular difficulties of our situation. . . ." He paused as he stood up and held out his hand and looked Berliner and me in the eyes as he added, "I know you can do that."

Later, when we had an iced coffee with Mr. Nho and his driver-secretary, who was waiting for us at La Pagode, we wondered if anything would really come of the meeting. Mr. Nho seemed quite happy about it all. So was his young secretary in the *aó dài* and black glasses, who was smiling too. It was all rather strange. We never heard from either of them again. Years after the war was over, I read in *The New York Times* that Mr. Nho had been made a member of the Saigon governing council in the wake of the North Vietnamese takeover. General Khiem, according to postwar revelations about the CIA, was the chief mover of heroin into and out of Vietnam.

But suddenly things were stirring. A few days after our meeting at the Ministry, Le Van Cu, whose exit and entry visas had expired, was authorized to leave on May 20, and three others—all from the Can Tho group—were sched-

uled to go on May 25. Since Cu was already waiting in a
Saigon hospital, Berliner stayed behind to complete the
linkups with the Air Force hospital plane and with COR
in New York. I flew to Can Tho to ready the others for
their transfer to Saigon.

Of course, it wasn't that easy.

When I got to the hospital in Can Tho and went to pay
my respects to Dr. Khoa, I learned that Huynh Van Tien,
the purported Viet Cong, had been carted off to a military
hospital where, although he could no longer walk, he was
chained to a bed. Furthermore, Khoa said, Chau Quynh,
the paralyzed Cambodian girl, had been sent home to die.
"They say that no one, not even in your country, can do
anything for paraplegics." Dr. Khoa went on to describe
the political situation he had had to deal with. Some of his
own staff not only supported the American surgeons in
the Tien case, in direct opposition to his medical examining
commission's recommendation, but there was a suggestion
that Dr. Khoa himself might have to be investigated for
his desire to aid "this VC." He asked me if COR wanted
to continue to evacuate cases from the Delta.

"Of course," I said. "As long as there are civilian casualties, we will try to help the ones who fit into our
charter." We were chartered by the Ministry of Health to
evacuate only war-injured children under eighteen years
of age.

Then Dr. Khoa mentioned Terres des Hommes, the
Swiss relief agency, very much like COR except they localized their reconstructive cases in one "peace village"
where their children lived together between surgeries.
"Mr. Balaban, if you can swallow your pride on this Tien
case, perhaps you and Terres des Hommes can divide up
the Delta for this kind of medical care."

I rose to go. "Dr. Khoa, thank you for all your trouble.
None of this is up to me, as you know."

He shrugged a rather Gallic shrug. *None of it was up to
him.* He did not want a police investigation. He had already

swallowed his pride. I thought I understood, but still I was appalled by his suggestion of forgetting about Tien and going on to "divide up the Delta." Was he thinking of me as a kind of road salesman for ghouls, or was he making a judgment—the kind that doctors are empowered to make—that a victory on Tien would so blacken COR that it would be effectively shut out of the Delta, whereas letting the boy die would put us back in Mekong medical graces and in the end save more children's lives? In any case, I sensed I had become a liability to Dr. Khoa.

Even so, he was protective. As I moved toward the door, he motioned for me to sit down. "Another tale, Mr. Balaban . . ." He gestured for me to sit down. "These doctors of yours are not all honorable men," he began. "The other evening they had goodbye dinner party. I learned that one of them complained about having one shrimp less on his plate than the others and that a fight broke out. Someone, *actuellement,* pulled a gun. Some are dangerous, Mr. Balaban. Drunkards, fools. Do not go out at night."

"What do they have against me?"

"They think you are a communist. Miss Dung, one of the young women who accompanied some children to Philadelphia, claims that what she heard there makes her believe that you are communists."

"Oh, God."

"Yes."

"And what do you think, doctor?" It was like his question to me, weeks earlier, about Negroes. Now, at least, we were both smiling, although there were so many absurdities floating in the room, I couldn't tell which ones were lighting our smiles.

"I think she felt she had to say such things to regain favor here with certain doctors on my staff. She wants a job."

"And what's this about a 'goodbye party'?"

"I have requested the team's dismissal, a month early. They are being pulled out."

"And what will you do for surgeons?" Most of Dr. Khoa's staff had either left long ago for France or the United States, or else had been drafted into the army.

"AID has offered me another surgical team. Australian. I said no. We would prefer Japanese. Anyway, no more Americans, Mr. Balaban. No offense."

"Oh, no. Thanks for the warning."

Another shrug. We shook hands and I went to find out about Chau Quynh. Denying Tien his recovery made a certain kind of brutal sense from a certain kind of brutal perspective, although one would not expect it from men who had taken the Hippocratic oath. But sending this girl home to die was beyond my belief. So I went looking for Louis Carter, the new Air Force surgeon who had taken over the case from Dr. Bowers even though we had left her in the hands of another AMA Volunteer Physician for Vietnam, Thomas Powell, who had since re-examined Quynh at my request on May 10 and had confirmed the necessity of her departure for "surgical fitting of an ileal loop and for detailed examination of the paraplegia." The Vietnamese nurse on the ward told me that Dr. Carter was in surgery.

I found Dr. Carter, a chubby man sweating profusely, just as he came out of the operating room. It seemed to me, at least at first, that the likeliest explanation for what he had done was that since he was new in Vietnam, perhaps he did not even know about COR or its plans to send the girl to Good Samaritan Hospital in Portland, Oregon. I introduced myself. Now some other doctors, including Major Hernandez, were filing out of the OR. No one said anything, but I could feel them listening as they took off the surgical masks and stowed their gear in their lockers. My hand hung out in the air in front of Dr. Carter.

Carter looked at me and said he knew who I was.

"But did you know that the girl was going to the United States?"

He started shouting at me. First he said that the girl

"did not deserve to go," and then that "no left-wing organization is going to get propaganda out of this hospital."

I waited a moment for him to subside. "Dr. Carter, she
was recommended to us by Dr. Bowers with Major Hernandez's approval."

Hernandez, who stood watching with the others, said
nothing.

"She also had the approval of Dr. Khoa's medical commission."

"Oh, yeah, you guys have been clever enough."

"Dr. Carter, you know better than I, but she will die
at home."

He didn't reply. I could see I was getting nowhere.

"May I say, then, that you take unilateral responsibility
for dismissing Chau Quynh?"

"Look, buddy, I don't care—you can tell the goddamn
Ambassador that I take responsibility."

"That's who I intend to tell." And with that I turned
and went out. Behind me, as the screen door closed, the
locker room surged with cheers and clapping for Dr.
Carter.

Where was the girl now, I wondered? Her father sol-
diered for a remote Special Forces company at Ba Xoai,
near Chau Doc on the Mekong border with Cambodia.
When he had understood that she would never walk again,
he lost interest in her, as if she were nothing more than
damaged goods. I remember him as perhaps the coldest
parent we had yet encountered, one who had signed off
his daughter into our care without much hesitation. Was
she dead already? A bladder infection caused by contaminated village water could kill her. Dr. Powell, the VPVN
replacement for Bowers, whose added recommendation
for Chau Quynh's evacuation had apparently caused him
difficulty, was waiting for me when I came out. He also
warned me to stay away from the surgeons. "They drink
a lot," he said. "Let's get out of here."

We drove to the Golden Pearl restaurant where, during

my IVS days, I used to breakfast, and where I had once
hatched plans with Gitelson. Dead only a few months,
Gitelson's fateful difficulties with his American colleagues
now seemed very much to the point. Despite the awfulness
of what had just transpired at the hospital and my concern
for Chau Quynh, as I entered the Golden Pearl for the first
time since coming back to Vietnam, I was cheered to see
two things: the sparrows hopping for crumbs on the aluminum chairs and fluttering up through the wired canopy
overhead, and, outside, the same portly government officials batting at tennis balls beneath rustly palms and
the big, cavernous banyan filled with chatterbox mynah
birds.

As we waited for our *café filtre* to drip into our cups
through blackened tin strainers, we talked about recent
events. Not only had I been threatened, Powell had been
threatened as well. He told me his account of the dinner
that Khoa had mentioned. In the doctors' view, I was "the
communist"; Samuel Epstein, a COR physician who had
been in Can Tho before us and who was a distinguished
toxicologist and cancer researcher at Boston's Children's
Hospital, was referred to as "that goddamn Jew."

"Why am I a communist?"

Powell lifted the lid of his coffee device to see if all the
water had seeped through the strainer. "I don't know,"
he said. "Something you said in *Newsweek* at Tet."

Powell, of course, had become a fellow traveler for helping us. In the view of some of the doctors, according to
Dr. Powell, we had come to Can Tho "to get us a VC."
He cited instances of their racism toward Vietnamese.
Considering the world he inhabited, Powell was brave to
be talking with me. How rotten his life must have become.
He had volunteered to come to Vietnam. Although he had
no obligation, he had abandoned his practice to spend two
months here. I realized that—like me in my early IVS days
at Can Tho—he must be dwelling now in pain and isolation.

What *I* felt was rage. Rage and a resolve to redress the

situation for both Chau Quynh and Huynh Van Tien. Now I even wondered if Viet, the boy who had gone blind, really had gone blind or if he too had been sent home merely to keep him out of our bloody, communist clutches. (No, I decided, we had, after all, been warned from the very start that we had only two weeks to get him out, and we had missed that deadline by a few days.)

After talking to Powell, the first thing that I did was to make a formal complaint with Dr. Khoa. There was no time to consult COR in New York or even Berliner in Saigon. My May 21 letter began:

> I wish to protest strongly, the dismissal of the patient, Chau Quynh, by Dr. Louis Carter. Dr. Carter's decision was executed against the wishes of the child's family, against the recommendations of your Technical Commission, and without the knowledge of the Committee of Responsibility, which had selected Chau Quynh for medical evacuation to the United States as recommended by Dr. Bowers and Dr. Powell with the approval of the American Medical Officer in Charge, Major Cruz Hernandez.
>
> As you may know, each of our cases is "invited to proceed on patient status to the United States by the Chief of Staff, USAF" in Washington, D.C. Chau Quynh, a paraplegic who was to be treated at Portland, Oregon, was authorized for evacuation tomorrow by the United States Air Force, and the Ministries of Interior and Health of the Republic of Vietnam. The Committee of Responsibility was prepared to do all that is possible for the girl's rehabilitation.
>
> I bring to your attention that she has been consciously and unilaterally denied this help.

I cc-ed the letter to Major Hernandez, made a copy for myself, and hand-delivered copies to Dr. Khoa and the Major, who took it from me with a glare of hatred.

Back in Saigon, I cabled COR about these events and

wrote another protest to Colonel Richard L. Coppedge, the Director of USAID Public Health. I made an appointment to see him. Coppedge had always been straight and fair-minded in his dealings with us and I had hopes that he would try to do something to retrieve the girl. I also sent a copy of this letter to Mr. Bishton, the U.S. Consul, who, if not sympathetic, at least had been appropriately helpful in moving the kids' passports through his office.

Meanwhile, on May 28, COR's executive secretary in New York wrote back:

> Just got your letter [to Coppedge] dated May 24. I am very curious as to what the result of the meeting of the 27th was. Did you get any satisfaction from Col. Coppedge? We have to really blow the lid off this Carter incident if for no other reason than to prevent its happening again. I am sorry we are in such a bind on C-22 [case 22, Huynh Van Tien] and consequently unable to blow the whistle on those within the Air Force and on those who initiated the initial fuss. . . . Ridgeway of the New Republic is planning to do a story.

On May 28, I wrote back to Needleman at COR in Boston:

> The evacuation will be set right regarding Chau Quynh, C21. I spoke to Col. Coppedge today, after alerting the Consul General, Mr. Bishton, to the seriousness of what Dr. Carter had done. Col. Coppedge agreed thoroughly that Dr. Carter had acted out of hand. He assured me that the girl would be located and that this sort of thing would never happen again. I take it he took some strong action.
>
> I was straight forward with Col. Coppedge and suggested that Dr. Carter's action regarding Chau Quynh might have resulted from his opinions concerning

Huynh Van Tien. Col. Coppedge said, yes. Their first
radio communication from Can Tho answered back
something about a 16-year old VC girl, confusing Tien
and Quynh.

Soon startling things began to happen. Copies of cables
sent to the State Department regarding Chau Quynh and
signed "Bunker" appeared in my APO mailslot. At first
I thought they had gotten there by gross bureaucratic error
and tried to return them to Captain Faircloth, the reluctant
overseer of our USAID-related privileges. "Nah," he said,
not looking up from his desk but showing me his shiny,
balding pate, wisped with carefully combed black strands,
"they want you to have them."

"Case rather complex," one cable ran. "Am investigat-
ing. — Bunker." I had met Ellsworth Bunker once, with
Dr. Wolff, and had had to sit there silently while Wolff,
only a few days in country, got bamboozled by Bunker's
aristocratic Yankee good-ol'-boyism as the career trouble-
shooter dropped the names of their common friends on
Nantucket as well as some from Harvard University Medical School and Massachusetts General. I never dreamed
that my current protest would get his attention. Stiff-
backed, and with the purest, coldest blue eyes, nearing the
end of his long, tough-dealing career, he seemed to me an
icy planet in distant orbit light-years from the civilian hospital wards of Vietnam.

Nonetheless, whether out of fear of tremendous bad
press or out of rectitude, or both, I was soon called by
someone at the Embassy and told that the Ambassador
had indeed investigated the Chau Quynh "tragedy" and
had ordered that not only would a helicopter go out to Ba
Xoai and retrieve Chau Quynh, but also that Dr. Carter
himself would officially readmit the girl at the Can Tho
hospital.

Only later did I see the lengthy Washington *Post* articles
by Nicholas Von Hoffman that sometimes directly quoted
my letters to Needleman:

Since the committee's honorary chairmen are Dr. Benjamin Spock, Dr. Albert Sabin, the inventor of the polio vaccine, and John Wesley Lord, the resident Methodist Bishop of Washington, D.C., our government has a tendency to regard each attempt to save a child's life as an act of treachery.

It follows that, although the Air Force has promised to supply free transportation for the wounded children, everything is done to prevent their coming. For more than a month now, Nguyen Hue, his exit visa in order, has waited for the medical evacuation promised by the State Department and the Air Force. Dr. Herbert L. Needleman . . . says that on one occasion a United States Air Force doctor refused the evacuation of Chau Quynh, a little girl paralyzed from the waist down, with the remark that, "No left-wing organization is going to get propaganda out of this hospital." On another occasion, a United States military doctor referred to Dr. Sam Epstein, a famous toxicologist from the Boston Children's Medical Center who works with the committee, as "that God damn Jew." . . . The policy is to hide the bodies, all the bodies.

On June 14, I went back to Can Tho. The American team was still at the Can Tho hospital, despite its supposed dismissal. But now so was Chau Quynh. She had been brought in by helicopter and was in bad shape. I stood by in the dank ward while Dr. Powell looked her over. He shook his head.

"You know, they are right about chances being dim for paraplegics with paralysis this high. . . ."

I shook *my* head. The point was that she had no chance at all in Vietnam.

"And this hasn't made her chances any better." He rolled the girl over slowly. The bedsore that had been a problem while she was in the hospital had now become a decubitus ulcer at the base of her spine. The ulcer was as large as an orange and raw to the bone. The shy girl smiling back at us could not feel it.

I never saw Dr. Carter again, which was just as well, but as Dr. Powell wrote his new assessment on her chart, I did see Carter's signature on the readmission sheet.

"You better get her out of here, fast," was Powell's final advice as he saw me out of the hospital.

I was scheduled the next day to fly out not only Chau Quynh but also Bui Thi Kha, the girl with multiple severe fractures and extensive infected flesh wounds inflicted when she was gunned down from a helicopter along with most of her immediate family, who were all now dead. After a bumpy ride to the airport in the hospital's ancient Peugeot ambulance, a ride that made Kha scream and moan in her full-body cast and left Quynh eerily silent, we met an Air Force plane out on the metal runway, especially detached from Saigon. The next day, June 16, 1968, Chau Quynh was flown to the United States, where her life was indeed saved.

By June 22, all of our thirteen delayed cases were in the United States. Huynh Van Tien never made it. Despite all the documents I held in my hands, including his passport and his American entrance visa, the Ministry of Interior finally reversed its approval of his leaving. He was, I was finally told in a static-crackling phone call from Province Headquarters in Can Tho, "a real VC." What he was, mostly, was a sixteen-year-old farm boy who was wounded in the only military action he ever saw. Sometime in late June or early July, according to Dr. Khoa, Tien died handcuffed to a bed in an ARVN military hospital. Dr. Khoa had sent over the ambulance and one of his doctors to get the boy back to his hospital, but was ignored. Tien was a wraith of bones at that point. He could not sit up, much less walk. The handcuffs were a form of torture. Because Tien was in a military hospital, we were not permitted to see him again, even when his frail old grandmother—the only family member who dared come near him for fear of police interrogation—tried to get our help. Like all those children, Tien was just a speck in the war, a bit unluckier, perhaps a bit more responsible, but just a boy nonetheless, an unschooled boy, just dust of life, *bụi đời* like the rest of those maimed children, a speck of human dust blowing before the face of Heaven.

12

Hanging Out
in Saigon

All of that mayhem transpired in less than three months—from early April to the third week in June 1968, when the last of those thirteen children finally lifted off the runway at Tan Son Nhut in a wide-bellied C-141 Starlifter fitted with rows of beds filled with mangled young Americans. Berliner and I, with the heat from the tarmac soaking up through our shoe soles, then got back on our scooters and puttered off behind the emptied ambulance as we turned back to work on the dossiers of our new cases. Only eleven weeks had passed since my return with COR—eleven jammed, enervating weeks that I recorded in intense detail, with a sense of fateful witness, in field notes and in a saved file of letters. Back home, Lyndon Johnson had announced that he would not run for the presidency; in Paris, the peace talks had begun; and, in Vietnam, General Creighton Abrams had just replaced William Westmoreland as commander. The slaughter of civilians had reached its peak.

An extraordinary energy had filled me during that time. The more the demands, the more energy I seemed to have for them. I was so wired that at night in bed my legs would often twitch and jerk as if yanked by strings. In those first few months with COR, I lived in a state so primed and ready to go that it was hard to wind down at the end of the day, and often I couldn't sleep. By my bed, I kept a yellowed ivory pipe and a bag of marijuana. Marijuana— as well as hashish, and even opium—had been legal in Vietnam not that many years before and, walking Saigon's streets or sitting in a movie theater, one often whiffed its distinctive smoke. Unlike many of my friends, I disliked marijuana because of the paranoiac and then depressive effects it had on me, but I smoked it sometimes to relax and put myself to sleep. "Ba Lang Nhang!" Kiet, one of the teenaged Buus, would sometimes yell down to my room as a puff from my pipe wafted up to the third floor and he saw an opportunity to tease me in earshot of the whole household of twenty souls settling to sleep, "*Trời ơi!* Ba Lang Nhang"—"Oh, *Heavens,* Balaban."

But even after I fell asleep, my head raced with dreams, dreams just a surreal shade off the actual. In one recurring dream, I found myself in an obscure, darkened back room of the Ministry of Interior, its narrow window shuttered, its floor stacked to the ceiling with dusty, elongated folders, each folder strapped with ribbon or a rubber band and printed "DOSSIER" in the habitude of the French *bureau.* In the dream, I would try to present a dossier which, when opened, turned out to be empty. I would then wake up, or think I had awakened, only to return to the same office, where I would present the dossier again, which again would be empty. Then I would again wake up, etc., *ad infinitum,* as if I had been sketched into an Escher drawing.

At dawn, as the unmuffled engine clatter from the mo- torized cyclos seeped through the louvers of my wooden balcony door and windows, I would get up, shave, and walk across the street where a man had set out some wiggly metal stools beside his breakfast cart. I would buy a big chunk of *bánh mì,* an aromatic, still-warm baguette, and a large glass of *cà phê sữa,* coffee with a dollop of Borden's

sweetened, condensed milk which the man measured out
and stirred in with a crude, gigantic aluminum spoon.

If we had time, Berliner and I—our briefcases lodged
safely between our feet on the floorboards of our scooters—would ride across town to a vast tin-and-tarpaulin
arcade of food stalls to get some *phở,* the Vietnamese breakfast soup, which simmered deliciously in huge brass caul-
drons twenty-four hours a day. We would gather our wits
there, hunkered over our bowls at a rickety aluminum table
amid other such tables set by the curb and packed with
ordinary folk, as the morning sun warmed our necks, and
as the traffic honked and rumbled by us in an engulfing
blue cloud of exhaust fumes, now and then pierced by the
traffic cop's frantic whistle as he stood by the traffic light.
Tiny blue-and-yellow taxis tooted past us through a sea
of bicycles jinging handlebar bells that—as the light
changed again and the cop again tweeted his whistle—
would be drowned out by loud, revving shark packs of
motorcycles zipping ahead of the heavier traffic of jeeps,
of two-ton camouflage-painted trucks blasting air horns,
of large-finned Embassy cars, of slow pedicabs pumped
by pith-helmeted old men, of three-wheeled Lambretta
jitneys sardined with peasants heading to market and children heading to school, and, finally, lost at the end of the
traffic tangle and about to be swarmed upon by the traffic
light's next release of vehicles, a *xe thồ mộ,* a blindered
donkey pulling a wooden cart with immense wooden-
spoked wheels, a clip-clopping throwback to the quieter
streets of prewar Saigon. The city was going to school, to
work, to war, cranking out an envelope of exhaust fumes
that would hang above the streets in the high branches of
the dying tamarinds until it finally dissipated in the predawn hours the following day.

Sitting there, Berliner and I would plan our day, keep
an eye on our scooters, sniff at the parsley and coriander
vapors from the beef boiling in the soup pots, and watch
the schoolgirls walk by in their white *aó dàis,* their silky

black hair sometimes so long that it whisked their bottoms as they went past. Sometimes, as I sat staring at the crowd, Berliner would read a Vietnamese daily and pause now and then to tell me who got arrested the day before, who got shot in what bar, and what new plan for pacification had been implemented. Since everyone around us was also trying to wake up and get something to eat before going to work, we went relatively unnoticed. Inevitably, though, someone would say, "Look, the Americans are using chopsticks," or "Look, he's putting in *nước mắm*," the clear, amber, pungent fish sauce that Vietnamese favor. But hardly anyone paid attention to us on those mornings, which were as relaxed and human, *as normal,* as any we had to spend.

Saigon, at that time, was the densest city on the planet, packed with more humans per square mile than Tokyo, New York, or Rio. Just thirty minutes away by air, deep in the Cambodian jungles around Siem Reap, in the stone temples of Angkor Wat, statues of Buddha and Shiva sat in the immense, centuries-old silence of a deserted city reclaimed by the forest, where the only sounds were the chirrings of insects and the cries of birds, where bats rustled in the damp stone ceilings and cockroaches perched on the gods' fingertips, their glistening heads shining in the shadows like painted fingernails. But in Saigon, in that press of troops, grafters, refugees, pacification hacks, and rootless post-colonial souls, it was hard to find a place to sit alone and think. My room at the Buu house was no good; even with the door shut, I could hear the smaller children running around the house, the yappy dogs, the older boys roaring in on their Hondas, Madame Buu shouting commands down from her bedroom sanctuary on the top floor, the older sisters rattling about the kitchen to put together two meals a day, which was no small feat in a family that large.

In the few free hours I had, I would sometimes go to the Botanical Gardens to hear the blind singers of heroic ballads, hunkered in the dirt by the bear pits, bending the pentatonic notes on their steel-string guitars. Or, I'd look at the cages of tropical birds, or watch the tiny Asian elephants being fed bundles of sugarcane and bamboo. Always, though, some panhandling boy or drunken ARVN soldier or passel of bratty kids would pester me until I had to leave. Then I'd go over to browse in the restricted library of the Société des Études Indochinoises, which was housed in the historical museum. The hushed library room, with its double tiers of bookshelves served by creaky ladders, reminded me of the family library where Anatole France's angels began their revolt. One could not talk in the library, but scribbled book requests on little cards. It was perfect in its quietude and in its civilized insistence on a life beyond the current war. I was delighted when I was accepted as a Société member.

Going outside from the cool, musty shadows of that Angkorian library into the hard sunlight was a double jolt. Back among the mildewed journals, I had been lost in the antiquity of Vietnam, in the symbols of its royal and religious architecture, in complexities of race and language of its sixty-some minorities, in ancient struggles against the Chinese invaders, in the colonizing of the South, in wars with Chams and Khmers, in the drastic mishaps of loony French adventurers among Stieng tribesmen, in their encounters with the Python Cult, and in their trials with the wily jungle "Kings of Fire and Air." Outside, on the sunstruck steps of the museum, beyond the Botanical Gardens' massive, wrought-iron gate, the choked, polluted street of the war-fattened city clamored like a madman hammering at the lid of a garbage can.

Just off to the left of the Botanical Gardens, museum, and zoo was a cordoned-off section of the city belonging to the Vietnamese Navy. The whole area was closed to public traffic—and had been since the end of World War II, judging by the immense overhang of healthy trees and the unmolested, prewar style of the French villas and naval buildings. Because I was an American, no one ever stopped me at the barricade.

Driving in there was like driving back in time. There were few shops and no traffic lights, no traffic jams, no cops, and no Americans. Street after street was shaded by huge, gnarly trees, and if there was litter it was the litter of aromatic leaves. Nearby, a sprawling Catholic nunnery took up an entire block with a church, chapels, a refectory, and a five-story dormitory whose vast decaying ocher stucco wall faced the street with gray-green blossoms of mildew. Not far away, I would sometimes buy a sandwich from a curbside food stall where the man sliced open a baguette, squirted the opened halves with something that looked like vinegar, shook in some salt flakes, then laid on duck pâté, strips of pork, lettuce, hot peppers, mint, coriander, and a heavenly sauce of his own devising. I'd eat it sitting on my scooter seat, taking in the smell of leaves, the clean, almost country air, the damp must from the rotting buildings, and wonder whether this is what Saigon would have been like if my country hadn't taken over the war.

In my work during that period, there was exhilaration and exhaustion; in my isolation, there were also friends, friends of such strange extremes that glimpses of them will always shuffle through my head, more real to me than those around me in my middle age: Lieutenant Trung, my former student, whose wife would bake a chicken in wine when I came to My Tho; Clyde Coreil, teaching Saigon medical students his version of Cajun English; Donald Duncan, the highly decorated ex–Green Beret who now wrote for *Ramparts;* and Jerry Liles, another ex-IVSer, who once drove a motorcycle all the way from Vientiane across Laos, Cambodia, and the upper Delta, through Pathet Lao, Khmer Rouge, Stieng, and Viet Cong turfs.

One Sunday morning, I sat in silence with Gordon Barclay, the senior surgeon of the British Pediatric Team, who organized a Quaker meeting that drew maybe three people.

That morning, he played a three-minute tape of the "dawn chorus" that his wife, Celia, had sent him from their rambling brick home outside of London, where all the English birds were chirping away so far from the war.

That very night, hanging out with former IVSers, we bought from a cigarette vendor a pack of Marlboros mixed with marijuana and nearly pure heroin. Then a half-dozen of us careened on Hondas and Vespas through the motorcycle packs in downtown Saigon, tooling past La Pagode and Givral's, the French-style coffee shops where long-haired Saigon cowboys and their petite girlfriends looked bored and naughty. Stoned, we woozed through monster traffic jams, wisecracking in Vietnamese to the Vietnamese, then stopped at the bars along Tu Do Street, where none of us could afford the drinks and we were cold-shouldered by the bar girls and bawled out. ("Why you come here no money?") Around midnight, we ended up at the plush Maxim's, reportedly owned by Ky, where one of the IVSers talked his way onto the stage and jollied the band in Vietnamese until he got them laughing and willing to strike up "If You Are Going to San Francisco," which he sang so well in an Andy Williams style that all of us were treated to drinks by a Vietnamese colonel hosting a big entourage.

Later, now drunk as well as drugged, traveling in darkness as our motorcycles scraped through alleys and over plank catwalks into God knows what demimonde of the city, still in tow with this same bunch of Saigon-smart friends, I remember sitting on the Honda as one of them walked up the steps to a darkened house and pounded on the door until finally a Southern voice drawled out, "Wha' you want?"

"I want to fuck!" our friend yelled back in with a kind of frat-rat mindlessness.

In seconds, the door crashed open and I could see a huge naked black man, his skin a satin glow in the dim lamplight, pointing an M-16 at our friend and asking, "You want to fuck this?"

"It's a mistake, man. We got the wrong house," someone said. Drunk and turned around, we had blundered into
the lair of one of Saigon's AWOL blacks.

"You got the wrong nigger."

"Look, man," I called up to the porch, "we're sorry.
We're getting out."

"Get," was all the guy said.

Later, after a final ride through the dead city, cooled off
at last after the day's heat, I remember collapsing in a bunk
at the IVS dorm, my head spinning out dreams in fast
forward until some guy in a top bunk—sleeping without
a mosquito net—woke up retching and gagging violently
because a sleepy gecko had fallen off the ceiling into his
snoring, open mouth. Another dawnsong.

I had two other friends in the British Pediatric Team,
John Clarke, a young surgeon, and Alex Clokie, who was
in charge of the British "sisters" at Nhi Dong. At some
point Alex and John started living together, and then I
actually had friends who had a real apartment where I could
go, now and then, for dinner or a drink. This was a real
treat. COR paid me only a little more than IVS, which
meant that I could only rarely go to the downtown restaurants and could get into places like the famous Brinks
BOQ restaurant only by sneaking in.

Alex and John, along with the Pediatric Team in general,
kept away from Americans and had a social life that re-
volved around the British Embassy and the medical staff,
which actually wasn't much of a social life, for like Berliner
and me, they put in eighteen-hour days. Maybe I was the
only American allowed into their company since our children were always parked in their hospital, and I saw them
almost every day I was in Saigon.

No one knew better than Alex and John what American
soldiers and American weapons were doing to the children
of Vietnam. Day after day, hour after hour, Alex and her
nurses struggled to make the wards a healthy place to
recover, initially taking the hospital, floor by floor, and

scrubbing it down, to the shock of the Vietnamese staff. Day after day, hour after hour, John Clarke was up to his elbows in blood and gore, performing so many operations with Gordon Barclay that his hands had started to crack and bleed from the constant scrub-downs with Phisohex. During the Tet Offensive, before either Alex or Barclay had arrived in Vietnam, just Clarke and the anesthesiologist had remained in the hospital, operating continually for three days and nights as a pitched battle raged nearby. When they could, they ate tinned food and slept on the operating tables, both of them sustained by a mix of British pride, duty, compassion, and valor that would have won them decorations in the U.S. Army, although, of course, few Army physicians ever labored so hard for Vietnamese.

Clarke, who was only in his late twenties, could be fun when he let off steam. Late one night well after Tet, he was driving home fairly drunk and managed to crash his Landrover into a tree, dislocating both his elbows. The Landrover was jammed up over the curb and onto the bole of the tree trunk. Clarke was lying collapsed over the steering wheel, popped-out arms dangling at his sides, when American MPs came along in their jeep, shone a light in, and demanded Clarke's ID.

"Sir," was Clarke's slurred reply from a state of what must have been the most extraordinary, hazy pain, "I am a British subject."

"Yeah, great. Let's see your ID."

"Fuck off, Yank." Clarke's public-school politeness took an immediate tumble as alcohol, pain, and embarrassment combined with every "third-party national's" irritation at the U.S. military's quite illegal intrusion into their lives (regardless of the state their lives were in).

Instead of dragging him out and clobbering him with nightsticks, the two MPs merely smiled at each other and got back into their jeep, where they sat listening to the radio as Clarke struggled to pull himself together. Now what would he do?

What he did was restart the engine; then, with his two dislocated elbows, he backed the Landrover off the tree and curb and started it down the street, somehow working the jerky gearshift in its stiff floor box, driving quite a distance across the city (with the MPs following in their jeep) until he finally got to the Nhi Dong hospital, where he crashed the thing into a wall, bashed his forehead, and fainted. Vietnamese nurses and an orderly ran out of the hospital. What had happened to Dr. Clarke, their always so proper and reserved surgeon?

The MPs drove away laughing.

On another occasion, Clarke and I were drinking beer one broiled, macadam-melting evening at the soup stalls that converted at nightfall to an open-air beer garden. The stalls were near John and Alex's apartment. Clarke called them "the puke stalls." Hanging out there at night was a bit riskier than at breakfast, for Vietnamese workers—who successfully suppressed a good deal of anti-American hatred by day—tended to let it out as they tanked up on Tiger beer and Japanese whisky in the tropical evenings, waiting for the city to cool off before going home to their cramped, overpopulated shanties piled together on the banks of reeking, pestiferous rivers and tidal creeks turned by the crush of refugeees into open sewers. An American drinking cheaply at the puke stalls had to know when to leave.

That night, Clarke and I were the only foreigners at the tables. Clarke's Landrover was parked by the curb. Beyond the curb, the thinner night traffic zoomed by at a fast clip. At our backs, U.S. Armed Forces Television was flickering bluish light onto the carousers, all of whom were male. A few women ran the concessions, setting up beers, chopping up blocks of ice, making sandwiches, and whacking cleavers down on hunks of Cambodian beef for tomorrow's soup rush. A man with a booze-blotched face and wearing a trench coat (in that equatorial heat!) kept grinning and winking at us in a conspiratorial way. Finally, he came over. He was very drunk. He wanted to buy us drinks.

Clarke said no thank you.

I translated that.

The guy frowned fiercely and offered again, calling across the tables to the woman running the stall. I noticed he was sweating with the effects of alcohol and the hot coat.

Again, Clarke said no.

Now the guy's smile disappeared completely. He said he was CIDG, a secret-police unit.

Clarke said that was just wonderful.

I did not translate this but said thanks anyway but we had to be going soon, and pointed to the Landrover.

"You go that?" the man asked, scoffing at Clarke's crashed-in Rover.

Clarke pursed his lips and made a rude noise at the guy in a kind of British raspberry.

I quickly quoted a proverb (*"Bầu rượu, túi thơ"*) to get a laugh and lighten things up at Clarke's expense: "Stomach full of wine, head full of poems." Clarke's raspberry was just his boozy kind of poem, right? Hey, we're all friends here.

But our mean little Inspector Clouseau wasn't laughing. Instead, he just grinned a kind of insane, forced smile. Then he opened his trench coat to reveal a .45 pistol in a shoulder holster.

We both stared at it.

Oh, God, I thought, an armed drunk, now we're in for it.

Then Clarke raspberried the man and his gun.

Operating on a kind of colonialist theory that one did not show fear to the natives because it encouraged them, I kept a blank face. I just hoped my English friend knew what he was doing by facing down this drunken goofball, who probably just wanted to impress us and later stumble home to tell his family he had chummed it up with some Americans, probably fellow spies, and bought them drinks.

At any rate, the guy then staggered to his feet, walked over to the Landrover, pulled out his pistol, which seemed immense in his little hand, aimed at a front tire, looked at us for a reaction, got none, and fired, shooting out the tire and nearly knocking himself down with the kickback. The commotion raised a hornets' nest of anger from the other drinkers who, joined by the women proprietors, started screaming at him to get out.

This made him adjust his sweltering trench-coat collar like Bogart in *Casablanca* and lurch off down the dark street.

"Him *xấu quá!*" ("very bad!") screeched our barmaid in pidgin English, as she treated us to another round of 33 beer.

Then there was my friend Steve Erhart, who after escaping the Viet Cong Tet siege in Hue was now writing a novel in his single room in the Saigon Moto Hotel, where Vietnamese whores and scam artists wandered in and out of his room along with the odd Filipino rock band trying to score smack. During the day, Erhart was an office manager at the RMK-BRG construction firm, from whose files he would later smuggle to the press the construction plans for the notorious "tiger cage" prison cells. At night, he inhabited the drug demimonde of Saigon. Somehow, despite this life, he managed to write, type, and publish his short stories in *The Atlantic Monthly* and *The Evergreen Review*.

Once Erhart called me at the Buu house and told me to come over right away to the Saigon Moto to meet "some people." These turned out to be three wounded AWOL GIs who had gotten hit in a recent Michelin-plantation sweep. After getting patched up, they had been given two weeks of rest before having to return to their unit. Instead, they headed for Saigon, which was off limits to most field troops. "Hell," one of them said, "I've been fighting for this city; why can't I see it?" One of the others, who limped along with the help of a cane, added, "So, like, what are they gonna do? Send us to Vietnam?"

Erhart wanted to write a news story on them and wanted me along so it seemed more like guys out on the town than an interview. They were wary. They had no reason to trust us and, besides, the MPs could pick them up any-time. Moreover, the three of them, with their worn boots and tattered fatigues, stood out from the Saigon military crowd. All of the Saigon warriors had their footwear spit-shined daily by Vietnamese "mamasans" who also pressed out their uniforms, which, if they got spattered, were spat-tered not with blood but with Bloody Marys. We put the three of them in a cab and directed the driver away from heavily patrolled, downtown Saigon to a Vietnamese res-taurant that had a Marseille-Sicilian cuisine. When we en-tered, the Vietnamese and foreigners looked up from their tables and nervously glanced away. The real war had walked in. Fortunately, the maître d' knew Erhart and gave us seats. I say "fortunately" because we didn't know what these guys would do if they were turned away. If you could sense anything about them right away, it was that they were worn and angry.

They had never been in a restaurant in Vietnam. One said he didn't know that Vietnamese could sit at tables or eat with knives and forks. He didn't mean that as a racist joke; it was real wonderment. His only sense of Vietnam and the Vietnamese had come from his months of humping the countryside, suffering ambush after ambush. In the Michelin plantation, they were not permitted to damage the rubber trees which provided cover for the Viet Cong who had ripped up their company, and their sense of Viet-namese came from seeing small black shapes fleeing into tree lines or from entering remote villages where the ter-rorized families froze before them. Back "in the world" none of them had objected to the war, although just one had enlisted. Now they had their doubts. One of them said, hell, he had no doubts, the war was "just a crock."

We had osso buco, pasta, and Algerian red wine. When we got out on the street, the MPs were waiting for them in two jeeps. The guys just shrugged. "It was worth it," one said. He meant the meal and seeing the city for which he was risking his life. I was glad to see the MPs were gentle, even apologetic, as they took them in. Apparently, they had waited in their jeeps while we finished our meal. The maître d' must have called; in a sense, he was just looking after his business. Really, you couldn't have people like that walking in.

When the MPs hauled them away, we followed the open jeeps on our scooters, watching as one of the soldiers, chatting with an MP in the back, slowly worked out of his pocket a cigarette pack of marijuana, which he dropped casually onto the street, grinning back at us. Erhart followed them on to the police station. I turned off and telephoned my parents from the USO to ask them to call the boys' families and tell them their sons were okay.

Another time, I was having a gin fizz on the Continental Palace's veranda with a friend from UPI who was waiting for the war correspondent Tim Page when Page stomped in from a field assignment dressed in fatigues and carrying an M-16, which of course wasn't allowed. Looking crazed, he pointed the thing at one of the Vietnamese waiters, who froze and nearly dropped his tray of china. Everyone on the veranda stiffened and fell silent. A couple of eraser-headed-Embassy-Marine types looked like they might jump Page just as the waiter began to beg, "Mr. Tim . . ." and Page squirted him down with what turned out to be an M-16 *water pistol*. This caused a roar of relief and laughter and a kind of chain reaction of Pagian lunacy, which I was seeing for the first time. The waiter set down his tray, grabbed the fake gun, and raced outside to the main downtown intersection in front of the National Assembly where a friend of his was the traffic cop. Then, in a slow saunter right out of the Westerns, the waiter—watched by the whole Continental veranda—stalked up to the cop. Suddenly there was a gasp from the veranda crowd and an "Oh, shit" from Page as the cop now started slowly for his pistol, all the while talking to his old friend who had evidently run amok and gotten some soldier's M-16. But then, before the cop could draw his gun, the waiter sprayed him. Now the Continental was roaring. The cop, pixillated by the same burst of dread and humor, yanked the M-16 away from the waiter, abandoned his traffic post, and ran up the steps of the National Assembly where two ARVN soldiers stood guard at the top. He squirted them down too. Indeed, if Page hadn't retrieved the water pistol then, it's possible it would have circulated through Saigon that way until somebody got shot by a real gun or Thieu squirted Ellsworth Bunker.

So it wasn't all bad. Well, if you thought of the beggar families rifling garbage cans behind the Continental while all this was going on, or of the leper clan that lived behind the stucco walls of the nearby cemetery where they were thrown scraps of food, or perhaps of the thousands of farmers driven from their homes and living on sidewalks in cardboard lean-tos, or of the thousands of civilians lying in hospitals, or the thousands who never made it, then it *was* all bad. Wars excite the best and worst in people. Wars test the character. In wartime, Erhart allowed, we're especially conscious of the Two Major Categories (i.e., life and death). Wars offer invigorating displays of the human soul. Wars call upon their participants and observers to reinvent, or to deny, their humanity. My friends responded to the war in diverse ways that were imaginatively far beyond the handful of clichéd roles that have been trotted out onto our TV screens. What my friends did— their humor, their bravery, their looniness, their theatrical play, and their humane hard work—buoyed me. "Happiness or misfortune are prescribed by the will of Heaven, but their source comes from ourselves." Certain misfortunes are a given; it's what you do with them that counts.

Like Gitelson and my CIA friend, Richard, these friends chose their own lives against the backdrop of the war, just as the sad Air Force doctors in Can Tho had chosen theirs. For me, witnessing this drama of the spirit was a wrenching privilege. I grew up in Vietnam. In this particular sense of growing witness and wisdom, it wasn't all bad.

13

TAKING
THE CHILDREN HOME

The work with the children wasn't so bad either. On the contrary. Despite our often brutal failures, it was wonderful to put the lucky ones on planes and know they were heading to the best medical care in the world. I never got used to their maiming but was undeterred by it. We were, after all, saving their lives.

On occasion, however, I was caught off guard. I remember once running up the stairs in Nhi Dong and turning a corner just as four little kids, the oldest no more than seven, ran up to me, each with arms amputated. My stomach did a flop as I reached for a windowsill to steady myself until my head cleared. Another time, John Clarke asked me to stay in the operating room while he worked on Nguyen Thi Thuy, an eight-year-old girl whose jaw we had repaired in San Francisco but which had become infected after her return to Vietnam. I watched as he slit open her scarred chin, so carefully reconstructed in the States, while she lay dead out on the operating table. I remember the unbearable click of his steel probe as he picked at her jawbone. When it was over, and he had discovered and removed an infected sliver of bone, he bandaged her chin and wheeled her into the corridor. I waited by her gurney for her father to come take her home. From past experience, I knew that Thuy's father was often drunk. I waited and waited. He never came.

Finally, I had to carry her like a limp Raggedy Ann down the steps of the hospital. As I walked over to the pool of cabs that sat at the curb, I was thinking, "Poor child. All this done to her, and no one here but me." I was weeping. I remember a woman coming through the main gate who regarded me with terror as she saw my tears and the lifeless girl in my arms: she thought I was carrying a corpse. When I hailed a cab to take us to the Buu house until I could collect her dad, I had to assure the driver that the girl was just sleeping. I never understood why Clarke wanted me to stay in the operating room that time. Maybe to probe the composure I usually kept.

It was experiences such as these that rattled me. When I could prepare myself, I could look at anything. And when I considered that my discomforts were a necessary part of the rescue, they seemed small and bearable. And, finally, when I was actually standing on an airstrip and seeing these cases off to recovery, I felt more happiness and empowerment than I ever guessed possible.

With a new COR doctor, Dale Purves, a first-rate surgeon from Massachusetts General, and with the hiring of Bui Thi Khuy, a university student who handled a lot of our paperwork and who could talk more intimately with the families, Berliner and I succeeded in evacuating still more cases, despite the obstacles constantly thrown up by the American and Vietnamese authorities.

What really came to bother both Berliner and me was the suggestion from our more radical antiwar friends in Saigon that not only were we creating a cruel, war-perpetuating illusion of American concern and responsibility (just look at our name!) but we were helping save these kids' lives only to corrupt them culturally in the United States and so make it impossible for them to live happily in Vietnam again.

In fact, we were getting unsettling reports from several of the COR chapters where children were convalescing near hospital centers in California, Colorado, Hawaii, the District of Columbia, Maryland, Massachusetts, Michigan, Minnesota, Missouri, New Jersey, New York, North Carolina, Oregon, Pennsylvania, and Wisconsin. Some of the children, we were told, were forgetting Vietnamese or refusing to speak it. Some would eat only American food. Some did not want to see the Vietnamese women we had sent along with them as translators and cultural protectors. I had had some training in linguistics at Harvard and Penn State and knew that, once learned, a language was hard to eradicate, but, from Saigon—tank-tracked flat by the worst aspects of American culture—Berliner and I could only speculate as to what was happening to these kids in the United States and what long-term effects it might have.

From Purves, we heard a story about Tran Van Quang, a twelve-year-old we had recently sent. We knew Quang as one of two handsome children of an overweight, funny, impossible nag of a mother who had lived with a French soldier more than a decade earlier. Her daughter was beautiful; her son, good-looking and brilliant. She was excessively proud of them both. Quang, in fact, had just won a national competition and a scholarship to a lycée in France. Just before he was to leave, Quang's mother sent him to say goodbye to his relatives in Phan Thiet. His bus, which was traveling a road closed by the Viet Cong, was blown up by a road mine. Quang was one of the few survivors. He lay on the road for at least an hour until GIs found him and took him to a nearby hospital, where he lost an arm and both legs. At Boston's Children's Hospital, a rather rich, goodwilled woman, who had read about Quang in the Boston Globe and had managed to get up to his room, tried to give him the eighteen-thousand-dollar necklace from around her neck, but was persuaded by Quang's Vietnamese convoyeuse that perhaps this wasn't the best way to contribute toward his medical costs.

What could such pressures do to these children? Were we wrong in helping them? My yardstick on the rightness of what we were doing, even assuming some inevitable cultural erosion and deracination, was that we were at least saving their lives. That mattered first. Later we could anguish over the spiritual damage to those lives. If we had left Quang in Saigon, once his mother had died he would have become a street creature, shoving himself along the sidewalks on a roller board. In Boston, we could stabilize his amputations, fit him with artificial limbs, and train him to walk by himself. Not to grant this chance to Quang—and to others in far worse condition than he—seemed obscene to me.

We started sending Vietnamese schoolbooks and records back to the COR chapters and to the American foster families that volunteered to take care of these children while they were between surgeries (which for some would take years). In those unforeseen spans of time, many of these good people became unable to bear the thought of returning to the war their injured foster children, who often had become a part of their families. Yet we were obliged to do just that. In fact, almost none of the Vietnamese families would have consented to let their children go if they had not had our word that we would return them. To make matters worse, the parents—who could neither read nor write, and who lived in the countryside without electricity or postal service—sometimes failed to send letters to their children in the United States, even if we had left with them a packet of stamped envelopes. We had a hard time convincing foster parents that this did not mean that the parents had abandoned their children—and, correspondingly, that now the foster parents were free to adopt the child. When each child was ready to return, Berliner and I made the arduous and sometimes dangerous trek into the Viet Cong–controlled countryside to locate the child's family before giving the okay to send the child home.

Families in Vietnam are intensely affectionate, large affairs. Not only are households with seven to nine children common, but those households, like the Buus' in Saigon, often include aunts and uncles, grandparents, and cousins. Families are imbued with a Confucian sense of obligation of parent to child, child to parent, and sibling to sibling. Rather than play with dolls, Vietnamese children play with their little brothers and sisters, for the older children usually take care of the younger children when both parents go off to labor in the paddy or the mother goes to the market.

These familial ties extend beyond this life. The proverb "Birds have nests; men have ancestors" plays on the word *tông*, which means both "bird's nest" and "clan." A person is nourished in the nest of his or her ancestors, who guide and instruct the living. Ancestral spirits reside in an altar in most homes. Ancestral bodies are buried in tombs planted right at the edge of the family's lands, so that their very flesh returns to the family soil, and so that the sight of these carefully swept and whitewashed tombs constantly reminds all toilers in the fields of their bloodline. It is a disaster for a couple not to have children, for who will carry the lineage forward and venerate the dead? Who will comfort the couple in their old age and burn incense for them after their deaths? "When young, you need your father; when old, you need your sons," goes another proverb.

This system of spiritual belief created around the family is the highest value of Vietnamese life. It permeates all social conduct. Even the dozen or so titles that Vietnamese employ in addressing nonfamily—"older brother," "little sister," "mother's brother," "father's older brother"— clearly imply family relationship or derive from family words that have been generalized. Our simple generic "I" or "you" would seem incredibly crude to Vietnamese.

Imagine taking a child out of this vibrant tangle of love and obligation. What if a child failed to return? For all our assurances to these families that we would ourselves bring back their children when they were well, Berliner and I were only operating on hope and faith in ordinary, decent persons in the United States who we had no reason to believe knew anything at all about the familial and cultural life these children came from.

At one point, I wrote to Robert Phillips, a doctor in Durham, North Carolina, about one of our cases there, a six-year-old girl, Pham Thi Huong, who had suffered a gunshot wound to her right thigh that had left a badly fractured femur, chronic osteomyelitis, and a draining wound. Now, after we had gotten her to Duke University Hospital, it seemed that the leg might be lost anyway. In addition, the child's foster parents were upset at hearing nothing from Huong's parents. I wrote to address both concerns:

> I am deeply upset about Huong, more so than for any other child we have treated. Perhaps this is because I brought Huong and her mother to Saigon and be-cause . . . I had to reassure the mother many times of the necessity of Huong's evacuation *if her leg was to be saved.* The mother and I knew that the leg would have been lost if Huong remained in Vietnam, and although I, of course, never told the mother that Huong's leg would be saved in the U.S.—and of course the mother asked this many times—this was the hope that the mother operated on.
>
> I got to know [them] well: I cared for them for a day and night's journeying and visited them nearly every day at the Children's Hospital in Saigon. I am still amazed at the mother's fearlessness and determination and love for Huong. She wrote us in Saigon that after her return to Quang Ngai that she cried whenever she made dinner and that the rice did not taste the same when she ate without Huong.
>
> I realize that I am writing this for Mrs. Herman-Giddens whom I don't even know except for your mention of her as Huong's foster mother. I would like

you to send this letter to her (and also the photos of us
in a Danang restaurant en route to Saigon). I want to
assure her that even if she and Huong never hear a
word from the family *that this is evidence of nothing.*

About a year later, after Huong's leg was indeed saved,
her foster parents actually did get a letter from the little
girl's family, which one of our Vietnamese social workers
translated:

> Since Huong was sent to the United States for the
> medical treatment, we have missed her very much, but
> we believe in your charity and we hope and are sure
> that some day our family will be united. We are just
> received a new information that little Huong is re-
> covering now and will return home. We are very happy
> to hearing this.
>   You have contribute very much to the care of Huong.
> We will never forget your charity and your kind-
> ness. . . .

When we finally brought Huong home, her foster parents
took the care to send a letter in Vietnamese with her, along
with pictures of Huong playing with their own children,
and a necklace for Huong on which they had engraved
their address, in case she ever wanted to know how to
reach them. "Tomorrow morning Huong will leave us for
your home," their letter began. "It is with sadness that we
must see her go for we will miss her. We are happy,
though, that she can return to you strong and healthy for
we know you love her and miss her. She has talked often
of you and her brother and sisters." The original of this
three-page report about little Huong to her Pham family
is in Mrs. Herman-Giddens' handwriting. How hard it
must have been to write. The photographs show an American family in love with their tiny visitor.

Just how hard it was for these foster families to return
the children came through again in a later letter that one

woman, a Mrs. J. R. Smurthwaite, wrote to President
Nixon after sending two boys home:

> Dear Mr. President:
> Living in our home for eight months have been three
> Vietnamese war-injured children brought to Oregon
> for medical treatment by the Committee of Respon-
> sibility. Coming to us after weeks of plastic and bone
> surgery were Nguyen Van Phuong, 11, Nguyen Minh
> Trung, 14, and Chau Quynh, a 16-year-old Cambodian
> girl—a paraplegic who will spend the rest of her life
> in a wheel chair.
> A month ago I bade the boys goodbye on a day to
> be remembered as the most anguishing of my life.
> Skilled doctors had done all possible to repair their
> seriously injured legs; Phuong and Trung were now
> returning to their families.
> Realization that the war might again engulf them is
> unendurable. Living with these children, experiencing
> their affection, their laughter, their quick responses and
> intelligence, was an experience we will always treasure.
> But having experienced this relationship we also as-
> sume responsibility for their welfare which must con-
> tinue unto all the days of their lives and of our own.

She went on to ask Nixon to call for a cease-fire and stop
the war.

So the children actually began coming home. It was for
Berliner and me both an immense relief and a consternation
as some of our fears appeared in the flesh. At the end of
May 1969, after a year of sending children to the United
States, two boys returned, Huynh Duc, fifteen years old,
and Ho Bau, eleven. They arrived on Pan Am because the
U.S. government, which had flown them out on Air Force
planes, now found there was no obligation to return them.
"No funds have been appropriated by the Congress for
this purpose," wrote William B. Macomber, Jr., then the

Assistant Secretary of State for Congressional Affairs, in a letter to Senator Charles Percy, who had inquired on our behalf, "and thus no agency of the United States Government can pay for the transportation of these children back to Viet-Nam." Frank E. Loy, the Deputy Assistant Secretary of the State Department's Bureau of Economic Affairs, was even more direct, writing Madeline Duckles in San Francisco that "there is a presumption that such transportation is not in the public interest." In 1968, when the issue first came up, William Bundy, then the Assistant Secretary of State for Asian Affairs, who had been fairly sympathetic to COR when Board members visited him in February of 1967, wrote Needleman that only those children in the States at that time would get a free return. He promised to create a special fund for these cases.

Duc was around the fiftieth child that COR had treated in the United States. He had been wounded when a GI at guard post went berserk one quiet morning and opened up on the village market with a machine gun. Duc had suffered an open fracture to his right forearm and severe gunshot wounds to his legs. Both legs required below-the-knee amputation. Duc, a country boy whose life was virtually ended at fourteen years, became one of Dr. Phung Tuan Hanh's Danang ward "children" until the surgeon recommended him to us for treatment at Kauikeolani Children's Hospital and the Shriner's Hospital for Crippled Children in Hawaii.

Ho Bau had also been evacuated from the Danang hospital on Dr. Hanh's recommendation. In June of 1968, a few months after the My Lai massacre, Bau was burned by napalm dropped from a plane in a free-strike zone near his house while he was playing with some other kids. He suffered third-degree burns over 25 percent of his body, right arm, and both legs. We had gotten him treatment in Boston, at Massachusetts General Hospital, and at another Shriner's Hospital for Crippled Children. Like Duc, Bau was also from Duc Duc (pronounced "Duk Zup," meaning "Virtuous Teaching"). While in the U.S., Bau had received a few letters from his mother (his father had been killed). Miss Bui Thi Khuy, the twenty-two-year-old woman who had worked with us in Saigon, served as Bau's companion, and had translated these letters as best she could:

Duc, Duc, Feb. 5, 1969

Dear Son,
Bau, we received many letters from you. But we couldn't send you a letter. Bau, I know that you are alone in the different people and country. I remember every day and night very very much. Each time I call your name in my heart, I feel sadness and I don't know whom I will talk to. The War separated us. The war took my good son away. Because the situation of the War, so I must carry on. The first and last letter I send to you. I don't know what I tell you. I always pray Heaven protects and gives you the good health. After you will return and live together with us. On that time the peace will come to my heart. Now I don't know when you come back. Today I write a letter let you know that we are well. Please write to me when you receive this letter. Miss Khuy, we are thankful and send you the best regards. Please our family send the best regards and thankful to Bau's foster parents for us. We will never forget them for their kindness to our son. Miss Khuy, please help my son write a letter for us.

Bau's Mother
Nguyen Thi Xung
DUC DUC Tinh Quang Nam
South Vietnam

Now, three months later, with Miss Khuy, who had returned earlier to Vietnam and would soon take another group of children back to the United States, I met the boys when they got off the plane in Saigon. Bau, except for his slightly scarred face, looked like a normal eleven-year-old who had just taken a long plane ride: tired, a little spaced out, and wide-eyed. He was very happy to see Miss Khuy. Duc, on the other hand, his hair thickly oiled, wearing a long-sleeved white shirt and a tie with a bright stickpin, arrived with two mammoth suitcases, a Pan Am bag, and a crated pedal sewing machine. He would not speak Vietnamese, he hoped our house had a TV, and he said that he intended to stay only three months, for he would be returning to live in Hawaii. As proof that his return was already in the works, he produced a card showing his honorary membership in the Coast Guard Club of Hawaii.

At the Buu house, Duc complained for the next several days that his stumps were sore from the chafing of his artificial legs and that he couldn't eat Vietnamese food. While he started to hang out alone in his room, Bau was already out in the alleys, where the Buu children, proud of their new friend, got him to introduce the neighborhood kids to Batman. In his room, Duc fiddled with his three radios and several watches. I began taking him out to lunch at working-class restaurants in Saigon. Once some men—unaware of Duc's lost legs—snickered at this boy who dressed like a middle-aged bureaucrat. Duc took notice. He got rid of the tie and pin on our next outing. Finally, he sold off most of his junk, saving only a radio and a few watches for his family. And when, gradually, he admitted that Vietnam looked "a lot like Kailua," I decided it was time to get him home. For some reason—maybe Miss Khuy's companionship—Bau had always been ready. Now the trick was how to reach their village in the contested mountainous region of Quang Nam Province. After telegramming ahead to their families, Miss Khuy, Bau, Duc, and I began the trek by flying to Danang with all their luggage and the pedal sewing machine, which was a good idea but weighed a ton.

At the Danang hospital, where we expected to link up with the boys' families, we found only Dr. Hanh. Our telegram hadn't made it. Dr. Hanh was immensely pleased with the two boys and with COR. We had done what we promised. Bau's face was almost normal, and he moved his burned limbs with ease where, before, there had only been hard keloidal scars and tendon contractions. Dr. Hanh had Duc walk around him on his new legs, grinning with pleasure as Duc walked proudly and without a waver. Back in Saigon, Duc had really had me worried about his limp and complaints of soreness. Now I knew he was going to be all right.

The only problem was that the parents hadn't arrived and we couldn't, of course, just leave the boys at the hospital. We had a lot to tell the parents about how to maintain Duc's stumps and artificial limbs and how to reach us if anything went wrong again. So we had to get to Duc Duc, but first we had to get to Hoi An. Even though the road to Hoi An had been cut by the Viet Cong, I begged rides for us out of the military airfield later that afternoon on a U.S. Army Blackcat Huey chopper flying to Hoi An. For Miss Khuy, daughter of Northern Catholic refugees, educated in a convent in Macao, and never before out of Saigon except for her Macao and U.S. trips, this was a frightening first.

When our chopper arrived, its whooping blades churned the runway grit into our teeth, blowing up Miss Khuy's *aó dài* so her flat little tummy showed as she held on to her straw hat and dark glasses with one hand and guided Bau forward to the chopper with the other, while the pilot waved us on to hurry. Duc could not run, and I remember setting down my briefcase, picking him up, and running with him, lifting him up to the door gunner, who hauled him in, and then running back for their luggage (the crated sewing machine, mercifully, would follow later, by armed convoy). Only when we were in the air did I remember that I had left my briefcase with my .38, my passport, and my money out on the tarmac. Getting the pilot to go back seemed hopeless and stupid. I fell into a huge funk. The only thing that made me feel better was when Duc told me he was sorry I had lost the briefcase with all my stuff. He said that if I hadn't had to worry about getting him on board it wouldn't have happened. This was such a simple, disarming thing to say that I could hardly believe he was the same greedy, self-centered, Americanized brat of a few weeks before.

Huey helicopters fly with their side doors open and hold about six passengers besides the pilot, copilot, and gunner, who sits behind a big belt-fed machine gun on a pivot post. Over the ocean, the gunner opened up at the water. The machine gun was deafening. I looked down at the waves but couldn't see anything; maybe he was shooting at a whale. Rather, I suspected that he was firing just to see the fear on Miss Khuy's face. In fact, she looked sick.

From Hoi An, we took another helicopter, which was resupplying Marine field units patrolling near Duc Duc. We flew for about thirty minutes over abandoned fields cratered like the moon, over bare defoliated mountain crests, over deserted villages, and over shining river loops. When we finally got to Duc Duc and hovered momentarily above its sea of brown thatched houses swelled by the flimsier shacks of refugees, I wondered how we would find the boys' homes, for Duc Duc was surprisingly large, and there are no street names or numbers in a Vietnamese village; moreover, we had just a few hours before the supply helicopter went back to Hoi An. If we missed it, we would have to spend the night in Duc Duc, either in the village, which would not have been safe for me, or in the Marine camp, which the pilot told me got mortared nearly every night and, anyway, would have been pretty rough on Miss Khuy.

Bau said he lived under a big pine tree. A Marine sergeant with a jeep parked by the chopper pad befriended us and, with all the luggage bouncing on the rutted mud roads, drove us around until we spotted, sure enough, an immense pine that stood out over one corner of the village.

Bau's mother was at market. His old grandmother was

home and she hugged him and seemed as bewildered as the rest of us as we waited for his mother to return. "You mean these kids was in the U.S. of A.?" the sergeant pondered. "I swear." A crowd of neighbors gathered. Some just touched Bau as if he were magic. He looked at me. He was frightened by the growing crowd. I asked Bau where he had been wounded, thinking he would point off in some direction and regain his composure by considering all the really frightening things that had happened to him. He pointed to an area about seventy-five yards from where we were standing. That was the Free Strike Zone. It was his backyard. Anyone could be shot there at any time.

While Miss Khuy was talking to the grandmother and Duc was sitting on top of the luggage in the back of the jeep, itchy to get to *his* home, Bau's mother came walking up the road. When a neighbor rushed down to tell her we were there, she threw her hands to her face and raced the thirty yards to her house, pushed through the crowd, and hugged her son, the one who had gone to "the different people," the one whose name she had said at night in her heart. Now, under the brilliant blue sky, she wailed, "*Trời ơi!,*" calling out to Heaven and weeping and, finally, just calling Bau's name. Bau, already rattled, looked at me as the bonds between him and the people who had repaired him started to dissolve and he was bewildered by what to do with this mother that he hadn't seen for a year, in front of these villagers that he could not remember by name. Then, under the sheer weight of his mother's love, he was overwhelmed and began crying and hugging her too. Everyone was crying. Miss Khuy was crying. She smiled through her tears when she looked over at me and saw that I was crying. I think even the leathery Sergeant was moved. Bau's minutes of burning, his pain and endurance, his mother's love, and the enormous distance that had separated them overwhelmed us all, a crowd of excited people milling about a jeep under a big pine tree in a raggedy village overswept by a brilliant sky.

It was getting late and we had to get Duc home, so after a few minutes, Miss Khuy spoke to Mrs. Xung and told her how to contact us if they needed help. Then Miss Khuy gave Bau a hug. She gave his mother some stamped, addressed envelopes, then we climbed back in the jeep and started out for Duc's house, guided by a neighbor who had climbed onto the jeep's hood.

Duc's father, Huynh Cat, who made rice paper for his living, was at their home near the market where Duc had been gunned down. His mother, however, had just gone to Danang in response to our telegram. When Duc saw his father waiting for us outside their house, Duc *jumped* down from the back of the jeep and strode over to Mr. Cat, whose smile grew wider as he saw his son grown older, looking rather like him, and walking. Still smiling, and without saying anything, he shook my hand while looking at his son, marveling at him, smiling at him, then nodding his head to me and Miss Khuy in thorough approval of how his boy had come back.

I felt just wonderful.

14

PRINCE BUU HOI'S WATCH

In early June of 1969, a letter from Lewis B. Hershey, Director of Selective Service, reached me at the USAID post office in the Mondial. "Effective June 24, 1969," it read, I was "released from the performance of civilian work contributing to the maintenance of the national health, safety, or interest under the Universal Military Training and Service Act." I had, in fact, served in Vietnam about a year longer than the average soldier. Reading my release, it did not occur to me that a soldier might have gotten decorated for what I had done (well, at least a Purple Heart) or that a soldier would have gone home with educational benefits, some guaranteed health care, probably even some back pay. All that stuck in my head when I got the General's letter was that *I could go home*. Only later did I think that not only had I really served my country, but my country had served itself by letting me do this work.

I was ready to go home. Despite all my displays of energy, I was depleted. I was also glad to return because I had been invited to prepare testimony on civilian casualties for Edward Kennedy's Senate Subcommittee on Refugees, Escapees, and Civilian Casualties. I had become an expert in Vietnamese misery. Over the months, I had assembled a devastating picture of the civilian slaughter, gathering my facts from meetings with Colonel Coppedge, the Director of USAID Public Health; with Dr. Vu Nghia An, the Assistant Minister of Health; with Dr. Isaiah Jackson, the U.S. Medical-Officer-in-Charge of the Danang Surgical Hospital; with Dr. Khoa from Can Tho; with Dr. Clarke from the British Team; with John Hayes, the administrator of the Children's Medical Relief Unit; with Mr. Trang Dat Hieu, the administrator of Cho Ray hospital; with Dr. Hanh in Danang; and with Dr. Barr, the regional health adviser for the IVth Corps region. I was ready to present the wretchedness of health care in Vietnam in which six to seven thousand civilian war casualties were *admitted* to hospitals each month, where thousands of others died before getting there, where others still were treated in Viet Cong facilities, and where, conservatively (I was using AID and DOD figures), 100,000 civilian men, women, and children were dying each year in the fighting. Indeed more of them were dying than were combatants of both sides. To make my quotations and numbers strike home, I described in some detail our last six cases. My figures were a far cry from the 127 civilian casualties that Robert McNamara, at the time of his Cambridge performance that propelled me to Vietnam, was acknowledging as the *total* number of war-related civilian injuries that he knew of:*

CASE BIOGRAPHIES

As has been known for some time, about 60% of the civilian war injuries are children under 16. This high

---

*Ironically, and sadly (for those he helped slaughter and for the pain he caused himself), McNamara had now come to a different view as well. In May of 1969, in an in-house memorandum quoted by Neil Sheehan in his A Bright Shining Lie (p. 685), McNamara wrote: "The picture of the world's greatest superpower killing or seriously injuring 1,000 noncombatants a week, while trying to pound a tiny nation into submission on an issue whose merits are hotly disputed, is not a pretty one."

proportion results from South Vietnam's relatively high child population percentage and from the obvious indefensibility of children in a war which rages about their homes. . . . It may be helpful to the Subcommittee to describe six children who were referred to the Committee of Responsibility during the last two months of my stay. These children are representative of many of the conditions which concern this Subcommittee.

CASE 74: A 12-year old boy whose upper and lower lips, jaw and mandible were destroyed after picking up a blasting cap—Vietnam is littered with such playthings—which he had found, together with several small mines and grenades, near the orphanage where he has lived since being abandoned by his mother. The boy's father had been killed some years previously. The mother could no longer support the family. The child will receive in Philadelphia long-term orthopedic, orthodontic, and plastic surgery which is entirely unavailable in Vietnam.

CASE 75: A 12-year old boy found by the roadside near Saigon with his hand destroyed and both eyes and ears perforated by grenade fragments from a blast of unknown origin. He cannot speak, see, or hear. No one knows where his family is. Until our discovery of and interest in this boy, he had been chained to a bed in a large orphanage near Saigon. Although there are two Vietnamese ophthalmologists in Saigon, the child had never been referred to them. In Boston, the child will receive delicate ear and eye surgery and rehabilitative training.

Even as I typed these awful bios on our office's ancient Royal, I knew I wasn't saying enough. I wanted to say what it *felt* like to encounter the first boy, who was dying of malnutrition because he couldn't get enough food through the small, hard, jawless hole that was now his mouth as he lay on a floor in the orphanage spooning in gruel, holding a hand mirror to see where it was going, because he didn't have any feeling there anymore. What it *felt* like to unlock the second boy from his bedstead under the hateful glare of an evil and stupid Vietnamese Catholic nun who had chained him there because she thought him crazy. I took him to Clarke, whose examination revealed that the reason this filthy, deaf, blind, speechless, mutilated boy had been butting his head against orphanage walls was that he had ear infections that were driving him wild with pain.

I wanted my words, like the infections raging in that boy's ears, to inflict pain on any American who heard them.

The evening before I left Vietnam, I remember wheeling down to the docks at the end of Nguyen Hue Street, not far from the elegant old Majestic Hotel, the floating My Canh restaurant, and the rough riverside, no-honkies strip of bars where black GIs hung out with the whores that catered especially to them. After locking my scooter inside the dockyard gate, ignoring as I always did the guard posted to keep out thieves and sappers, I climbed on board a commercial freighter that looked emptied by shore leaves. Carrying a new briefcase, with a new .38, I crossed the gangplank and the first deck to get to the ship's river side. A crewman passed me. I gave him a stiff hello, as if I had important business and damn it he'd better not interrupt me, and then I saw no one.

Now, with the upper decks between me and the Saigon traffic, I could hear the tidal river slapping the boatside. For a while, I stood at the railing looking at the muddy water, at the bobbing snags of swamp stuff that drifted by, at the little ferries puttering back and forth to the village on the other side, and at the palm trees overshadowing the huts on the opposite shore. Then I reached into my bag and pulled out my new, stainless-steel .38 Smith & Wesson. It had belonged to Sean Flynn, now missing in Cambodia with his reporter pal, Dana Stone. Jerry Liles, who somehow ended up with all their stuff, had sold it to me for twenty dollars.

With my left hand clutching the rail, I reached back and lobbed the gun into the river. It disappeared with a satisfying plunk. Then I threw in my box of shells. As a CO, I had been a bit of a flop, and it was good to see the gun gone and out of any use.

The next morning, I started home on Air France, through Bangkok and Teheran, and finally to Paris, where I stopped to visit the National Liberation Front offices on the Rue Laverrier near Montparnasse. Berliner and I, having often feared for our safety when we escorted returning children to their homes in the countryside, had pieced together in Vietnamese a description of COR to give to the Viet Cong whom I was now going to meet. I had never met any VC except the men who had kidnapped me briefly during my first month in Vietnam. Indeed, no one Berliner and I knew—except Gitelson—had met them.

Just outside their Mission across from the Luxembourg Gardens, a French cop stopped me with a *"Monsieur?"* as I reached to ring the bell. He held out his hand and asked for my passport, positioning himself between me and the Embassy door as he looked at my picture, then glanced back at me, and finally gave it back. With a smirk that indicated he knew I was a nut, he stepped aside. He motioned me to ring. Now I saw there was another cop, in a car parked by the curb. When the Mission door finally opened, I introduced myself in Vietnamese. This startled both the cop and the Viet Cong diplomat. Dressed in a dark-blue suit, he cocked an eye at the policemen as if to say, "I don't know who he is; stick around," but nevertheless let me in.

Once inside, I offered my *carte de visite* and our description of COR. Still responding in French, the Viet Cong diplomat told me to have a seat; then he disappeared down a hall and through a door. A man who appeared to be

addressing envelopes smiled up at me from behind a desk
that sat beneath a huge picture of Ho Chi Minh. On another wall was a poster with three women holding AK-
47s on a blood-red background; below their bare feet were
the words "CAMBODGE VIETNAM LAOS VICTOIRE." Finally, the first man came back with two others who offered
me tea. Despite the summer heat, all three men were neatly
dressed in suits and ties with vests or sweaters. They were
small men, whose outfits might have come from the boys'
department at an American store. We sat down at a coffee
table. A maid brought a pot of tea and some crockery cups
right out of the Saigon market. As they poured tea and
passed about cups, I couldn't imagine their small hands
gripping AK-47s, although almost certainly some of them
had done that once. They were calm and curious. I was
sweating in my jacket and tie. Outside in Luxembourg
Gardens, even the chestnuts were wilting, and the pigeons
perched listlessly by the medieval fountains.

As we talked, they were amused by my Vietnamese and
repeated some of my phrases to one another. Unlike most
foreigners who thought they spoke Vietnamese, I had
learned the tones accurately and could be understood. But,
unwittingly, I had learned the dialect of the Mekong Delta,
not the more proper speech of the North. This was apparently amusing to these men, only one of whom was a
Northerner. One of them, noting my IVS stint, volunteered that he was from Can Tho. I said something *de
rigueur* about the beauty of the Ninh Kieu district. I realized
that there was little reason for them to think I wasn't a spy
of some kind.

At last they referred to the sheet of paper I carried, and
I told them about the Committee of Responsibility and
about my special concerns. They shook their heads sym-
pathetically and then ended our talk by saying that Vietnamese would take responsibility for their own affairs and
that I should go home and use my experience to help stop
the war. I don't think they had ever heard of COR. Perhaps

they too thought I was a nut. When I was shown the door, one of them patted my shoulder in the same way that someone had reassured me that terrifying day in Cao Lanh nearly two years before.

From my meeting, it seemed evident that the Viet Cong had never heard of COR, and that led me to my other mission in Paris: to meet Prince Nguyen Phuc Buu Hoi, the former Ambassador–at–Large in Vietnam (under Diem) whose cousin had been, at the same time, the Minister of Health in the North. Dr. Buu Hoi, who had once built a small nuclear reactor at Dalat (which during the war was still used for teaching), had until recently been head of the Institut du Radium just outside Paris. He had also been a research colleague and friend of Samuel Epstein, one of our Board members and the COR doctor who had riled up the Can Tho MILPHAP team. My first encounter with Buu Hoi was a postcard he sent me from the Hôtel Riviera in Aix-en-Provence, complimenting me on a short poem set on the Binh Thuy River that I had had published in *The New York Times,* and which Sam must have sent him. Buu Hoi, whose given name—like those of all the Nguyen royalty—was part of a poem written by an Emperor ancestor, was a complexity of delicacy and hard will, a rotund man with poor health and Coke-bottle glasses, who nonetheless had a powerful effect on intellectual Western women. He was also, as I later learned from *The Pentagon Papers,* one of the cleverer players in the war, suffering the vilification of his countrymen without protest because in the last days of the Diem regime he had been authorized by Diem and his brother, Nhu, to begin secret peace negotiations with the North. Buu Hoi had in fact nearly arranged for a truce in 1963. Then the assassinations of Diem and Nhu ended all hopes of a separate peace that would exclude American participation.

Originally, I was going to meet the Prince, as Sam liked to call him, to discuss the possibility of COR's offering medical aid to civilians in the North. But in the time since

Buu Hoi was supposed to have carried our intention with him to Hanoi (and presumably had gotten a reply), he had died of a sudden heart attack that was brought on, Sam and some of his other friends believed, by the suicide of one of Buu Hoi's oldest friends, a distinguished French scientist in his eighties who had concluded in a farewell note that the world was going to hell, then leapt from his balcony. Buu Hoi, who had maneuvered through the cataclysmic colonial depression, through a French medical education, through World War II, through the Japanese occupation, through the abdication of his Emperor-uncle, Bao Dai, through the rise of the Viet Minh, and through the wars against the French and then the Americans—all the while pursuing his extraordinary talents in science as well as his clever avenues of diplomacy—seemed to slow and collapse inward with his elderly friend's suicide, the suicide note piercing his chest like a montagnard's dart.

So now Buu Hoi was dead himself, and I was coming to offer respects and to find out from Patricia Boshell, his good friend, editor, and secretary, if he had gotten any response from Hanoi about our proposal. I had actually met Buu Hoi twice—once at the top-floor Pan Am Building restaurant in New York, where he was dining with the Indochina historian Ellen Hammer, and then along with Sam Epstein at the San Francisco Airport restaurant where immediately upon seeing us Buu Hoi apologized profusely for having foolishly carried my Hanoi proposal in his suit pocket. It was my proposal in the sense that I was its sole signator: the COR Board could not risk the accusation of "trading with the enemy." After all, we had children in the United States to look after and get home, as well as more to bring out with Air Force and Embassy cooperation. I, however, if the proposal were discovered, was a mere employee that COR could disavow. Anyway, that was our rationale for my drafting the letter, which indeed, as Buu Hoi explained, had been found that day in his suit jacket and taken from him as he cleared customs.

Now, nearly a year later, the day after my meeting at the Mission of the Liberation Front, whose representatives seemed oblivious to COR's existence, I took a taxi to Patricia Boshell's apartment on the Right Bank's Villa Ségur. Although he had been dead for months, Buu Hoi's things were still all around the apartment: mementos, photos, books, little *chinoiserie*. On Patricia's fireplace mantel I noticed a photograph of her in a white dress and sun hat along with the Prince, Ngo Dinh Diem, and Henry Cabot Lodge, all in white linen suits, with Lodge towering above and smiling down upon the chubby little man we liked to call "the Churchill of Asia."

I looked at her with real surprise.

"That was taken," Patricia said, "the day before the assassinations. We had to flee Saigon. If the French Ambassador hadn't intervened for us, I don't know what would have happened to Buu Hoi." She went on to tell me how Buu Hoi then became, purely on the authority of his own gall and lineage, the Vietnamese Ambassador-without-portfolio to Madagascar until he was able to organize the Institut in Paris.

Then she reached up to the mantel and took down a man's watch, an old Omega from the forties.

"You take it," she said. "He loved your poem about the Binh Thuy."

A few days later, at the beginning of the crowded flight to New York, a young woman with two small boys asked me and the woman next to me if we would change seats with her and her eight-year-old son so they could be next to her other, seven-year-old son.

"If you don't want to, just say so." She smiled when she noted my hesitation. She was seated across the aisle. Her one son was at her right; the son in question was across the aisle in front of me, on her left. She wanted to sit right behind him. The woman next to me pretended she hadn't heard the request.

Handbags and passengers were still pushing through the aisle. I had just sat down and had gotten my luggage stowed and I did not feel like moving. I said that if she didn't mind, I would stay where I was.

She said "Okay," and then, in sudden tears, she lit into me. "People today are so unfeeling, so selfish," she said. "If you had children, you would understand!"

Puzzled, I looked at her. If she had reached out her arm, she could have touched the son that she wanted to sit behind. I thought of the children who had littered the village battlefields to be picked up, perhaps, by U.S. helicopters, children who perhaps died en route in filthy bullock carts and three-wheeled Lambrettas, who perished in field hospitals for want of an IV or antibiotics or a doctor's presence, children whose parents would never know what had happened to them. I thought of the children I had evacuated, children separated from their families by years and by ten thousand miles of silence. This American woman's distress seemed selfish and absurd, but, I supposed, on her terms quite reasonable. I then realized she was suffering a personal tragedy of a kind that no longer made sense to me. I guess I should have been delighted in some way that she could reach adulthood, even motherhood, with such a limited sense of tragedy. But personal tragedies common to middle-class Americans in the sixties were pretty easy to come by, weren't they? Michael's acne; Debbie's crooked teeth; Granny's demise. And, more importantly, did they open up Americans to the pain of others? The war I had come from was evidence in reply. Year after year of slaughter in their name and yet most Americans managed to ignore it. I thought of saying all this to her. Instead, I just said, "I understand."

And then I was home, home being a cabin in the woods outside Penn State where I was to begin teaching in the fall, but since I had enough money to last until January, I asked if I could start then. In the meantime, I walked the

Allegheny woods, wrote a blurry account of my year, and ventured off now and then to Boston where I joined the Board of Directors of the Committee. Clyde wrote me from "Jeddah, the Desert, Nowhere," sending some money for a four-year-old girl who had had the side of her face blown away and was now in Los Angeles. The Clarkes wrote from Sheffield, where John was doing surgery and Alex was carrying their first baby. Erhart sent stoned, Asian boosterisms from Indonesia, after abandoning his ethereal wife, Crystal (who had learned traditional Lao dance and was now trying to translate Vietnamese poetry), to John Steinbeck IV, the author's son who having been discharged from active duty in Vietnam was now gathering his "lysergic Buddhist" friends on an island in the Mekong Delta run by a comical Taoist monk. I wanted to be with them.

I bought a scythe and mowed part of the meadow to the road, cutting paths along the creek down to blueberry bushes where bears sometimes could be found munching berries in the evening. I spent hours, days, walking the trails, discovering the fern thickets where deer bedded down near the creek; I spooked grouse out of hawthorns and tangles of fox grapes; I marveled at the quietude of jack-in-the-pulpits and lady's slippers deep in the untrod woods behind my rented cabin.

I had been hired to teach grammar theory to education majors who needed a smattering of linguistics for their teacher certifications. I tried to prepare for my classes, but couldn't keep my mind on the books. The summer wore to a close, and still all I thought about was Vietnam. I tried to talk to my new colleagues, mostly thirty-something men who had gone from prep school or high school directly to college, then to graduate school, and then to teaching. Maybe they had worked summer jobs. But that was it. That was their worldly experience. I sensed that I made them nervous. They made me nervous. At parties for new faculty, I had a hard time locking on to anybody's conversation. At one party, my long-haired host took me aside to say that smoking marijuana in front of everybody wasn't cool. I remember being awfully embarrassed. My sense of the current scene had been formed by reading *Newsweek* for the past two years in Vietnam; I thought everybody smoked dope. I was twenty-six years old and had nearly nothing in common with anyone I met. Instead of mingling, I stood by the record player, trying to catch up on the rock-and-roll I had missed in Vietnam. I bought records and took them back to the cabin, where I sat on the screened porch and listened.

I waited on the mail and word from my Vietnam friends. From Clients' Mail at the Bank of New South Wales in Australia, I heard from David Tichbourne, who had been a repairer of heavy hospital equipment in Vietnam, a job that he took in order to gather firsthand facts against his country's participation in the war. Tichbourne was schizo-phrenically split into a dead-serious, tediously ranting antiwar activist and a beer-drinking goofball. I had nick-named him Aardvark as if, in some sense, that beast ex-plained this duality. The name stuck among our friends. Characteristically, Tichbourne appended this P.S. to his otherwise earnestly serious letter:

> I'd like to know! Did you really drop your trousers and show your ass to those army guys at the hospital in the Delta? I remember reading recently that some-where in China during a demonstration not so long ago the mob showed their contempt by using this ges-ture, and the article said that its an old Chinese insult. Did you do it for this reason? . . . I'm anxious to know.
>
> Ardvark

Around the same time, Sandra Johnson, who had been captured and then released by the North Vietnamese who had taken Hue during Tet, wrote from Cambridge, Massachusetts, that she

> remembered Hue as a paradise lost, where monuments and moonlight, poetry and personal affection were the vivid elements of daily life. Perhaps this was an illusion created by linguistic inadequacy and political repression. Yet in my mind I like to believe it was truly so. Sometimes I think my life's most fertile urges are those that seek to recreate this lost (imagined) Hue.

Sitting on the cedar-plank bridge above the bright creek chattering through the hollow, I realized, to my horror, that I missed the war.

Maybe it was just Asia that I missed. Maybe I was just experiencing revulsion for America. At the end of the sixties, especially after what I had witnessed in Vietnam, I began to think that maybe I wasn't going to be able to live with my fellow Americans. Martin Luther King and Robert Kennedy had been assassinated the year before. General Curtis LeMay wanted to bomb the Vietnamese "back into the Stone Age" with, if necessary, tactical nuclear weapons. At the university just over Bald Eagle Mountain, a handful of radical students marshaled a feeble demonstration down College Avenue and some of my rural neighbors went after them with ax handles which they swung at the marchers from the beds of passing pickups.

My friends kept writing for me to join them. From Steve Erhart, now floating around Bali pursuing petite women and trying to write magazine articles, I got a bookmailer full of opiated marijuana and a letter extolling the virtues of Asia beyond Saigon and asking:

> And what of your plans? Are you thinking of returning to Asia when school lets out? Verily, I say, life is much better here. One gets a distorted pic-

ture living in Vietnam; life is not altogether normal
there. But in a country without war and without too
many Americans, it's very good. Cheap. Lots of grass.
No harassment by soldiers, police, angry negroes,
troublesome whites of the right and left, and all those
hyper-tense contemporaries that litter the American
landscape.

. . . Please write. My mail still comes to the American consulate in Surabaya, where I will visit from time
to time from my mountain retreat a few miles to the
south.

Was he nuts sending stuff like that? From the cabin's
peeling porch steps, I looked up from the letter to the
bright autumn meadow where, here and there, raspberry
canes were turning purple, Queen Anne's lace was withering up into dry cups, and scraggy heads of joe-pye weed
were nodding over the graveled drive. I felt far away from
anything that counted, from anything urgent, from what
Erhart called "a life lived between the two major categories, i.e. Being Alive and Being Dead."

My sense of estrangement came in big whacks. Almost
as soon as I had gotten home, I had received a letter from
Miss Khuy in Saigon. She and her family had taken in Dao
Thi Thai, the teenaged girl who had been scalped by propeller blades when her family's boat got knocked over by
mortars, and whom COR had treated in Boston. She was
now learning to read and write and to be a seamstress
before finally returning to her family near Can Tho. Khuy
would soon be leaving with another group heading to the
United States. Just before I had left, I had asked Khuy to
tell me the report on Tran Van Quang's mother. (Quang
was the trilateral amputee in Boston whose French father
had deserted the family.) After Quang had left for Boston,
his mother had started visiting our office in Saigon complaining of pain and weariness. Neither Berliner nor I believed her complaints because she was always complaining
about something, but finally, to shut her up, I had arranged

a referral for her with a surgeon at the Seventh-Day Adventist Hospital in Saigon. Now Miss Khuy's letter said that Mrs. Rot had been diagnosed with lymphatic cancer. "I think she is going to died soon. Last week Dick and I helped her got in Cancer Hospital in Gia Dinh."

"This morning Dick and Jerry [Liles]," she continued, "went to the Police asked for my Passport. Hope, I will leave soon. Dick choose three more wounded children. They might go to U.S. We are busy as you was here. What are you doing there? Hope see you soon."

But I never saw her again. A few weeks later, I got a letter from Berliner saying that, while riding her Honda near the central market, Miss Khuy had been crushed by a drunken ARVN soldier running a red light with his two-ton truck.

Miss Khuy's death made me feel incredibly useless and even more alone. Useless, because even the little that we seemed to have accomplished in Vietnam was now unraveling. More alone, because increasingly I realized that I really had no one to talk to about Miss Khuy or any of the other memories of Vietnam that occupied my thoughts.

When winter came, I found myself still walking the woods talking to myself about distant events, plodding the snow drifts in yellow boots whose metal clasps jingled as I pushed past the snow-packed hemlocks to the black creek that, like me, kept its own conversation, wriggling out of the ice under gloomy skies. Standing in my plowed driveway, I heard clutches of oak leaves rustling around me. As I looked back to my empty cabin in the hollow across the creek, logs snapped in the fireplace, shunting puffs of blue smoke up and out the chimney, against the dark pines and the foggy hillside. Rendered mute, my memories a turmoil of lost friendships and spilled blood, I looked back at the empty cabin and realized I was enduring a kind of exile. Like poor Raleigh pacing The Lie in his tower, I saw the heavens above me as "high, far off, and unsearchable."

One morning when I had finally started teaching, I was having breakfast and reading *The New York Times* before walking up to my class (who were in junior high when I went to Vietnam) when I read on the fifth or sixth page that the village of Duc Duc had been caught in a crossfire and burned. Duc Duc. The Village of Virtuous Teaching toward which Miss Khuy and I had labored so hard to return Bau and Duc. I wondered what had happened to them, especially Duc who couldn't run. If they had somehow escaped, then the best I could say for our efforts was that we had saved their lives and returned them home so they could become homeless. Were all our efforts just so much more American folly? Who could know? With my thoughts sparking like tracers, I finished breakfast, walked up onto campus, and taught my grammar class. I talked about allophones, minimal pairs, and immediate constituents. All the while, I thought I would explode with grief. At my wrist, the Prince's watch was ticking like a bomb.

PART THREE

THE RED CLOTH

YOUNGER HUMANIST FELLOW,
NATIONAL ENDOWMENT
FOR THE HUMANITIES

15

DUKING IT OUT
OUTSIDE
THE ROYAL HAWAIIAN

In front of the bank windows, on a side street off palm-lined Kaulakaua Boulevard near the big pink Royal Hawaiian Hotel and the jungle-motif outdoor mall just up from the Waikiki beaches, a skinny kid in jeans had grabbed a blonde teenager by her wrists and kept raising his other hand to hit her as she squirmed in his grip and seemed to be pleading something. Inside, tellers and customers paused from their banking chores to watch through the sunny plate-glass windows as the boy raised his hand, the girl flinched, and then he unclenched his fist as he shouted some muted accusation. Slowly the people in the bank turned back to their business. A Hawaiian doper and his hippie girlfriend.

It was August 1971, and my wife and I were in the Bank of America on our way to Vietnam. All that summer, we had been staying in a dive motel in Waikiki while I studied Vietnamese seven hours a day at the university and Lonnie hung around the Manoa campus or the tacky beach near the motel, a jammed strip taken over by low-budget tourists, knots of tough Hawaiian teenagers strung out on drugs, and phalanxes of Nikon-toting, pale-skinned Japanese businessmen who wanted snapshots of themselves with bikini girls. I had a Younger Humanist Fellowship from the National Endowment for the Humanities to return to Vietnam and collect on tape whatever remnants I could find of the oral poetic tradition known as *ca dao*. The Fulbright Commission had just sent me travel funds and now, just one day before leaving for Vietnam, we were trying to cash their check. The problem was, of course, that I didn't have a current account with the bank (although I still had a passcard from its Saigon branch), and the check was for twelve hundred dollars or so, the cost of one round-trip ticket from Philadelphia to Saigon. As the argument outside continued to draw glances at the window, our teller was starting to sound apologetic about my check. Then the girl's scream pierced the thick plate glass, stiffening the backs of everyone inside the bank as the boy started to slap her in earnest.

"Stay here," I said to Lonnie. Her straight blond hair pinned up in circling braids, she was just twenty-two years old and looked impossibly young. Her blue eyes widened in fright as I left her in line with our papers and went out after the girl, who now was being dragged into an alley.

Outside, in the shock of sunlight, I could see that lots of people seemed to be ignoring the commotion of the couple as the girl screamed "Let me go!" and the guy—obviously someone she knew—yanked her along.

"Excuse me," I called as I caught up to them, "I know it's none of my—"

With only the pause that it took for him to let go of the girl and turn around, the boy punched me straight in the jaw. I collapsed to the sidewalk and, as I fell, the back of my head hit a parking-meter pipe. *That* nearly knocked me out, but just for a moment because as I was shaking the tweety-birds out of my eyes, I discovered that Lonnie was helping me get up. Ahead, I could see the guy still dragging the screaming girl into the alley.

He was a skinny kid, brown as teak, with lank long dark hair. This time when I caught up to him, I didn't say a word but just spun him around by his shoulder and popped him in the face.

To my surprise (I hadn't done this sort of thing before; even as a kid, I had fled from fights, much to the shame of my friends and older brother), HE WENT DOWN. Not knowing what to do next, I jumped on him, keeping my weight on top of him for fear he'd get up. Then I discovered I was punching his face so hard and so often that it ballooned into a kind of cartoon face as I exhausted all the punch in my arm. Literally. My arm went weak. I couldn't punch anymore. Now I was frightened that he would really kill me, so I pressed down upon him as he whipped his head left and right and cried "Let me up! Let me up!" and his dirty-blonde girlfriend in her cutaway jeans was yelling "Stop!" and trying to pull me off him.

"Get 'er away," I bellowed to Lonnie, and I hunkered down close to the guy's beady, drug-drained eyes and heard him garble out, "Er 'urting me." My thumb was in his mouth. My last punch had been so spastic that my right thumb had landed in his mouth. Suddenly I was afraid he'd gnash down on my thumb, so I tucked it into the side of his left cheek and then, with my own mouth almost next to his ear, in a huge surge of evil inspiration, I said, "You're fucking right. I'm going to rip it to your ear," and with that I began to pry the full force of my thumb and fist against the corner of his mouth until indeed it began to rip apart in my hand.

"My 'owf!"

But I kept ripping until my hand was slippery with blood and both Lonnie and his girlfriend were pulling on me and yelling for me to stop.

When I got up and left him to go back to the bank, he was thrashing about on the sidewalk holding his face as his girlfriend knelt beside him, whimpering. And when I walked back into the bank with Lonnie—my clothes grimed and stuck with sand and gravel, my right hand crimson with his blood—a bank clerk gave me a clutch of Kleenex, some guy yelled "Way to go," and our own teller, who had been about to say no to cashing my check, now pushed a pile of greenbacks at me and said, "You're crazy. They're all on uppers and downers or something. His girlfriend probably likes it." Then she remembered to shove my Fulbright check over for me to sign.

"Well, he should have hit her at home, then. I didn't want to have to watch it."

She smiled and said to Lonnie, "You've got a brave husband, honey, but you better get him out of here fast. Those guys travel in packs."

Luckily, we were out of Honolulu the next morning. On the Pan Am flight to Guam, Tokyo, and Saigon, as Lonnie snoozed on my shoulder, I couldn't forget the fight. How could I do that to someone's mouth? Just rip it open and, moreover, *take pleasure—take power*—from letting him know I intended to do that just as I did it? I tried to scan my current feelings, looking for some shame and remorse. I wasn't the least bit sorry. Something new was at work in John Balaban.

Flying away from Hawaii, I felt a stab of worry for myself and for the girl sleeping on my shoulder. Lonnie had never gone farther from Pennsylvania than Ohio. Now she was flying with me to Vietnam. Though we had talked about going for hours and hours, until now, until after the churning violence of the fight, I hadn't really calculated— hadn't *felt*—the enormity of her trust in me, or its weight. Nixon's "Vietnamized" war was running full-tilt, and we were heading into it. I wasn't just looking out for myself but for someone who had no experience of the place. Our—my—plan was to go up to Hue where I'd teach English Something-or-Other at the university, using Hue as my base for venturing out into the countryside with my tape recorder to collect folk poems. Erhart had written me that with the withdrawal in July of all U.S. forces just below the DMZ, the whole Northern border looked shaky.

Back in June, *The New York Times* had begun publishing *The Pentagon Papers,* revealing the enormity of the government's folly and deceits in Indochina. Yet the war went on. Nixon, who had run on a platform to end the war, now sent it into Cambodia. Nothing seemed strong enough to stop the war, not marches or media outcry. COR's maimed children had barely caused a ripple in the public mind. When Lonnie and I decided to go, it seemed like the only honest thing to do for citizens of a society raging at itself as it killed hundreds of thousands of anonymous little people halfway around the world. Those people weren't anonymous to me. From my point of view, the best thing that I could do now to help stop the war was gather the poetry made by ordinary folk in Vietnam and bring it before Americans. However insignificant this effort might be, the more human Vietnamese seemed to Americans, the harder it might be to slaughter them.

Besides thinking like two citizens of the sixties, we were also two youngsters in love. Now, as our plane nosed across the Pacific, I pondered how practical and safe the plan was. Especially now, since we had just learned in Hawaii that Lonnie was one month pregnant.

We had met in March of 1970, during my first few months of teaching at Penn State, and after six months of my odd self-imposed exile at the cabin. The first time I saw her, Lonnie was a student volunteer at a rock-concert benefit to raise money to pay the hospital costs of COR children. I remember her dancing through rows of students, holding out a can and shaking its contents of quarters and dimes in tune to the music booming from the stage amps in seismic cascades. She was so pretty and full of herself that, with the benefit as pretext, I tried to talk to her in the rock-and-roll din. She said she was the friend of someone on our local COR committee and had wanted to do something more than march in demonstrations. I don't remember my excuse but I got her phone number. The next morning, with more gall than I ever thought I could muster, I called her.

"Do you want to have lunch?" I asked.

"Sure. When?"

"Well, how 'bout today?"

We sat most of that afternoon in a booth at the local
diner. She had such a soft voice and so soothing a manner
that it surprised me to hear her talk about sitting in at Old
Main during a recent antiwar demonstration (the university
was a big Navy contractor), then getting shoved out of
the building and down the steps by the police, and finally
having to pass through a gauntlet of howling frat rats who
spat on the demonstrators as they went by. After lunch,
she drove home with me to the cabin.

She never left. A few days later, we went to her apartment to get her toothbrush, her schoolbooks, and some
clothes. She left some of her stuff there in case her family
called, but our life together began that day in the misty
hollow where we walked my old trails and talked and
talked.

As spring arrived in full force, the creek flooded into
the front yard and I had to park my car on the other side
of the bridge. On mornings when Lonnie had to be in class
and I was free, I'd put on my boots and carry her piggy-
back through the icy freshets meandering through the front
lawn, slopping forward, laughing, until I was wading
knee-deep in the freezing runoff. Then, with the torrent
of spring-melt rushing against my legs, I would ford the
bridge—its cedar planks all surged over and slippery—as
Lonnie clutched her arms about me and hung on, squealing, until we'd made it across and I'd set her down on
higher ground so she could walk up the lane to where my
car was parked.

We got a pup from the local pound, and later, in May,
a dozen newborn ducks with tasseled heads. I built them
a shed by the stream. Quacking their route upstream,
they'd come home each evening after a day of dallying on
the creek, their pompom tassels shaking as they waddled
up the bank into their shed, safe from foxes, coons, and

skunks. Later in May, after the last frost, we broke the hard clay by the side of the cabin and worked it into a garden. Soon the rabbit-wire fence was overwound in bright twirls of yellow nasturtiums.

I was already trying to translate *ca dao*. Crystal Erhart, Steve's ex-wife, had sent me Nguyen Van Ngoc's *Tuc Ngu Phong Dao,* a collection of folk poetry and proverbs collected in the North during the 1930s. Working with a young Vietnamese at Dispatch News (Dispatch was the independent, mostly ex-IVS agency that first discovered the My Lai massacre), Crystal had tried some translations, but she didn't know Vietnamese and wanted me to help. I had never even heard of *ca dao* but realized when I saw the poems that this was an oral tradition that no one in the West had even heard of. Hoping that Vietnamese culture would survive long enough for me to record this loveliest of its aspects, I applied for an NEH fellowship and waited that summer and fall for a reply. When it came, I got a year's leave from Penn State. In Vietnam, it could matter that we were legally man and wife, so Lonnie and I decided we'd better get married.

Why. Why did I go back? Why did I take my young wife? To that place whose horrors I knew with directest authority. All I can say now, as I think of myself sitting in the plane worrying over the same question, is that it seemed impossible not to go. So much had happened that year that it became *impossible* to sit still in our idyllic green dell in the Alleghenies. Almost daily, for months, the press exhumed some further details of the murder, rape, and sodomy of the 504 noncombatant men, women, and children at My Lai. At the end of April, Henry Kissinger and Richard Nixon (the guy with the secret plan to end the war) invaded Cambodia, destroying yet another Asian people in inimitable, ignorant, American savagery. A week later, the Ohio National Guard shot four students protesting at Kent State. At Penn State, the howling frat rats were now spitting on state troopers sent to restore order. All-American, apolitical fraternity boys and sorority girls, who had only months before abused antiwar demonstrators, now were battering the police buses in a hail of bricks and stones as the cops fled for their safety.

Sitting still was once again intolerable. Garden and ducks, dog and creek were left to others. In a logic that made sense only then, we were heading to Vietnam.

16

TWIGGY AND STEVE

It was a late afternoon in August when our plane scraped down on the tarmac at Tan Son Nhut. Lonnie and I stared through the Plexiglas oval at the busiest airport in the world, at the headquarters of MACV, "the Pentagon East," at the headquarters of the Vietnamese Air Force, of the U.S. Seventh Air Force, of the 834th Air Division, of the 460th Tactical Reconnaissance Wing, of the Third Aero Rescue and Recovery Group, of the 315th Troop Carrier Group, of the 505th Tactical Control Group, of the 1965th Communications Group, and of the Combined Document Exploitation Center, where important prisoners were interrogated and where tons of captured documents—diaries, graphs, maps, trajectory tables, letters, communiqués, leaflets, certificates, and decorations—were photographed and analyzed for intelligence. A maze of guard towers, perimeter roads, mine fields, cement bunkers, barbed-wire berms, runways, hangars, garages, staging areas, barracks, gymnasiums, bowling alleys, PXs, chapels, swimming pools, cafeterias, messes, ammo dumps, tank farms, warehouses, movie theaters, mortuaries, stockades, and God knows what else emerged through heat vapors as our plane taxied in. A Vietnamese woman behind us retched into a paper bag while her AID husband chatted to a fellow passenger about one of her cousins, who on a previous flight had been shot by a sniper firing straight up from the end of the runway and, would you believe it, the bullet went straight through the cousin's seat, traveling up his spine, and tearing out through the top of his head.

Out on the simmering runway, the War Machine appeared before my wife's eyes as our plane taxied past rows of aircraft parked in steel-and-concrete reinforced bunkers: past Cobras and Hueys, past F-100 Supersabres, F-4 Phantoms, tiny Dragonfly jets, past massive, lumbering Hercules troop carriers, and antique, prop-driven Skyraiders. Armed men in olive drab dotted the stretches of cement and the weed-killed flats: flyweight, helmeted Vietnamese and beefy Americans, whose fatigue shirts were blackened with sweat as they stood guard duty off the baking runway. Shirtless, beet-red boys were lolling around armored personnel carriers whose surfaces must have been hot enough to fry eggs; other boys were scrambling over planes, or running forklifts, or guiding planes out of their bunkers, waving them onto side runways. "Golly," Lonnie said, her forehead pressed against the plastic window as she stared at the war's nerve center, Pentagon East, quivering in the tarmac heat. A dense damp aroma was seeping into the cabin as the pilot cut the air conditioning and our Boeing trundled up to the terminal. Then we stopped rolling, the engines died, and finally a stewardess opened the door to Vietnam.

Past customs, in the caterwaul of Vietnamese con men, taxi drivers, privileged clans of war profiteers saying their goodbyes to relatives, mean-mugged MPs, couriers, airport cops, and private chauffeurs, I was delighted to see Steve Erhart sitting on his motorcycle with a little blue-and-yellow Citroën taxi and driver in tow.

"Ooh, look what you brought us," he said, grinning at Lonnie, shaking my hand. Tall, handsome, charming, Erhart was a classic bipolar manic depressive who dwelt in hilarities and obsessions, his high moods swinging him abruptly to the brink of suicide. Recently, he had done everything he could to dump Crystal, his lovely and loving wife, who finally gave up on him. This left Steve free to chase bar girls. Every now and then, he'd send me a photo or a slide of some pretty bar girl posing in her panties before an armoire mirror, her doubled image perhaps meant to suggest that this wasn't soft porn but real art. Along with the photos came Steve's exclamations about freedom and love. Then, when he and Crystal were finally divorced, and after she was remarried and pregnant, Erhart decided he wanted her back. When that proposition became absurd even to him in his mania, he had taken off in severest self-loathing to Indonesia, living on his savings and odd bits of journalism. Now that Crystal and her husband, John Steinbeck, had gone home to New York with their new baby, Erhart had returned to Saigon, to heroin, and to bar girls. He was writing a brilliant, convoluted biography about heroin use which he called *The Skag Journal,* as well as a screenplay in which a USO dancer (he pictured Ann-Margret) falls in love with a Green Beret officer involved with the Saigon underworld, etc. He had just published a story in *The Atlantic Monthly,* "Her Perishing Cunning Flesh," a not-very-fictional account of dropping acid with a bar girl, actually his newest flame, Twiggy. He worked now as an office manager with RMK-BRG, the construction firm that built everything in Vietnam from roads to "tiger cages," those cramped torture cells in which Viet Cong sympathizers were imprisoned until media outrage drew a Congressional delegation to the Con Son prison island where they found men and many women confined in these cement boxes into which the guards routinely urinated or tossed quicklime onto the prisoners through the barred lids; some of the prisoners had been blinded by the lime. Like My Lai, the tiger cages became one of the scandals of the war. What only a few of us knew was that Erhart had secretly provided the first proof of the tiger cages, leaking the actual construction plans and contracts from his company's files. His actions amazed his friends, who had watched Erhart progressively disappear into his unique, selfish universe of words, ironies, dope, and sex. When I heard about Steve's pilfering those files and giving them to the press, the news was even more surprising than his legendary standing on top of a tank to film the explosion of the Lai Khe ammo dump for VISNEWS, the British news service, for which he also moonlighted as a stringer. The Lai Khe footage—filled with rockets and tracers screaming past the camera—was explicable if you knew about Erhart's suicidal periods and his perfectionist interest in the camera he was just learning to master. But the tiger cages? No one guessed he cared enough about other people. The few times he had worked with me during my COR days, Erhart had kept any burgeoning seriousness in check by referring to his tasks as "the burned-baby business." No one guessed he cared that much about Saigon prisoners, about mere politics—that is, cared enough to risk his job, which was his only tie to his peculiar life in Asia.

He was happy, even delighted, to see us. Though he had no desire ever to return to the United States, he hungered for American publication of his fiction and odd reportage. Back home, I had helped him publish articles in *The Atlantic, Harper's,* and *The Evergreen Review.* I had found him an agent at Curtis Brown, Ltd., and an editor at Houghton Mifflin that liked his work and wanted a novel from him. He was beaming as he helped the taxi driver load our stuff into the little cab. Steve had no other friend as loyal or, at least, as reliable as me, and he could see that Lonnie, with her uncommon good looks, would be an asset to his demimonde of Saigon, an underground community that included antiwar and establishment reporters, "third-country national" contractees, an AWOL black restaurateur, various Vietnamese scam artists, a Korean spook, one or two black-marketeers, some naughty truants

from the exclusive Madame Curie girls' school, an elec-
tronics smuggler who employed Liles, assorted photog-
raphers, some Vietnamese and Filipino rock artists, one or
two peace activists, plenty of uncategorizable misfits, and
a handful of do-gooders of various nationalities. All these
assembled from time to time in the Tu Do bars, on the
hotel verandas, in the field, or in Graham Greene's old
apartment, where a few close friends still gathered to
smoke opium.

"First we get you settled," he said, clapping his hands
together like a cruise hostess, "freshen up, say howdy to
the Buus, take a nap. Jacqui"—Madame Buu's eldest
daughter, who ran the house—"will wake you at 8:00.
You'll have a little dinner. And then I'll be by."

"Then?" I asked, keeping an eye on the taxi driver, who
had an Atlanta Braves cap which he was now using to flag
down another cab: his was now filled with our luggage,
including my almost irreplaceable tape recorder and por-
table typewriter.

"Then . . . let's see, we've got to get you wheels. You
can use Clyde's Lambretta tonight. He won't want to come
with us."

"Steve, where are we going?" Lonnie asked.

He grinned his whitest, toothiest smile. He was thirty-
three, with crow's-feet creasing his eyes. Lonnie's sheer
youth and innocence must have jarred him with excitement. "Why, we're going to show you the town! You
can't just have some dumb pajama party at the Buus'. Not
on your first night in . . . the center of the universe!
You've got to meet the folks! Press the flesh. Liles! Twiggy!
You've got to meet Twiggy."

"Oh, okay," Lonnie said.

But I wondered. I hadn't met Twiggy, Steve's latest
amourachée, but I knew his idea of a night out on the town
might well be dropping acid and stumbling about the dark
streets offering money to the various deformed and leprous
beggars who haunted the sidewalks. You know: looking

into your own soul reflected in their bewildered eyes in order to examine the *possibility* of generosity untainted.

Dispatched by Steve, Jerry Liles appeared around 9:00 on the big Triumph cycle that he had smuggled in from Laos. Steve was right about getting us wheels: Clyde Coreil, who was back from Arabia and teaching at the medical school, and who kept shy of Steve's crowd, was happy to loan us my old Lambretta before retreating to his own room at the Buus' to smoke dope, grade exams, and listen to his recording of whale music.

So, with Lonnie wrapping her arms around my middle, the Buu dogs, Lena and Ti-Ti, yapping at our tires, and Jacqui smiling as she locked the house gate behind us, we took off after Liles, who was already ripping ahead of us through the snarls of traffic down Tran Hung Dao Boulevard, past the circle at the Saigon market, past the Two Ugly Soldiers statue until we finally pulled up onto the sidewalk in front of the King Bar, paid a kid to watch our bikes, and went inside.

Even though the King had a playing-card motif—the front door was a painted king of hearts—inside it was more or less like all the bars on Tu Do Street: you walked into darkness as blasts of rock-and-roll, gusts of cigarette smoke, and scents of hairspray, beer, and cologne rushed out to greet you. An older woman proprietor sat behind the bar. A dozen or so Vietnamese women, their miniskirts slit up the side, their halter tops or plunging dress fronts showing off their tits ballooned by silicon, huddled against young, hulking Americans in various states of drunkenness. *Di mèo,* "Go catting." Even the girls who were lighting cigarettes or squeezing some GI's thigh watched the door like cats. And when Lonnie walked in, the whole bored, hot-to-trot feline assembly purred and flicked its tail.

"*Trời ơi!*" exclaimed the proprietress. Her Cheshire-cat grin was a gleam of gold fillings.

The only Western women seen in the bars—and these were rare sightings—were the odd French reporter or foreign nurse larking with friends. Most of the women of the war effort looked like Martha Raye, and what social life they had took place in private apartments, in the Brinks Officer's Club, or at Ky's restaurant-nightclub down the street, Maxim's. *At last,* one could almost hear the bar girls purl in chorus as they turned away from their soldiers and stared, *the real thing, let's check her out.*

Liles led us to a booth, where he introduced us to Twiggy, Steve's girl, and to Sherry, her associate. Whereas Sherry was aglow with bonhomie and shook hands with all three of us in that one-pump French way, Twiggy looked up like a sulky teenager.

"Hey, Jerry, what you do? You almost miss my dance. Where's Steve?" Now she patted the cushion next to her for Lonnie to sit down.

"Him number ten," Sherry consoled her.

"Business errand," Jerry said. He blinked and sat down next to Sherry. He didn't like confrontations.

"Business, shit," Twiggy said, "he out chasin' smack."

Her tough-guy talk, which sounded both Southern and black, was as striking as her looks. Unlike the other girls, she had decided just to look herself: no surgically rounded eyelids, or silicon-straightened nose, or padded tits; no heavy makeup. Even her jet-black hair was left straight. Her nose was long, flattish, and *tonkinoise.* Her teeth were remarkably white and even, though there was a slight gap between her two front teeth. She was confident enough to look like what she was—a skinny Vietnamese teenager who knew how to handle herself. Twiggy.

One of her sidelong glances gave two of the girls at the bar permission to come over and squeeze in with us. They nodded politely at Jerry and me but feasted their eyes on Lonnie. I could hear them mumble some question to Twiggy, who nodded at me. The music was so loud, hardly anyone could be heard. Then one of the women started patting the blond fuzz on Lonnie's arm; another touched her fine blond hair. One of them, "Suzie," who had a kind of Mary Tyler Moore flip and bags of blue eye shadow, kept looking at Lonnie's breasts. I was afraid she was going to fondle them. Now, on either side of Lonnie, there were two bar girls stroking her arms.

A bit wide-eyed, Lonnie looked at me, but before I could intervene, Twiggy told the girls in Vietnamese to cut it out and said to Lonnie, "They jus' think you too beautiful."

Lonnie smiled at them and then excused herself to go to the john. As she walked down the length of the bar, I wondered if I shouldn't go with her, what with all the drunken soldiers.

"She be okay," Twiggy said, watching as Lonnie moved away past the startled, lonely, boozed GIs who gawked at her.

I saw Twiggy studying the way Lonnie walked: Slowly. Her arms straight down at her sides. Her fingers loosely curled. Her chin up. Her body conscious of the Janis Joplin booming from the tape deck.

"Hey, man," Twiggy said, taking a swig on her bottle of San Miguel, "your ol' lady is pretty cool."

There were three GIs sitting near us at the bar. When Lonnie came out of the john, one of them shouted "Ten hut" above the music. The three of them then jumped to their feet, backs straight, and formed a file. With the first guy shouting commands, they marched toward my wife. I got to my feet and heard Liles mutter "Uh-oh" as he too got up.

Now everyone at our end of the barroom was watching the three soldiers as they marched up to Lonnie, executed a sharp left just before her, and came to a halt with their backs to her as she sidled behind them and hurried up the aisle.

The three stood before the bar's fishpond, created by a little waterfall running from a grotto in the wall, and, on

command, reached down, unzipped their flies, and started
pissing in the water.

"*Trời ơi! Ghê quá!*"—"Good God, how disgusting!"—
screeched the lady behind the bar, raising her shrieks above
Big Brother and the Holding Company. And then, to the
urinating soldiers, she yelled, "What you do, kill my
fishy?"

When they were done, the soldiers zipped up their flies
and broke into hoots of laughter. As they shuffled back,
they sneaked glances at Lonnie to see her shock, to see the
shock on her face, the shock that might record her recognition that any trespass of homegrown beauty into their
place of piggery was unforgivable. Then they stumbled
back to their seats, where their bar girls playfully slapped
their blotchy faces and told them they were "too bad" and
would have to pay the mamasan something extra.

Liles blew a sigh of relief. Tanned, with movie-star good
looks, he kept himself perpetually cool, calmed out, on
smack. His financial means were more or less a mystery;
like his best friend, Erhart, Liles had made a home in
Saigon. From time to time, he took considerable but carefully calculated risks with his life—stringing as a reporter
beyond the protections of U.S. Army surveillance, hiking
into the VC countryside for COR to locate the parents of
a child ready to return from North Carolina, drifting alone
in the dank shooting galleries up in Hue and Danang,
where his fellow skag hounds were mostly drunk, gun-
happy, suicidal ARVN renegades. But nearly being called
on to help rescue my wife had eradicated whole days of
careful composure. "Oh, boy," he said, "it's going to be
fun having Mrs. Balaban along."

When Steve finally came in, a Vietnamese rock group,
the CBC, was already wailing on the little stage opposite
the pissed-in fishpond. Between the deafening amps, their
petite lead singer pulled deep Joplinesque chords from
somewhere in her sparrow's body. Twiggy was already
on stage with them, writhing left and right in the slow

parts, shaking it up in the fast sections, with her miniskirt
twinkling its silver tassels. She shot Steve a dirty where-
you-been-motherfucker glance.

Steve looked disheveled and out of sorts. He nodded to
us, sat down, and finished Twiggy's beer. He motioned
for another. When he turned to the bar and held up the
emptied bottle, you could see he had a bloody welt on the
back of his head. His shirt was scuffed and ripped in one
place.

"Bump your head?" Liles asked.

"Aw, I'll tell you later." Turning to me and Lonnie, he
said, "She's been taking lessons." He was also encouraging
Twiggy, he had told me after the ride in from Tan Son
Nhut, to study piano and voice. He was teaching her to
read and write. He was trying to civilize her. He wanted
to marry her.

Twiggy's big dance was "Proud Mary." Her main terp-
sichorean principle was speed. By the end of the song, she
was a vibrating blur of jerks and shakes, spinning around
the stage like a speeded-up film, hopelessly out of sync
with the beat, her arms whipping up and down like a
sprinter's, her little butt a paroxysm of shimmy.

Steve was beaming, turning to us every now and then
for our approval.

"Yeah," Liles said. "Yeah."

"She can really move," I offered.

Sherry was aglow with pride in her friend.

"God," Lonnie whispered to me, "she's like a mosquito
out for blood."

When the dance was done and Twiggy came over, she
was flushed and happy enough with her debut so that she
merely carped, "Hey, man, where the fuck you at? You
almos' miss my dance." Then she saw the bloody patch
on Steve's head, grabbed his head in both her hands, and
demanded to know how it had happened.

"Dope dealers, my dear. It's a jungle out there."

He said he had been struck on the head with a piece of

brick or a bottle, a bit from the Oort Cloud of debris
streaking at him as he had raced away from a gang of street
kids who had come to the aid of a polio-crippled friend of
theirs who had just stiffed Steve on a buy of heroin.

"You were hitting the Cripple?" Liles asked. He studied
his bottle label with a smile of vast amusement.

"Yeah, damnit, he stole my money." Now Steve saw
the humor in the situation and broke into a grin, then a
wince, as Twiggy daubed a whisky-soaked bar towel at
his bruise. "I couldn't discriminate just because he's crippled. We're building democracy here, Jerry."

"What did you do to him?" asked Lonnie.

"Well, he told me to come back this evening. I did. But
he wasn't on the street corner. So I drove around until I
found him, but the little rat tried to scuttle off on his
crutches. He didn't have the stuff, so I grabbed him and
said, 'All right, where's my money?' He said he didn't
have it. So, you know, things got rough. . . ."

Lonnie didn't know.

"Well, eventually I knocked his crutches away just to
give him a hint of retribution and he fell back against a
wall and started cursing me and screaming for his friends,
so I slapped him a couple of times. Then this horde of little
bastards—you know," he said, turning to me, "bike-mice,
shoeshine boys, door pimps—start yapping and yelling
and chasing me."

"You a bad mother," Twiggy said, giving him a smile,
a hug, and a big kiss. "Baby, you like my dance?"

17

PHOENIX ISLAND

Goin' up the country, girl, do you want to go?
—*Canned Heat*

The next morning we were on the road to My Tho. In an orange bus with yellow dragons painted on its sides, its rear doors sporting a huge, toothy, smiling black man and the words "Pour les Dents Blancs—Denta Trice," we were careening out of Saigon into the country. The bus was jammed with peasants in *nón lá* leaf hats, many of these farmers barefoot, some toting clutches of chickens cinched together at the feet, or bunches of *bưởi,* the local grapefruit, or pungent breadfruit, or crocks dribbling smelly *nước mắm,* the fish-sauce flavoring. Down on the floorboards or stowed up on the overhead racks were ducks in wire cages, and trussed piglets. Under a broad Delta sky, we were heading into the country enveloped in squawks and chatter, in human sweat, in a cloud of fumes and red dust. We had stayed the night before at Steve and Twiggy's place, stoned and jabbering until we finally fell asleep in heaps on reed mats, convinced by Steve that the best way for Lonnie to fathom where she was . . . was, well, to jump right in.

We had Twiggy's fat old trusting mama in tow. Only

two weeks before she had come over to their place to clean
it up when they were out, had worked up a fierce thirst,
and had innocently drunk Kool-Aid from a pitcher laced
with LSD that had turned her into a hallucinating pow-
erhouse Mr. Clean genie. Now all of us—Mom, Twiggy,
Lonnie, Steve, and myself—were on a pilgrimage to the
Delta, first to My Tho just forty miles southwest of Saigon
and then, via two Mekong ferries, to Phoenix Island, haven
for Ong Dao Dua, the Coconut Monk, who preached an
eclectic blend of Taoism, Buddhism, and Christianity as
well as a more immediate political message of truce, rap-
prochement, and an end to the war.

The trip was arduous but not unsafe. The My Tho road
was pacified during daylight, a dusty two-laner weaving
through villages and rice fields, the route shaded by palms
and eucalyptus, strewn with checkpoints and military
camps, with cement bunkers and guard posts at all the
bridges over the flat, muddy creeks. Forty miles, but a
two-hour trip. The rough part was the traffic, a snarl of
military convoys, trucks hauling foodstuffs into the capital,
fall-apart buses, Lambretta jitneys, and mule-pack motorcycles, all of which drew to radiator-boiling halts at the
roadblocks until waved on by the Saigon troops. Freed en
masse after a convoy went by, the whole side-swiping
scramble of vehicles came bucking right out of the chute
and jockeyed for the lead. Then the motorcycles that had
been air-horned off to the side by the big trucks and buses
in the fast stretches claimed the vanguard and the cleaner
air that came with the pack lead as the dust-stirring, black-
exhaust lumberers were left behind.

At the bus stops, Lonnie got a double-dose inoculation
of culture shock. Clamoring vendors who reached into the
glassless bus windows to hawk their trays of sugarcane
slices, baskets of French bread, chunks of raw, fermenting
pork in banana leaves, packs of Bastos, Melia, and Salem
cigarettes, tangerines, and Juicy Fruit gum, pinched her
arm and pulled her hair. "Hey, you. You, buy," they'd
say, slapping at Lonnie until Twiggy's foul-mouthed barks

reduced them to wide-mouthed gaping. One undaunted teenaged girl ("Probably a VC," Steve observed) called back, "You number ten, shit American." Steve told Lonnie not to take it personally, getting a laugh out of her that made him wink at me as if to say, "She's doing fine." Sometimes the freak frenzy visited upon Lonnie was almost funny, as one woman held up her infant son outside Lonnie's window and said, "You buy babysan." That made the whole crowd laugh. Then the mother (who now wanted to show Lonnie how much she loved her little naked boy) held him up above her head and swallowed his itsy-bitsy penis in her mouth until the sleepy boy woke up in smiles and added his laughter to the crowd's.

Finally, grimed by the road and chewing tangerines that were Twiggy's mother's treat, we reached the Mekong ferry, a huge white boxlike affair, a leftover from the French plantational empire. My Tho sits upriver above two of the main branches of the Mekong's easternmost fork where the river is as broad as the Mississippi. The ferry shunted us across that awesome brown expanse to a village on the other side of the river where we had to wait for a small wooden boat to take us to Phoenix Island, where the Coconut Monk presided. The Monk, his real name Nguyen Thanh Nam, was a crooked wisp of a man whose own parents had been wealthy enough to send him to Paris in the 1930s to study chemistry and agriculture. Instead, Mr. Nam came back mystic, took a vow of silence, climbed up to live in a banyan tree, and gathered a following. Now, to the irritation of the Saigon government, in the midst of the war, he preached pacifism and compassionate regard.

Twiggy's mother was pretty excited about the Coconut Monk. She had had a rough life, grubbing in Saigon, married to a man who early in their marriage had gone flat-out goofy and for years had just sat in a darkened room in their small hovel on the edge of town. One of her daughters had married an American and was living in Canada. That brought in some money, but in order to make ends meet, when Twiggy was twelve, her mother had sold her to a Chinese merchant for the equivalent of $150. "Chinese man," Twiggy informed us cheerily as if her mother's selling her into prostitution had been merely a sort of bad practical joke, "like cherry girl. Chini' think it make him strong." Whatever her resentments, Twiggy was sweet to her mother. And though our My Tho trip was just a lark for Twiggy (who was far too street-smart to get tied down to anything as intangible as religion), she tried not to laugh as her mother insisted on rehearsing Steve, Lonnie, and me in the protocols of kowtowing as we stood on the muddy bank under the broad Delta countenance of Mr. Sky, clasping our hands at our chests, bowing, bringing our hands to our foreheads, then down to our chests, and then to our foreheads again as, nearby, a dog lapped up fish scales by the water's edge.

Our next, much smaller, wooden boat glided toward Con Phung, Phoenix Island, taking us beyond any vista of city or road or blockhouse, as the silty Mekong stretched around us. When river breezes momentarily carried away the chatter of our engine, we could hear a soft gonging floating across the water from the distant island palms. Twiggy's mother now became positively agitated in a religious sort of way. To show her reverence, she clasped her hands together and placed them to her heart. This seemed to amuse some of the Coconut Monk's followers on our leaky little boat: men and women—and even children—in maroon *aó bàba* pajamas that the sun had faded to various shades of brown. Some of the men's shirts had long since lost their original fabric and were now just patches on top of patches. The women wore their hair tied up in buns like most older Vietnamese women, but the men wore turbans cut from the same cloth as their religious duds. One striking young man—perhaps for Lonnie's or Twiggy's benefit—undid his turban to rewind his shiny black hair, which fell to his knees before he wrapped it up again in his maroon headscarf. But mostly the Phoenix Islanders seemed to pay the rest of us little attention. They were straight-backed, dignified people, talking quietly among themselves, aware of us, but unfazed by our presence. While Lonnie and I sat pressed together on a little wooden bench, I could feel her relax at this new manner of reception.

As our boat rounded the head of the island, however, all of us visitors—including Steve who had been there before—were stirred by the sight of huge pillars looming above a fifty-foot cement circle set on pilings above the river. On top of the pillars, apparently cut from steel and painted in brilliant colors, were immense placards of deities: the tallest of these showed Christ and Buddha. Buddha's arm was draped over Christ's shoulder, and the two seemed to be floating along in philosophical talk. Near them were the Virgin Mary and Quan Am, the female Bodhisattva of Mercy, walking hand in hand. Then, a laughing, potbellied Hachiman under a golden parasol, his begging bowl slung against his enormous bare belly, his bare feet resting on a globe of the planet. Below the various deities were fluorescent-lamp florets spreading out of three-foot ceramic lotus buds. Below the lotuses, the pillars were entwined with gigantic, light-bulb-eyed, plaster-of-paris dragons. At the bottom of the pillars and all across the prayer circle were perhaps a hundred men and women bowing soundlessly on the yin and yang halves of the circle.

As our boat approached the dock just below this prayer platform, we could see the sources of the gonging in two bell towers, each housing an immense brass bell rung by two men swinging battering rams on rope gantries hung from the roofs of the towers. A very big bell with a deep, soft resonance and a smaller one with a higher pitch were being worked in careful counterpoint as the now prostrated followers rose, kowtowed, fell to their knees, sat back, kowtowed, and rose again in continuous repetitions. All of them faced the head of the island where, beyond cement catwalks and underneath some more pillars (something like ship masts, complete with crow's nests), was an immense

relief map of Vietnam upon which a small bent man, supported by what seemed to be a shepherd's crook and wearing a Cistercian bib and what looked like a tonsure, was
carefully stepping along the length of the country.

"Wow," I said, looking at Lonnie who, two days before,
was fending off marauding Japanese camera-clickers at
Waikiki.

"Ong Dao Dua." One of our shipmate monks said the
Coconut Monk's name to us so that we would know to
join them in kowtowing, which indeed Twiggy's mama
did and continued to do long after they stopped and our
boat tied up. When the boatman cut the engine, all we
could hear were waves washing the landing and the gong
and ring of bells.

With some islanders offering helping hands for Twiggy
and Lonnie and their luggage, the two of them made the
leap from the rocking boat deck onto the plank jetty while
Steve and I—planting one leg on the dock and the other
on the boat, and each taking a grip on one of Twiggy's
mother's arms—tried to maneuver her off the boat and
safely onto shore. She was enormous: nearly two hundred
pounds of double chins, flabby arms, inner-tube belly rolls,
and ham-slab buttocks. It took a while to get her to agree
to make the jump. All of us were laughing, including the
monks who had come down the cement steps to steady
the boat—all of us, that is, except Twiggy's mother who
continued to look terrified until, on Steve's "Heave-ho,"
we landed her. Then she was beaming with beatitude.
Beaming as if all the sorry exhaustion of her hustling,
corrupt, Saigon-stinking life had been relieved and she had
just entered the Pure Land of Amida Buddhism. For a few
moments all of us were having a marvelous time watching
her as she took in the peaceful village, the monks, and the
towering statues. She walked forward in a happy trance
until—to our sudden horror—she walked off a plank gang-
way and (as Twiggy screamed "Mama!") disappeared from
sight.

We all rushed to the catwalk. From down below where

the river usually flowed, Twiggy's mom looked back up
at her daughter and at the crowd of maroon-robed islanders, grinning wildly. Luckily, the tide was out and she
only fell into the stinky, gooey tidal muck of the Mekong
shoreline. In that awful moment, she must have remembered her recent bad luck with the Kool-Aid. Whatever
her thoughts, she opened her muck-caked lips to speak,
but said nothing. Instead, she held out her mud-packed
arms, regarded them, touched her oozy fingers to her hair,
the front portion of which was plastered in slimy mud;
then she looked down at her legs, sunk into the muck up
to her crotch, tried a couple of times to work them free,
failed, and then just sat down. I was afraid she'd start
sobbing or have a heart attack.

"John . . ." Lonnie said.

Oh, God, I thought. The stuff really stunk. But I looked
at Steve who already had his shoes and socks and pants off
and was wiggling his way in his underwear toward his
future mother-in-law, alternately comforting her in Vietnamese and breaking into burlesqued "*Trời ơi! Trời Đức
ơi!*"'s that finally got her smiling. Some nearby islanders
who were putting in a coconut-trunk house pylon—the
muddy men wearing only shorts, their long hair tied up
in big topknots—slopped over toward Steve and helped
him pull the old water buffalo out of the mire and onto
the hard-packed dike at the shoreline. Then island women
came with buckets of water and washed her down. Twiggy
and Lonnie helped, and when the old woman was clean
enough to enter a house, they took her away for a bath
and clean clothes.

And that was how we marked the afternoon of Lonnie's
second day in Vietnam, and how we first passed through
the fateful portal at Phoenix Island over which hung a
mammoth sign that read "CHRIST AND BUDDHA PAGODA."

18

HEAVEN, HUMANKIND, EARTH

Soon after our return from Phoenix Island, Lonnie and I flew to Hue, where I was supposed to teach grammar and linguistics at the university. We looked for a house and found we could either rent a French villa (with requisite guard and cook) for an unaffordable $250 per month, or rent a two-room bungalow with a cold-water tap and a Hitachi kerosene stove for $35 per month. There wasn't any middle ground. Both ends of Hue's wartime real estate market seemed unsafe in that desperate city, which at Tet Mau Than had seen hundreds of its citizens murdered and dumped into mass graves by the Viet Cong and—after the city was retaken by U.S. Marines—by an avenging Saigon regime. This was the city where Erhart had first hidden from the Viet Cong and then held out with a besieged ARVN battalion for the rest of the offensive. This was the city where Sandra Johnson was captured, to be returned unharmed nearly a year later. The city from which Gary Daves and Marc Cayer, two other IVSers, had also disappeared during Tet; they had not been heard of since. This was where the MACV and AID Americans were found executed at Tet. After sixteen years of an American military presence, it took only one look to see that anywhere in Hue—with its poverty, shaky defenses,

anti-Americanism, and violent crime—we would always
be easy marks. So, much to the annoyance of university
officials, we returned to Saigon, choosing to live at the
Buu house while I did my Hue teaching once a month in
marathon stints, as did most of the Vietnamese staff, flying
in from Saigon and flying out four days later.

But what I was looking for in Hue—live remnants of
an ancient oral-poetry tradition—could not be found in
Saigon. Early on, I brought back to our apartment one of
the blind singers I had seen at the zoo playing for piasters.
He came with a boy—maybe his son—who led him by
the hand and carried the old man's six-string steel guitar,
and for an afternoon I taped his singing and his bent-note,
blueslike strumming, but what he turned out to be performing was really an altogether different oral form called
vọng cổ, nostalgic legends of princes and princesses. *Vọng
cổ,* as the blind bard's instrument might suggest, was a
relatively recent oral tradition. What I was interested in
was something much, much older. *Ca dao,* I knew from
Nguyen Van Ngoc's anthology, were lyric—not narra-
tive—poems in the first person, and they were brief, usually only four lines long. *Ca dao,* which were composed
by ordinary peasants, who passed on the poems orally,
had existed through the millennia, from the distant origins
of the Vietnamese when they called themselves the Lac and
lived in diminutive agrarian kingdoms in the deltas of the
Red and Black rivers of the North. If *ca dao* still existed,
they would be an amazing index to the continuum of
Vietnamese humanism. But did they still exist? And
where would I find them now?

In Saigon, I found a folksinging group called Du Ca
Mua Xuan (Sing Out in Springtime) which purportedly
sang *ca dao:* about eighteen college-age kids—mostly privileged children of Northerners who had fled south in
1954—singing folk poems *in chorus* and accompanied by a
church-basement piano. Their Western-scaled renditions
had about as much to do with *ca dao* as "Kumbaya" or

"Michael Row the Boat Ashore." Like most city dwellers, these youngsters were simply cut off from the countryside by the war. And as was true of my late friend, Miss Khuy, their country homes in the North were places of mythology, not memory. Moreover, the Southern countryside was foreign to them. Gitelson would have known it better. So, when I clicked off my tape recorder in despair and asked the group's leader if he thought *ca dao* still were being made by peasants in the countryside, he shook his head with a forbearing "no" at my typical American misunderstanding of the Vietnamese condition. There I was: I had received from the National Endowment for the Humanities a year's salary to record a poetic tradition that no longer existed. I was in a real fix.

But *ca dao* was very much alive outside the city. What I found almost by chance on subsequent visits to Phoenix Island was that as long as there were Vietnamese living in the traditional rice-growing rhythm of the land, they sang *ca dao. Sang,* because the poems were not written down (the people who made them could not read or write); *sang,* because the poetry's tight formal structures organized the accidental musical tones of Vietnamese words into a natural melody line sung by a single person offering his or her voice to the cricket-churning backdrop of the Delta. No guitar. No piano. No chorus. Nothing but an unstudied voice offering its plaints of love and yearning to the trees in the family orchard, to the baby being rocked in a woven hammock, to the river sliding off into the horizon. This singing of *ca dao* joined with the rhythms and rhymes to make these delicate, vanishing artifacts—more than any monsoon-crumbled monument—the clearest record of Vietnamese culture.

Thiên. Nhơn. Địa. Heaven. Humankind. Earth. On one of my early trips to Con Phung, one of the island's white-haired elders gave me a heart-shaped pin by way of his blessings. Stamped inside the heart was a circle. Inside the circle were two overlapping circles. The top circle was marked "Heaven," "Thiên"; the bottom circle was "Earth," "Địa." The ellipsoid where they overlapped was marked "Nhơn," "Humankind" or "Man." Vietnamese humanity dwelt in proximity to Heaven and Earth and, indeed, derived from their contingency. Wherever these two realms of Heaven and Earth joined in equal parts, the ancient oral poetry of Vietnam had a place of nurture.

So Phoenix Island, not Hue, became my main place of work. In Hue or anywhere else in Vietnam, I would have been viewed as a freak or as an imperialist marauder. But among the Coconut Monk's serenely dignified followers, I could talk to Vietnamese as equals. I was a listener of poetry. In Vietnam, this is a sufficient, culturally plausible identity. To Vietnamese farmers who all knew this poetry—I never found one who did not—my poetical interests were perfectly reasonable, and so they sang to me what they knew. What they knew they had heard when their mothers sang *sau hè,* "behind the house in the orchards"; what they knew they had heard sung by their fathers as the whole family broke from the rigors of the rice field to drink tea in the shade of the tree line.

My additional, great luck in gathering *ca dao* at Con Phung Island was that its people came from all over the Mekong Delta to follow the Coconut Monk and to evade the war. Stuck in the middle of the Mekong, the island was bypassed by the war, as if a core of humane calm emanated from Phoenix Island to pacify violent adversaries. No one brought arms to Con Phung. The war raged at night on both riverbanks (sometimes close enough to be heard on my *ca dao* taping), but the war never came to Con Phung. And so, luckily for my project, the Coconut Monk's followers had brought with them the regional poetic traditions of the entire Mekong Delta. The war would keep me from traveling up flat, meandering creeks and rivers to villages in Kien Phong, Kien Tuong, Ba Xuyen, Bac Lieu, An Xuyen, Go Cong, Vinh Binh, Kien Giang, Chau Doc, Sadec, Dinh Tuong, and Phong Dinh, but the war also had brought farmers from these provinces to Con Phung, and there, through the sanction of the Coconut Monk, I could record their catalogues of songs. Poem-songs of seduction and lost love, of duty to the king, of honor to parents, of the wisdom dwelling in beasts and birds, of the philosophies of fish, of the wedding of Mr. Rat, the funeral of Mrs. Egret, of pleasures of hard work, of displeasures in marriage, of sacrifice for one's country. What a privilege my year was, sitting with these families as they paused from boatbuilding, or sewing, or gathered around in the evening before the glow of kerosene lamps singing of their world and of the world of their ancestors.

Imagine the reverse—imagine a Vietnamese walking up to an American farmhouse and knocking on the door, introducing himself, and saying, "I wonder if you would sing me your favorite poem?" Instead of being driven off with a shotgun, I was welcomed. From September 1971 to May 1972 (mostly on Con Phung but also at Binh Thuy, at Ban Me Thuot, and at Hue), I asked ordinary Vietnamese to sing into my microphone and, with varying degrees of suspicion, delight, and amusement, they did.

Two factors made my taping possible. The first, of course, was the blessing of the Coconut Monk, who liked my having been a conscientious objector. An S-shaped man, perhaps in his sixties, he had shaved his head except for a long braided pigtail which he used to circle his crown (displaying it like a tonsure) or, sometimes, bunched under his chin as if it were Christ's beard. It was all his own peculiar show on Phoenix Island, and since he had taken a vow of silence, that show was mostly a melodrama of visual symbols, although occasionally he scribbled out notes, as he would now and then during our audiences which took place up in his tree-fort perch at the prow of the island. He set down community rules within the reach of Delta farmers. They could marry and have children, but mothers had to leave the island to have their children (where there was no doctor, anyway); followers had to wear the garb of the island and had to refrain from killing animals and eating meat, even the fish abounding in the river. They had to take part in the arduous praying in the circle, unless excused for work.

But the Coconut Monk spoke best through symbols: the palsy-walsy Christ and Buddha and other deities; his tonsure and yellow bib; the tamed monkey and bear that lived together near the prayer circle on a vegetarian diet; the great brass bells cast from spent artillery casings; the relief map that he walked each day from Saigon to Hanoi and back again; and his salvaging of a Korean barge sunk by the Viet Cong downriver, which he had towed up to Con Phung and on which he intended to build a conference hall for peace talks. In all these marquees of the human spirit the Coconut Monk had created something like a Taoist theme park with a Coney Island touch. Indeed, he promoted a festival atmosphere on Con Phung because he knew that it would draw the attention of ordinary Vietnamese. If they came to amuse themselves and laugh, all the better. His instruction was right out of the *Tao Te Ching:*

> *When the man of highest capacities hears Tao*
> *He does his best to put it into practice.*
> *When the man of middling capacity hears Tao*

He is in two minds about it.
When the man of low capacity hears Tao
He laughs loudly at it.
If he did not laugh, it would not be worth the name
  of Tao.

Yet, Ong Hai, "Older Brother," as the islanders called
him ("Coconut Monk" was more or less a name of derision
given him by outsiders because his diet consisted mainly
of coconuts), for all his otherworldly goofiness, was regarded by the Saigon authorities as a threat. He was permanently confined to the island. His monks, when they
ventured off the island to run errands in My Tho, were
picked up by the police and imprisoned for draft-dodging.

But sometimes the Coconut Monk slipped away, as he
had the year before with the help of John Steinbeck, whom
the Dao Dua had dispatched to Saigon as a kind of advance
man to organize the press for the Monk's unauthorized
visit to the U.S. Embassy where he intended to present to
the Ambassador a coconut squiggled with a naturally
formed character for peace. The coconut was the perfect
Taoist symbol—round, female, dark, secretive, nourish-
ing—and it was the Monk's primary stage prop that day
as the wizened old man, creeping along the cordoned-off
boulevard with the help of his shepherd's crook, con-
fronted a company of ARVN soldiers sent to block his
way. He "talked" his way through them (in some quirk
of bad logistics, it turned out that the company's captain
was from the Coconut Monk's province of Kien Hoa) and
actually got up to the doors of the Embassy—the now
chained and padlocked three-foot doors—while a helicopter gunship hovered overhead and U.S. Marines who were
huddled behind sandbags trained their BARs on this little
bantam. Finally, an Embassy official emerged to say that
the American Ambassador was unable to accept gifts while
abroad but if Mr. Nam would mail his coconut to the
Smithsonian Institution in Washington, D.C., it would be

kept there until the Ambassador's retirement from the foreign service.

Having wrought his gentle havoc, having made his theater, the Coconut Monk smiled his impish smile to the white man in the suit, pointed one finger to Heaven, and turned back.

He was no fool. The communiqués and press releases that he sent to the outside world through the young reporters that he drew to the island made far more compassionate sense than anything said in Washington, Saigon, or Hanoi. "The Vietnamese country," began one of his letters to President Thieu, urging the creation of a peace conference at Con Phung,

> has experienced more than twenty years of war, the result is: millions of people killed, millions wounded and crippled, deserted homes, uncultivated gardens and rice fields destroyed by bombs and bullets, all moral values betrayed. And this war will cause innumerable more pitiful situations for our country if Peace is not brought about quickly.
>
> In this very dark condition of human history I am very heartbroken and feel compassion for all living creatures who must bear many sufferings because they can't stop their unscrupulous enmity, anger and ignorance. Following the examples of Buddha and Christ, to redeem all living creature's sins, I (a poor monk) made a vow to sacrifice my body (to live an ascetic life and to be on a vegetable diet until my death) to pray for peace day and night by kneeling between Father Sky and Mother Earth, with the hope that people will awaken early and quickly turn the right way: carry out a vegetable diet, do good things, avoid doing evil to soften their Karma gradually and liberate themselves from the rule of metempsychosis, use compassion as a means to cancel out resentment. Only in this way can we stop resentment and all living creatures can stop bearing their confused sufferings.

One day, after I had made several recording trips to the island, I had to ask him something and found none of his lieutenants around to take me up to see him. So, unannounced, I climbed the ladder to his perch and found him sitting there in his crow's nest high over the Mekong with his back to me, to the ringing bells, and to the bustling village he had founded.

"Ong Hai," I called to him.

When he turned to see who was calling, I was embarrassed to see that tears were streaming down his cheeks, that he had been weeping as he sat in his vigil over the river.

"Dạ, thưa Ông, xin lỗi," I said, begging his pardon for barging in on him like that.

He smiled, touched a finger to a tear at the corner of an eye, and pointed up to Heaven.

19

THE RED CLOTH

Ngồi buồn nhớ mẹ ta xưa:
Miệng nhai cơm trắng lưỡi lừa ca xương.
Nhiễu điều phủ lấy gía guơng.
Nguơi trong một nước phải thương nhau cùng.

Sad, idle, I think of my dead mother.
her mouth chewing rice, her tongue removing
    fish bones.
The Red Cloth drapes the mirror frame:
Men of one country must love one another.

—Ca dao *sung by Mrs. Bui Thi Cu,*
        seventy-six years old, in October 1971

The other reason I prospered on Phoenix Island was Le Van Phuc, a melancholy twenty-three-year-
old monk who had taught himself English by listening to
Armed Forces Radio and the BBC World Service, and who
served as the Coconut Monk's English translator. By the
time I got to Phoenix Island—well after Steinbeck, Tim
Page, Sean Flynn, and the other lysergic journalists had
departed—Dao Phuc had become bored with translating
proclamations, had become cynical about journalists, and,
finally, had become skeptical of the likelihood of the

Monk's achieving anything but a jail sentence. Phuc's melancholy derived in part from the withering effect the war had on all peasants his age who could foresee little in the way of a future except death on a battlefield. Anytime Phuc—his name means "Lucky"—left the island, he could be picked up by the police. To top it all, his mother was nagging him to get married despite the hopelessness of his circumstances. So, when I showed up with my green Harvard bookbag stuffed with my tape recorder and dictionaries, Dao Phuc brightened up and took on my project in much the same way I had: as a worthwhile pursuit in face of the war, a small attempt to save *ca dao* before it disappeared with the rest of Vietnamese culture, as a means of making the ordinary Vietnamese human to the English-speaking world, particularly that part of the world which was raining bombs upon them. At this point in my experience with the war, I saw collecting these poems and translating them as the only sensible political act I could perform. The COR office was now out of the Buu house and in another part of Saigon, and I was glad for that. I just could not bear getting lost again in such a sea of hopeless misery. Once I chaperoned three kids with harelips and cleft palates to a surgical unit in Saigon, but I was out of "the burned-baby business." Looking at those three tots, with their white teeth poking through their rabbity split upper lips, made me think of Thomas Whiteside's *New Yorker* articles on Agent Orange. What had they drunk that I had drunk? What dioxin, picloram, arsenic had knitted in my cells, in Lonnie's, who drank the Mekong with me, in Lonnie, pregnant in Saigon? My job was gathering poetry. Somehow, in an idealism earned by my hospital endeavors, I hoped that the poetry would save lives.

Since Phuc knew nearly everyone on the island, I simply tagged along as he led me to his neighbors. One of my first encounters was also one of my strangest. Dao Phuc wanted me to meet a Sister Lien-Huong (Lotus-Essence) who sold herbs for a living, and who, although he said she could not read or write, could compose perfectly metrical poems while in a sort of sibylline trance. Phuc led me through a maze of shady paths until we came to the bamboo monkey bridge that offered a wobbly entrance to her house raised on coconut-tree-trunk pylons above the river. She had just two small rooms. The walls and the roof were bamboo thatch. As I followed Phuc across the wobbly poles, fearful of dunking myself and my recorder in the tidal goop, she stood in her front door. She was an unusually tall woman, maybe in her mid-thirties, her long black hair shot with gray and tied up. Her large hands were rough; her large face, weathered. She stared at me boldly as I followed Phuc up to her door. Maybe because her eyes were set too close together, her stare was a bit unnerving. I had the feeling, as I stood there and Phuc introduced me, that she was about to break into a grin and laughter. A pungent, complex aroma wafted past her from the bundles of herbs she had hung from her rafters.

With the three of us still standing in front of her door, she sang her poems in a high, cracked voice, her eyes half closed. When she was done, she wiped her mouth with her hand.

I asked her my standard first question: "How did you learn to sing?"

She said she started singing when she was about twenty-seven and living in a Cao Dai nunnery in Tay Ninh, just north of Saigon.

"What preceded your first poem?" I then asked; although this was not part of my list of simple questions about each singer's age, place of birth, size of repertoire, and means of creation, there was something odd about Lien-Huong. All of the people I had hitherto recorded had sung from childhood. None could remember just when they had started. Only Lien-Huong sang exclusively about the Buddha.

"What you say, Mr. John?" Phuc asked.

"Well, what was she doing—what *happened* to her to make her start singing all at once like that?"

When Phuc rephrased my question in more accurate Vietnamese, she looked at me nervously. And then, after a pause, she told Phuc something that I couldn't follow but which embarrassed him.

"She say she was in a period . . . for several years"—here Phuc paused to find the English words—"of insanity. When she got the power to sing about Lord Buddha, her mind cleared."

Until she was about eleven, she went on to tell us, she was paralyzed on one side. A famous wandering monk, Ong Su Gua Ban Khoai (the Monk Who Sells Potatoes), came along, and her parents begged him to cure her. They were not rich, they told the monk, but they promised him anything of theirs he wanted.

When the Monk Who Sells Potatoes picked a leaf from a pear tree and gave it to eleven-year-old Lien-Huong, her paralysis disappeared. Her parents asked him what he wanted. He said he wanted her. After that, she said, she followed him around for about two years until, after her first menstruation, he left her at the Cao Dai nunnery in Tay Ninh. She never saw or heard of him again.

When she was with him, she said, he could make himself look like a fool, or a leper, or a blind beggar. In the guise of a blind beggar, he would often set up by the roadside a little grill on which he roasted potatoes. Peasants, seeing that he was blind, would sometimes steal from him. When they did, he would launch into a sermon in verse about the realms of hell, startling the peasants and causing them to consider their ways.

The Monk Who Sells Potatoes. Ever since Buddhism began its journey east through Indochina, there must have been Delta people, men and women, filled with doctrine and pieces of doctrine, wandering about the countryside. History knows few of their names. Dao Phuc later gave me a photograph of a painting of the Monk of the Western

Peace, a Delta peasant born in 1849 whose prophecies were believed to have averted a plague. The Coconut Monk was just the latest in this long lineage.

Phuc was as curious as I to enter this peculiar world of the Mekong Delta. Once we finished taping on Phoenix Island, we planned to try recording among the militant Hoa Hao sect in the upper part of the Delta; then we planned to cross the border into Cambodia and go to the legendary Seven Mountains where anchorites still dwelt in caves. It was fairly peaceful across the Delta in that fall of 1971. If the Coconut Monk sent word ahead for us, we thought we could do it.

Our plans were a pipe dream. The farthest Phuc and I journeyed together was to nearby My Tho where his mother made him go to consult an oracle about the right time for him to get married. I wanted to see what an oracle was, so one morning at dawn, we climbed on board a big two-deck wooden boat belonging to the Island. About fifty islanders were going to sell their produce at the My Tho market, as they did every day. Cold mists swirled off the river. Egrets and bitterns flapped off from marshy islands before our noisy engine, an ancient tractor motor that some French plantation owner must have imported in the thirties.

At around mid-river, a U.S. Riverine Patrol boat began to overtake us. For some reason (maybe because he just couldn't hear very well down there by the engine), our captain did not stop our boat when the patrol raised its siren. We kept going. Phuc and others were on their feet shouting down to the captain, but before he could even fathom what they were trying to say, the patrol boat started firing across our bow, the bullets skipping the waves about ten feet in front of our prow. Then everyone on the boat started shouting and hopping up and down like ants on a griddle.

With our engine now cut and our big, unwieldy craft

drifting in the river, the gray, steel-clad cutter came up alongside, cannons trained on us, decks bristling with sailors aiming M-16s and pistols and shouting pidgin English and unintelligible Vietnamese. All the people on board fell silent and sat down in their seats.

The first sailor to board stopped dead when he saw me sitting in the back with Phuc. I was dressed—minus the turban—in the maroon pajamas of the islanders. I could see a light bulb flicker with dim wattage as this guy figured he had captured one of the fabled Russian advisers to the North Vietnamese. He elbowed another sailor, who took note.

"Just be polite, Mr. John," advised Phuc. He gave them his ID. I gave them a Card of Identity and Registration (American Foreign Service Form 225A), which I carried instead of my precious passport. It had "Foreign Service of the United States of America" printed in large type on its cover, and now the sailor seemed to take me for an Embassy spook.

"You know that the Geneva Conventions forbid a foreign army to detain noncombatant citizens of another country?" I asked.

"You know best, sir," the guy said, actually winking as he handed me back my card. Then he looked at me more closely. I carried my stuff in a cotton bag that Crystal Steinbeck had sent me from India. Over the months, Lonnie had sewn all sorts of amulets onto it: tiny cloisonné Thai bells, a reverse swastika symbolizing the Wheel of Dharma, a stamped brass peace sign, a Hindu mala bead, a picture of the Coconut Monk encased in a medallion of clear plastic, the Thiên-Nhơn-Địa pin—stuff like that. "You know," the sailor continued as he seemed to take a new fix on me, "we were upriver one day in VC country, and we went down this narrow inlet and found this hootch where there wasn't supposed to be any, so we sneaked up on it, and you know what we found?"

I shook my head.

"These two long-hairs. Hippies. Vietnamese hippies. I mean, they were sitting at a table drinking tea out in this free-fire zone—nothing but crickets, craters, and VC— and they were just kind of laughing and talking. It blew my mind. I mean, they weren't VC or nothing, from what we could tell. They didn't even run when they saw us, just started laughing again. They looked kinda high. I felt bad, but we had to take them in."

"Why?"

"Draft-dodgers." He circled his .45 above his head and signaled his men to leave. When their gunboat pulled away, Phuc recited the first two lines of a poem we had translated:

> Sad, I blame Mr. Sky.
> When sad, I laugh. Happy, I cry.

The next lines went:

> Not a man, in my next life
> I'll become a rustling pine
> on a cliff in the sky.
> Fly with the pines, cool and lonely.

That was the only bad time I had in my lone travels. On another visit with Twiggy, Lonnie, and Steve, I was even able to stop a fight with a proverb I had picked up from my research: Người khôn ngậm miệng; người mạnh khoanh tay. "The wise man," I said to a young cyclo driver who was about to square off with Erhart over the price of the fare, "shuts his mouth; the strong man folds his arms." To my amazement, the young thug cut the throttle on his rage and merely scowled at me in resentment before stalking over to his cohorts across the street at the riverside pedicab park, telling them what I had just said. "Dao Dua," one of the older men said to him by way of explanation. "Christ, Balaban," Erhart commented, "you're really tapped into something. Pretty soon we'll just walk across the water to Disneyland."

I *was* tapped into something. As Phuc and I recorded over the next months, and as I made other recordings with the Muong minority up in the highlands, or consulted in Saigon at the Summer Institute of Linguistics with a missionary-linguist, David Smith—perhaps the world's foremost authority on the history of the Mon-Khmer parent language family of Vietnamese—and, finally, as I found myself coached up in Hue by an eighty-year-old former mandarin, Le Thanh Canh (one of the singers I recorded through him had been his former palanquin-bearer during the last emperorship), I realized that indeed I had tapped into something. It was nothing less than a record of Vietnamese humanistic belief, a record that I could trace back at least one thousand years, to the time when the Vietnamese language separated from its country cousin, Muong, a record that probably went back unbroken to the Mon-Khmer four-syllable singing prayers that were being created in Southeast Asia centuries before the Christian era.

In Hue, I recorded the former palanquin-bearer, his mandarin, a riverboat merchant, and a high-school teacher; in Ban Me Thuot, drinking reed alcohol and smoking horribly strong Lao black tobacco until my lungs ached, I recorded songs that were an archaic parallel to *ca dao*. On Phoenix Island, I taped children, mothers as they sang to their babies, a Viet Cong deserter, a number of farmers running hand plows behind water buffalo on the Island's farm holdings across the river, an Island shipwright, the Coconut Monk's cook, and old Mrs. Cu, who paused from her sewing to sing for me the poem about the red cloth, the poem that led me later into that courtyard in imperial Hue where I secretly watched those indecipherable trance-dancers wheeling about, their faces veiled in red scarves. *Mặt trời,* the "face of Heaven." The mirror, which was traditionally part of the family altar, represented Heaven. And the red cloth? Surely, the human heart residing close to it.

I gathered something like five hundred *ca dao* that year, mostly from the men and women of Phoenix Island. Most of these songs had never been written down, not even in Vietnamese, and to transcribe them I had to play them back again and again in our apartment in Saigon, realizing as I did so that the calming Island bells had so penetrated the singers that they punctuated their line endings with the bells, that they regulated even their breathing to the big bell's soft tolling.

A line from one of my taped poems went: *Đừng giữa Trời anh nói không sai,* "Standing before Heaven, I cannot lie." Conscious of Heaven, one is filled with clarity and compassion. Surely such revelatory moments can occur in a laundromat in Detroit as well as in a flooded rice field shaking with sunlight. But for ordinary Vietnamese dwelling in such a moment of spiritual consciousness, their culture also gives a means of expression. And so, across the centuries, in their singing of *ca dao,* peasants have made a record of their reaching toward Heaven, of their reaching out toward one another. For the better part of a year, I glimpsed their Heaven in its bright mirrors of poetry, heard its summonings in its bell, the *"chiêu-ẩn am,"* the "temple bell that calls one to seclusion," ringing in our realm between heaven and earth.

20

TWO FINCHES

On Nguyen Hue, down from the white-washed, *fin-de-siècle* Saigon City Hall, the dividing strips in the center of the wide boulevard housed a string of newsstands. Farther toward the river, kiosks sold species of bamboo, bougainvillea, orchids rooted on bark chips, slips of jackfruit, jasmine, and tamarind, buckets of cut flowers, and potted jungle plants. Still farther down the boulevard, one could find caged monkeys, rare turtles and civet cats, along with domesticated mutts, and all sorts of tropical birds chirping and cawing in handmade bamboo cages: parrots and canaries, of course, but also weird raucous birds—drab bulbuls, secretive drongoes, scarlet flowerpeckers, thumb-size chartreuse-and-green bee eaters, lorikeets, and finches.

The red finches stole our hearts; Lonnie and I kept two in a cage that we hung before the window in our apartment. When the morning sun sifted through the slats of the shutters, the two birds sang and sang and made the room cheery.

Then one disappeared. I couldn't figure out how it could have gotten out of the room even if it had managed to wiggle through the bamboo bars of its cage until I noticed that, at the top of the outside wall of our tiny kitchen and shower room, vents were fashioned in the brickwork.

In the days that followed the finch's flight, our other
bird became so listless that finally we thought either of
giving it away (since we didn't have many more months
left in Vietnam) or of buying it another companion. Then,
for a number of days it revived, chirping away and cocking
its head toward the balcony window. I thought the sparrows outside had aroused it with their songs. A few times,
Lonnie even thought she heard another bird answering
ours and looked out through the bars of our window, but
saw none. And then, after a week or so of excited singing,
our little bird settled back into the solitary silence of its
perch.

One morning, intending to shake out a dusty broom, I
opened the balcony door we kept locked against the increasing street crime. We hadn't opened the door in
weeks—it was one of those accordion shutters that was a
devil to lock—and as I pulled it screeching across its run-
ners, I saw the escaped finch lying on the dusty balcony
tiles, quite dead. It was so sad; we realized it had flown
away only to hover just outside its mate's window, trying
to call it away or to get back in.

We were off on our Honda looking for a baby's outfit
for a college friend of Lonnie's, and had pulled up just in
front of the poncho-and-parachute arcade attached to the
storefronts at the corner where Le Loi joined Cong Ly near
the central market, across from a downtown military post
guarded by a gun placement. Neither of us had any money
on us (Lonnie's university, which we were counting on
for piasters, hadn't paid her in months), but Lonnie wanted
to stop and take a look at the kiddie clothes hung up on
screens facing the street. Noting the soldier sitting in his
cement-and-wire guardhouse across the divided boulevard, I let Lonnie off, yanked the bike back up on its
kickstand, and locked it. Actually this area was a kind of
market overflow specializing in cotton clothing. We saw
the prettiest dress for a baby girl and told the seller we
would come back for it. She thought we were trying to

get her to drop the cost, and so, as we walked out to the street from under her tarpaulin, she kept dropping her price until I was laughing and finally turned and took out my wallet and showed her it was empty. *"Nghèo Mỹ,"* I said, "Poor Americans," and she laughed too, repeating my silly oxymoron to her associates, who laughed because it was rare to see Americans there, especially one who spoke Vietnamese.

Lonnie had already gone ahead and was straddling the motorcycle seat, waiting for me. As I turned to step from under the sidewalk arcade, I was kicked in the small of the back so hard it sent me flying hands-and-knees onto the street. I looked over to Lonnie and, as I straightened up and turned around, saw a teenaged street tough smirking at me, hands on his hips, from under the tarp where I had just been standing. He pointed a finger at me, daring me to respond.

I didn't know what to do. He wasn't much to worry about—just a skinny sixteen- or seventeen-year-old. I could tell he was drunk because of the booze blotches under his eyes. I didn't want any trouble with Lonnie there. She was pregnant. But in the same instant (really, all this— kick and turnabout to the pointing finger—had occurred within two or three seconds), I looked again at Lonnie still seated on the Honda and realized he could kick her in the back when I got on to drive away. I must have said something like "Fuck it" as that last thought flooded my head with rage and I went for the kid to settle fast whatever this was.

As I lunged to grab him, Lonnie screamed, "They've got a chair!"

They? Chair? And then in the corner of my eye, I saw another boy hiding off to one side behind the tarpaulin flap. I lurched back just as the metal chair swung down, not on my head but on my right index finger, which snapped. When I reared back, my left hand flailed up to ward off the chair and somehow ended up with it.

Now both boys were gaping at me in surprise. The

women sellers started screeching and grabbing at their
goods as I raised the chair and cracked it across both punks,
whereupon they dropped like does and just as quickly
scrambled to their feet in a terror to race away. I could
have gotten away then, but I was now fiendish in anger.
Still clutching the chair, and now sprinting after the boys
who were knocking people down in the narrow passage,
I chased them until, to their bad luck and mine, they ran
smack into a soup vendor trundling through the narrow
alley of stalls with her wooden yoke of steaming double
basins of soup. Just before they tumbled into her, the boy
who had kicked me called out to three older toughs who
were sucking noodles at a stall just behind the soup lady.
These boys, I saw in that millisecond, had dispatched the
other two to take me out and lift my wallet. It was just a
mugging! But if a word from me earlier might have
stopped things then, all that was happening now was unfolding too fast to check as my two assailants crashed into
the yowling soup vendor who careened backward into the
noodle stall sloshing her boiling soup on herself, on the
boys who had stumbled into her, and onto the three other
thugs who were knocked off their tinny stools and scalded
by the soup. As I came skidding to a stop, they all lay
before my feet.

I brought the chair cutting down on all five. *All five.* I
heard a bone crack as one boy got the brunt of my stroke.
Then, still holding the chair, I ran for my life back up the
bazaar.

As I was about to jump onto the Honda, it was already
too late. The first bottle hit me on the head, and then I
saw one hit Lonnie. "Get out of here," I yelled at her.
"Get a cop!" I motioned down the boulevard to the city
center. The soldier across the street was just watching from
behind his machine gun. Then, as a hail of glass was falling
all about us, I looked back and saw the five boys, including
one who was holding his arm, running into a pharmacy,
sweeping whole trays of bottles into their hands, lobbing
them as they ran toward us.

The market people were screaming, but none were intervening in our behalf. "Go!" I shouted to Lonnie, who, bless her, did not want to leave me. But we had an agreement: if ever we got into a tight situation, she'd let me call the shots—if I said fight, she'd fight for her life; if I said run, she'd go for help. This was run. After all, we were in downtown Saigon, with White Mice cops at every corner, with patrolling American MPs and their Vietnamese Canh Sat counterparts, and with thousands of civilians milling about.

As Lonnie ran out into the traffic and disappeared down the street, the shopkeepers were closing their shop doors to keep the thugs from gathering up more of their merchandise to throw at me. I still had the chair, and held it up as a shield. I took a Jergens bottle on the forehead, but for the time that was it for the bottles. Then the boys closed in. (I say "boys," but I could see they were old enough to be in the Army.) They were afraid to come too close because of the chair, which I kept swinging.

I got out in the middle of the street to attract as much attention as I could. Now the kids had circled me, one even jumping the steel median divider to get behind me. The traffic was honking by us, but no one stopped. I had to keep turning around, wielding my chair as one of them would feint in from the front and another would lob something at me from behind. I was so tired from swinging the damned chair that at one point I leaned against the median, chair down, feeling like a deer run down by dogs. Then the traffic light released a new swarm of traffic toward me and across the median I called to an older GI and his Vietnamese girlfriend driving an Army jeep into town. I wanted to vault the median but knew if I did the kids would get me from behind, maybe with a knife, before I got over. I remember seeing the middle-aged sergeant's eyes widen as his lane of traffic slowed, putting him right next to the fight, and he heard me call out to him, "For Christ's sake, give me a hand or go get the MPs." His girlfriend slapped at his wrist holding the steering wheel

and he goosed his engine and drove on. Same thing with
the Vietnamese watching. No one was going to help. The
shopkeepers, I suppose, knew the kids would come back
to settle up.

I was facing a hard-core bunch of vicious but—luckily—
cowardly thugs, the ones who slit purses with razors in
the market place or who at night thumped on lone GIs too
drunk to walk. They lived on these streets. No one in the
crowd was going to help me, but everyone would watch.
I remember swinging the chair as one kid jumped in with
a karate kick and—in the second my swing left me exposed—another kid dived in to swing at me with his board.
The board was jagged on the edges and it caught me across
the stomach, ripping through my shirt and slicing my belly
across the navel. The crowd oohed.

Then I saw Lonnie coming back up the street, literally
pulling a Vietnamese cop by the arm and, as they got
nearer, reaching for his gun. He slapped at her hand and
reluctantly unholstered his weapon.

"Police!" I shouted in Vietnamese, and the boys looked
down the street.

Some of them turned and ran, but an older one, one of
the three who had been eating noodles, pointed a finger
at me and said, *"Chết rồi,"* "Dead now"—i.e., "You're
dead"—and I knew this wasn't ever going to be over as
he sauntered off slowly through the crowd, which made
no attempt to stop him.

I had a cut on my scalp, a broken finger, and a superficial
slash across my stomach. Lonnie, who was holding me
and shaking with sobs, had saved my life. But now I realized that my getting hurt and nearly killed wasn't the
bad part. The bad part was the fear of what would happen
next: the vengeful pointing finger, the *"Chết rồi."* We had
to drive past that intersection daily to get back to our house
off Tran Hung Dao. If I stopped at the traffic light there
enough times, I could bet that one day one of those kids

would rush out of the arcade to put a knife in me or Lonnie.

We went right away to talk to Erhart, who got on his bike as I climbed on back to ride through the area to see if we could spot the kids. And we did, or at least got a glimpse of one of them running away into the market. Then we stopped and Steve just shook his head, agreed that it was bad, and suggested I go talk to Kevin Buckley, the young Bureau Chief for *Newsweek*. (Mert Perry, my pal and the Bureau Chief at Tet, had died of a heart attack.)

"Kevin knows a lot of people," Steve said. "Maybe even the kind of people you might need."

I didn't know Kevin that well, but liked him a lot. We all—Twiggy and Steve, Lonnie and me—had had a disastrous dinner at his house once, with Kevin's friend Frances FitzGerald miffing Steve with what he had taken to be a slight to Twiggy, and once Kevin and I had talked a long time about the U.S. Ninth Division in the Delta— Kevin was preparing an exposé on the Ninth's own My Lai–like slaughters (similar to their shooting up of Cai Rang above Can Tho) over a period of several years. Once, I had run into Kevin by chance in the dining room of the Auberges des Pagodes at Angkor Wat, and after that, when I got home to Pennsylvania, I called his parents in Connecticut to say I had seen him and he was fine. Kevin was more than fine. He was bright and funny.

When I went to see him, he too thought we were in trouble. I asked him if he knew anybody that could scare these kids into leaving us alone. Hesitantly, he suggested that he could arrange for me to see a certain Captain Huan, who sometimes fed information to *Newsweek*.

I did see Captain Huan, or rather Captain Huan came over to Kevin's to hear about my trouble. The Captain didn't see it as much of a problem. For $250—$50 per head—he would have each of the boys killed.

Kevin looked at me in horror, not knowing what I'd say.

Murder. How far had I come from my pacifism? *Why,*

I now wondered, hadn't I tried to *speak* to the first boy? It had worked in My Tho: The wise man shuts his mouth; the strong man folds his arms. Even with these thugs, I could have tried *something*. All I did was go for him. And then everything I had done subsequently (*why* did I have to chase them?) had turned the robbery into a vendetta.

"Couldn't you just threaten them?" I asked. "Slap 'em around so they know we mean it?"

The Captain smiled politely, showing off some nice gold uppers, and shook his head. It didn't work that way. He had his own plausibility to maintain in the underworld.

"Well, thanks," I said. "Thanks anyway, but I don't want to kill anybody."

The only thing I did was buy another .38 and pointedly drive by the place several times with Steve. Then I looked up a Marine guard at one of the Embassy annexes who had once asked me to translate a love letter from a bar girl. I asked him if I could go out with the guards to their firing range to sight in my new weapon. When we went, I took Lonnie with me. A gunnery Sergeant helped me sight the thing in on some sandbags, found it shot low, filed down the front post, and then watched approvingly as I proceeded to blast out the bull's-eye on my target at fifty yards. I showed Lonnie how to use it. And when I went up to Hue to do my teaching a few days later, I left the gun with her. I had to go. I was giving exams.

When my Hue stint was over a few days later, I found Clyde Coreil waiting for me at Tan Son Nhut Airport. "Clyde, my mysterious friend," I said, "what are you doing here?"

"It's Lonnie," he said.

"What? Clyde, what?"

"Well, it's not bad. . . ."

Clyde couldn't bear to tell anyone anything bad, so his reticence now was double agony. I punched his shoulder. "For Christ's sake, what?"

"She's losing the baby. I took her out to Third Field Hospital. She's going to be okay."

"What happened?"

"Nothing happened. She just started bleeding. I'm sorry, man."

One morning before I had left for Hue, Lonnie had complained of cramps. She said that when she had run away to get a cop she had been certain she'd come back to find me dead, and that when she thought that she felt an ache crease her belly as she ran down the street searching for help. Later on in the day when she said that, on the slim basis of my Fulbright travel grant, I bullied our way in to see the Embassy doctor (who was not authorized to see us because we weren't "official"). He told Lonnie not even to think about it. "My God, young woman," I remember him saying, "in old times women got thrown from horses and still had healthy babies. Your bad fright won't make a bit of difference. Do you feel okay now?"

"Yes."

"Well, believe this old doctor. It won't make a difference."

But a week and a half after the street fight, in the U.S. Army's Third Field Hospital, off Tan Son Nhut, where Clyde had rushed her in a taxi, she lost the baby. A young Army doctor from Georgia, nicknamed Peaches, helped her through the miscarriage while I wandered the hospital grounds crazed with grief and remorse, convinced that the fight had caused her miscarriage, and ashamed that I had not been nearby when she was in pain. I kept thinking of our two finches, calling to each other at the shuttered window.

PART FOUR

AFTER
OUR WAR

21

WHAT
WE CARRIED HOME

When Lonnie was well enough to travel, we took a long vacation in Malaya, traveling by train from Kuala Lumpur to Fraser's Hill in the mountain jungles of the old tin-mining districts. From there we went on to Penang, where we stayed at the Lone Pine Inn—still governed by Victorian etiquette—on the island's north shore, looking off into the Straits of Malacca. The other guests were British, some on honeymoons. We ate three-course breakfasts—porridge and finnan haddie and scrambled eggs—served to us by immaculate, deferential waiters at palm-shaded tables set with ornate, engraved silverware. Then we would sleep on the beach before returning to our table for a six-course lunch. There was a 4:00 tea. Dinner at 8:00. In the afternoons and evenings, we'd walk the beach watching the huge iguanas basking on boulders and, later, the moon barely riding above the wave crests. In the mornings, mynah birds held court on the tiled roof under our hotel-room window. In the afternoons, an Indian snake-charmer brought his baskets of cobras to entertain us. We were so young that—feeling the healing power of all that sleep, wave-washed silence, and good food—we thought we had banished our recent pain. We were young. We would have other children.

But Vietnam had marked us both indelibly. When Lonnie's university finally paid her after I threatened a lawsuit, they paid her all at once and toward the end of the school year in so many packets of devalued piasters that we had to carry away her salary in two suitcases. A large part of that money, as well as my Hue University salary, we simply gave away in the rain one night in Hue, when it was our exhausting bad luck to be in the city as it seemed about to fall to the regular North Vietnamese Army which had routed the Saigon troops north of the city at Easter, 1972. We had come on one last trip to see the imperial tombs and the old royal city. That day, as we walked the monuments with Vietnamese friends, the aerial and sea bombing that stopped the North Vietnamese advance started thudding in the distant mountains and by evening, as heavy rains fell, the poor minority tribes who lived in the mountains had to flee their homes and go to the strange, foreign city for shelter. Whole families, whole clans—barefooted men, nursing mothers, toddlers, and bent grandparents— had left their ancestral villages to escape the bombs and were walking into Hue in their single-file style. *Mọi,* the Vietnamese called them, "savages." We doubted they'd even be given shelter from the rain. Holding a pistol under my poncho, I stood by as Lonnie gave away our money in the drumming downpour, returning to me several times to take more from my hidden satchel and weeping as she told me about one old man who did not even seem to know what she was handing him. For us, it was play money. We were going home.

For the next sixteen years we were childless. The cause for this was so much a mystery to our doctors that finally we thought that, if the fight hadn't caused the miscarriage, maybe one or both of us had become contaminated with dioxin, the teratogenic toxin that was a lethal element of the Agent Orange defoliant that America had sprayed on the forests unaware that, subsequently, dioxin would enter the food chain, where it is still, two decades later, causing

stillbirths and deformities in Vietnamese babies and in livestock. Lonnie had drunk the Mekong on Phoenix Island
our second day in country. "How could you take her to
a place like that?" my outraged friend Vida once asked me
many years ago, and her words stung my face as red as if
she had slapped me.

Tận nhân lực; tri thiên mệnh: "Venture all; see what fate
brings." That is my best, though uncertain, reply. The
human realm of "red dust" is the realm of *samsara* where
calamitous changes overtake us, even those of us who may
be consciously pursuing their fate before heaven. That pursuit brought Lonnie into a classroom in Saigon where in
her exquisite youth and beauty she taught four hundred
students how to speak English, dividing them into man-
ageable sections, and taking seriously their instruction. She
must remember herself doing all that and telling her sol-
dier-students, who arrived on dusty Hondas, to stow their
M-16s by the classroom door. If she remembers the fight,
she must remember how she saved my life. Fate brought
her, bless it, Steve and Twiggy, and the Coconut Monk,
and the beautiful songs that she heard sung by the Monk's
followers on that magical island in the Mekong. As it does
to many marked and tested by Vietnam, fate brought her
a fuller sense of herself. So I don't know, we have regrets,
we have no regrets. "Happiness or misfortune," to repeat
the Buddhist nun's words from *Kieu,* "are prescribed by
the law of Heaven, but their source comes from ourselves."
It's not what happens to you; it's what you do with what
happens to you. *That* is our human aspect which Heaven
watches, for in that moment we are creating our fate.
Wouldn't it have been in some sense a greater risk to have
stayed home, hunkered down safely in a university when
fate was calling us to venture all? *Đi ra cho thấy mặt Trời
mặt Trăng* is a line from a poem that a twelve-year-old girl
sang to me: "Go out and see heaven's face, and the
moon's." Everything realized and written in this book
results from such a venture.

As the years have passed since the end of the war, much of my life has been threaded through the needle of Vietnam. The poems I brought back, I made into a book. Some found their way into a novel of John Barth's. Others became part of a documentary. As the war ended, and hundreds of thousands of Vietnamese fled to the United States, I have heard from them from time to time as they have discovered in my small collection of *ca dao* one of the few scraps of their culture they can lay their hands on and give to their Americanized children. As the war ended and the hard line softened in Hanoi, allowing moments of communication, I was even sent—through an intermediary at the Smithsonian—a scholarly study of *ca dao* that quoted my book as a source. And as I sat typing the last sentence, the phone rang and someone from National Public Radio in New York called to ask me if I would sing some *ca dao* on the air. I will. It's part of what I can do now. I know the poems by heart.

By the war's end, COR had returned almost all of the children in its care, though we did not return any orphan who wanted to stay. In 1975, we had paid our hospital bills, shut down our offices, and had a little over one hundred thousand dollars in the bank. The question was: Did we have any further role in Vietnam? While doing research at the Bibliothèque Nationale, I visited the Provisional Revolutionary Government's Embassy in Paris and asked them how COR might continue. As before, I got a polite reception and COR got no answer of any kind despite a follow-up letter from Dr. Needleman. Finally, The Committee of Responsibility to Save War-Burned and War-Injured Children had a last meeting in Boston at which it voted itself out of corporate existence, writing a check to the Ministry of Health of the Democratic Republic of Vietnam for the balance of our account and stipulating that the money be spent on the care of paraplegic children. Only Mr. Sky knows if it actually was.

But what of those children? What happened to children like Duc and Bau into whose lives I had come like an emissary of fate? After Saigon fell, we never heard from any of them for nearly fifteen years.

And what of my friends? Richard, Dr. Khoa, Clyde, the Coconut Monk, Steve, Twiggy, Buckley, Liles, Dao Phuc, the Buus, Trung, John and Alex Clarke, Crystal and John Steinbeck? As I returned to teaching in the middle of Pennsylvania, they became more real and dear to me than anyone I could meet as I now re-endeavored as an academic. I did not even dare to write the Vietnamese, lest such contact with an American cause them trouble with the new regime which was revealing a far less human and more communist face than any of us, except poor Trung, would have guessed.

Fate keeps bringing its returns. It brought Erhart's death from colon cancer at the age of thirty-five. He died in Bangalore, India, on his way back to Vietnam to see Twiggy, to give her, at least, if not his name, then his small worldly wealth. In Bangalore, he was hoping—half-seriously, but hoping—after all the National Health Service chemotherapy and painkillers, to be cured by Sai Baba, a then popular guru.

I had flown to London to see him before he started back to Vietnam with John Steinbeck in 1974. Steve was staying with Steinbeck and Steinbeck's new flame, Rosie Boycott, at her house in Shepherd's Bush which she shared with her fellow editors from the brash new magazines *Sparerib* and *Time Out*. Seeing Steve again was a shock. His yellowish flesh was now shrunk to his very bones; his very bones bulged out at the joints in knobs of cancerous calcification. On that last morning I saw him, he stood wrapped in a towel in the opened door of his Kensington Hilton room (reserved on a credit-card bill he would not live to pay), handing me a paper that made me his literary executor. "Just in case," he said, winking. Behind him on

the tousled bed I could see the model and photojournalist
Marie-Laure de Decker, who, in the current issue of *Newsweek,* was rumored to be the woman President Valéry
Giscard d'Estaing was sneaking off to see, leaving a sealed
letter at the Elysées Palace giving his whereabouts in case
of nuclear war. She had flown in from Paris to say goodbye. I looked at Marie-Laure sleeping with her back to the
door and then I looked at Steve, at the wreckage of his
bones, and shook my head in disbelief.

"I'm the only man who didn't try to fuck her in Vietnam," he explained, adding, "I knew that would get her
sooner or later." But it was more than that, as of course
he knew despite his sarcastic reduction. He was probably
the only man who had really befriended her in Vietnam,
after she photographed the man aflame on the government
lawn, after the cop smashed her Pentax to the sidewalk,
after she had more or less given up on doing anything
useful there. Steve had befriended her despite all the difficulties this caused him with the jealous Twiggy. And
now she had flown in to say goodbye by fucking his dying
brains out.

Later that morning, Steve, Rosie, and John were off on
Air India. At the airport, some of their friends from *Time
Out* sang them a chorus from *Hepatitis,* a musical that one
of them had written about hippies flocking east: "The
burning ghat is where it's at."

A total of 8,744,000 Americans—men and women, civilians and military—went to Vietnam, twice the number
engaged in World War I, half the number engaged in World
War II. No wonder this war won't go away. It lives in
varying degrees of intensity in all those heads. The average
age for an American soldier in Vietnam was nineteen. As
Steinbeck said, they grew up in Vietnam.

Some years ago, I was in Boulder, Colorado, to see
Steinbeck at the Tibetan Buddhist center where he had
lately taken refuge. We were walking outside as the Red

Zinger Bicycle Classic zoomed by us. We were talking—
of course—about Vietnam, and specifically about Post-
Traumatic Stress Syndrome, which John had just written
about for a magazine.

Often enough over the years, I have found myself at a
window with tears in my eyes as I suddenly, without ex-
pectation, have been greeted by the naked nine-year-old
thrashing on the stainless-steel operating table with his
eardrums blown; often images from my COR days come
floating up on mental backwaters: the napalmed mother
and her lovely infant daughter with the blackened arm; the
pajamaed girl throwing her thigh over her old father to
keep him warm as he lay dying beneath her; my carrying
little anesthetized Thuy in my arms down the steps of Nhi
Dong hospital; watching a doctor unwind the turban of
gauze from Thai, the scalped teenager. But somehow, if
I believed at all in the existence of PTS, I thought of it as
something that applied to GIs, like shellshock or battle
fatigue. As Steinbeck and I spoke, however, a troubling
thought overtook me. "John, do you think *we've* been
damaged by Vietnam?"

"C'mon, Balaban, you're too smart not to have realized
that."

But I hadn't. I thought all that flashback stuff was soap
opera and whining. And now, twenty years after these
events, I can't imagine how I could ever have thought I
could look on that carnage of children and not be hurt
forever by what I saw.

Four years ago, when my daughter was only a few weeks
old, I remember holding her and rocking her in our living
room as Lonnie was doing the evening dishes and we were
waiting for the Halloween trick-or-treaters to ring our
doorbell. My daughter was so small that as I held her
sleeping against my chest her tiny feet barely touched my
belt, and her fragrant peony head snuggled just below my
chin. I was so happy that I started crying to myself, big
tears streaming down my cheeks, and suddenly I heard the

chorus of Soeur Anicet's orphanage infants crying in the cribs. It was real, and all around me. In that bewildering moment, the doorbell rang and I got up, with my little girl still sleeping against me, to open the door to an evil little midget in Green Beret togs, jump boots, night paint on his cheeks, penlight for reading maps, and a rubber knife for slitting throats belted to his seven-year-old waist. For a moment, I thought he was part of a hallucination.

"Trick or treat?" he said.

"How you doing, soldier?" I gave him a Mars bar from our tray of candies. I looked into the darkness beyond the kid and saw his father, also got up like a Green Beret. "You shit," I hissed at the father, who grabbed his son's hand and hurried away.

Affected, I'd say, not damaged.

Affected, filled with memories—like almost every conscious person who went there—memories that are sometimes more real than current reality, memories of moments in which we were marked and tested. Elusive memories, for despite their power, they often hold back in the vagaries of time certain key details by which we might judge more objectively what we did. In recent years, I met up again with Kevin Buckley, who went on from Vietnam to become a Nieman Fellow at Harvard, then editor of *Look,* then of *Geo,* and, most recently, of *Lear's* magazine. We had dinner and talked about Alexander Shimkin, another one of those IVS rare birds (antiwar, yet the son of an Army colonel to whom he was deeply attached). Shimkin junior, despite his politics, was probably more expert in the deployment of both sides' military hardware than anyone at the Pentagon East. Shimkin, stringing for Buckley, was killed while reporting the rout in Quang Tri Province, just north of Hue, at about the same time Lonnie and I were ordered out of the city and put on a special CIA Porter Pilatus that zoomed up from the old citadel.

After dinner, Kevin and I joined his wife, Gail, and we

all went to Mass. For them, it was a usual and necessary part of their lives; for me, it was a first time. Later, back at their apartment off Central Park, with Gail gone to bed, we stayed up all night talking and drinking until Kevin finally asked, "That Vietnamese Captain I introduced you to . . ."

"Captain Huan?"

"Yeah. Well . . . what *happened?*"

"Oh," I said, not really sure what Kevin meant but seeing him immensely troubled by his question, "nothing happened."

"Thank God," he sighed.

"You mean all these years you weren't sure whether or not I asked Huan to kill those kids?"

"I'm afraid so."

"No-no-no-no." I laughed and took a gulp of wine, horrified at the guilt he must have entertained for so long. Poor decent Buckley, already steeped in grief for Shimkin.

"And something else." He poured himself another glass. It was 3:00 A.M. "Why did you think you could ask me about something like that? I mean, did I have that kind of image as someone who . . ."

"No. Remember—Steve told me to ask you."

"Well, then, did *he* think I could arrange murders?"

"Kevin, *no.* He knew that you knew nearly everything going on in Saigon, that you'd have connections to informants who might know what to do. None of us suggested murder. Huan did."

"Whew," Buckley said, shaking his head.

If this were fiction, I'd bring Gitelson back to life, or have Richard step out of that Red Zinger bike-race crowd from the anonymity of his CIA retirement and tell me who killed Dave. If this were fiction, I'd have Erhart beat his cancer through Sai Baba and go on to marry Twiggy, moving them to Orange County, where they'd run a Saigon-style coffee shop as he wrote his own fiction. If this were fiction, I'd free the Coconut Monk from the house arrest in which he languishes under the present regime. All of the COR cases would go home healthy to prospering families. But these accounts, despite whatever my flaws of remembrance, happened as I told them. These affairs, as it says in *Kieu* after the heroine's enormous tribulations and her wanting to "tear down the sky for justice," were *cho hay muôn sự tại Trời*, "all decided by Heaven."

22

AFTER
OUR WAR

In the twenty or so years since my Can Tho teaching, my fieldwork for the Committee of Responsibility, and my year of journeying the countryside collecting *ca dao,* I have become an academic teaching in an English department at a large state university in a small college town. Vietnam is less naturally a part of the conversation of University Park, Pennsylvania, than I suppose it might be elsewhere across the United States—say, in any factory, police force, shipyard, prison, or farm. My peers, after all, managed not to go. My current students were about five years old when the war ended. Finally, I have almost no contact with the few Vietnamese students here—mostly science majors—although once in a while some nearly deracinated soul will wander into my office hungry for a sense of his homeland. In this college town full of barber shops, boutiques, and beer halls, there's a mom-and-pop grocery run by a former Vietnamese diplomat and his wife, and I sometimes go in to buy *The New York Times* (which I search for any Asian articles bylined by Steven Erlanger) and to chat with Mrs. Binh in Vietnamese, although my abilities in that language lessen with each year.

I've learned to try to keep Vietnam out of my conversation, although this is difficult since most of my moral, political, and religious views are based there. I am appalled at the possibility of sounding like an American Legionnaire telling war stories, and even if I were to evade that kind of beer-belly boorishness, summoning up Vietnam— among those whose moral, political, and religious views derive from elsewhere—is a bit like bad manners. It's like talking about yourself. Amiable talk develops from shared experience. In certain ways, I've learned I'm out of it. At the university, some of my colleagues have even suggested I stop writing about Vietnam, since it's not part of my departmental duties. For them, as for most academics (despite Dante's "The proper subjects of poetry are love, virtue, and war"), *our* war, just fifteen years over, is dead history. So, like most who have returned home, I find it best to keep Vietnam to myself.

No wonder so many of us—dwelling in charged, middle-aged silences—want to go back to that lost continent still sending live transmissions on our special-pay channels.

As I started on this book, I got a letter that began:

> Dear Mr. Balaban:
> Although you do not know us, we have in our home a photograph that you made over twenty years ago. Your photograph has meant very much to our family. You were very kind to send us that photograph and we are very happy to send you now, even after all these years, a photograph in return.

The letter was from a Mr. and Mrs. Herman-Giddens in North Carolina. They were the foster parents of Pham Thi Huong, the tiny girl who had been shot through a leg that was barely saved at Duke University Hospital. The photo I sent them was of Huong in her mother's arms on the airplane journey we took together from Danang to Saigon, a journey that must have been incredibly bewildering for them, since neither mother nor child had been in a city before the little girl's wounding forced them to the Danang hospital. The photograph the Herman-Giddenses sent me was a snapshot of Huong, now a grown-up woman, a bit plump, favoring one leg, wearing pink pajamas and leaning toward a blossoming shrub.

Huong's photo was my first echo back from the silence that had swallowed up all of our returned COR cases after the fall of Saigon.

Then, in the next few weeks, I got a clipping from Dr. Needleman, a clipping from the *Los Angeles Times* picturing a smiling twenty-one-year-old Nguyen Thi Bong. I had last seen her as an infant with a huge hole in her face, the day I put her in an ambulance on the way to Tan Son Nhut. Now she was a pretty and unusually articulate coed at UCLA.

Also around that time, I got a call from a woman at KQED in San Francisco. One of the orphaned COR boys was going back to his home village to be *married*. They were going to film it. Was I the one who had handled his evacuation in Saigon?

Mr. Heaven was giving me some nudges. Winks.

All these years, I had sweated about the final rightness of our intervening in these children's lives. Now, in the liberalizing climate that began in Vietnam in 1986 with the "new thinking" of the reformist Communist Party General Secretary, Nguyen Van Linh, I wondered if I couldn't go back and see for myself. *Find* the children. See what had happened to them. In my notebooks, I still had many of their addresses. In Vietnam, country people stay put.

23

RETURNING

Northwest Airlines Flight #7, bound for Tokyo, stopping in Seattle, connecting in Tokyo with NW Flight #27, bound for Bangkok, seems part of another world even before roaring off the snow-flurried runway in Philadelphia. Along with the Japanese businessmen returning with some piece of America in their attaché cases, a Thai Buddhist monk in saffron robes sits nearby with his hands folded in his lap. Next to me, by the window, a long-legged guy sits with his bony knees bunched up, decked out in jeans, in tooled leather boots, and sporting a Stetson with bushy feathers in its hatband. He hands me his card and asks where I'm headed. I look down at his card: Doug MacArthur, Breaking & Training, Tam Bren Arabian. A horse head and spurs are drawn on either side of his name. He says he just brought an Appaloosa out to Connecticut and is going home to his ranch on the Yakima River. He puts out his hand.

"Oh, I'm going on," I say, shaking a callused grip that tells me he's what he says he is.

"Tokyo?"

"No, Bangkok."

"Whoo-ee, Bangkok. Whatcha doin' there?"

"Well," I say, mindful that I have four hours of flying

with this talkative cowboy before we land at Seattle, "I'm going to Vietnam."

His face darkens. "I wouldn't want to go there."

"Why not? The war's over."

"Kid brother was killed there."

"Sorry."

"Whatcha want to go there for?"

It's hard to explain. The Christopher Reynolds Foundation and the American Friends Service Committee, which have been trying to send me for years, have finally been given the go-ahead by the Vietnamese government to sponsor my lecture at the Vien Van Hoc, the Institute of Literature. I am carrying with me, in excess baggage, thirty-five copies of the four-volume *American Literature* edited by Cleanth Brooks et al., along with an assortment of other books like A. J. Poulin's *Contemporary American Poetry*, Irving Howe's collection of essays *Politics and the Novel*, and F. O. Matthiessen's classic, *American Renaissance*. I am also to continue on to Saigon, now Ho Chi Minh City, and from there to Can Tho, where I taught for IVS. Penn State's free-spirited graduate-school dean, a distinguished scientist who liked my project right off, has kicked in a couple of grand so I can travel into the Mekong Delta to meet some of the COR children, if they are still alive. To meet them, I will travel down dusty roads and rivers forbidden me during the war. I am returning, partner, to have a looksee at the face of Heaven.

Some eighteen hours later, we are landing in Bangkok. I have watched *Honey, I Shrunk the Kids*. I have read Francis Fukuyama's prophetic essay ("The End of History?" *National Review*, Summer 1989) predicting the complete collapse of the Soviet empire, the worldwide triumph of "American-style" liberal democracy, and a somewhat dull, politically homogenized planet after this last ideological challenge to democracy has been dumped on the trash heap of history. In what is already *yesterday's* stopover at the

Seattle airport (after saying goodbye to Mr. MacArthur—who must now be feeding carrots to his Arabians at his snowy ranch near the Yakima), I watched the TV monitor in an airport bar as the hard-line Czech government crumbled to Havel and Dubcek. How is this playing in Vietnam?

The man now next to me—a small Asian who has actually been on the flight all the way from Philadelphia—stirs from his sleep as the cabin lights go on and the Thai stewardess hands out customs and emigration cards. Soon he asks me to help him fill out his card, shoving it over onto my seat tray. I see that he is thirty-eight and a U.S. citizen, that he has listed his occupation as "truck drive," and that he is Vietnamese by birth. He's confused about the transit questions. I ask him in Vietnamese what's his final destination, and he blinks back in surprise and discomfort (why does this American know Vietnamese?), then braves it out and answers "Saigon." Saigon, not "Ho Chi Minh City." In his answer, I can guess his politics. Soon we are talking. He was thirteen at the end of the war. At twenty, he served in the Vietnamese Navy on the river near Can Tho and then at sea, up north, near Haiphong, waiting for another Chinese invasion. This is his first trip home.

An Asian man behind us perks up at our conversation and starts talking to Mr. De in Vietnamese too speedy for me to understand. He too, it turns out, is going home, but he is going home for good. He has spent only seven months in the United States and even though his family went broke paying bribes to get him out of Vietnam, he wants to go home. He says they don't know he's coming back. He says he didn't dare tell them. Moreover, he doesn't have a passport of any kind. The Immigration and Naturalization Service authorities in Seattle, his last port of call, have given him a travel document and a warning: if he goes to Vietnam, he will never be readmitted to the United States.

Mr. De and I look at each other in horror. Mr. De's

fingers make a crazy-person motion at his head which this Mr. Long cannot see because of the seat back.

"Didn't you like it in the U.S.?" I ask.

Oh, no, he says, he liked it a lot. He had a dishwashing job and was even singing with a Vietnamese group. He pulls out an advertisement for the group's performance at a recent Thanksgiving dinner at a Holiday Inn in Orange County. Mr. Long is in the photo, wearing a tux, a cummerbund, and a preposterously large bow tie.

"Well, why are you going home?"

"*Nhớ nhà,*" he says. "Homesick." The Vietnamese phrase bespeaks a condition as profound as unremitting depression. *Nhớ nhà:* "remember house," remember the orchard behind the house, remember the smell of your family, the fragrance of the rice grown in the local water, the perfume of fruits, the pungent fish sauce, the dense aroma of tropical mildews, the light shaking through coconut sheaves, rain on banana leaves, walking in a crowd where tropical sunlight glints off shiny black hair, the river sounds, the birdcalls. Mr. Long says that all he could ever think about were the parents and wife he left behind.

"Children?" Mr. De asks him, and even though Long answers no, Mr. De shakes his head in commiseration. Long is now less crazy to him. Mr. De understands *nhớ nhà.*

I help Mr. Long fill out his landing forms. He is twenty-eight; his occupation, he insists, is "singer."

"Do you have an entrance visa for Vietnam?"

He says no, grins, and almost laughs at his own haplessness. I look over at Mr. De who just keeps shaking his head sadly. We both know that Long is headed for trouble. The Thais don't like Vietnamese, period, and will not cut him a break lest they end up with one more unwanted refugee. Moreover, without even talking to De, just by looking at him, I can tell that he too thinks it doubtful that the Vietnamese consular authorities will let Long back in, even should the Thais let him out of the airport to apply for an entrance visa.

How many Vietnamese are there, I wonder to myself, ordinary people like Long—refugees who made the trek to the promised land, squandering their families' wealth to get on boats that might sink or be boarded by pirates, to linger, if still alive, in squalid camps, only to find after several months in America that they want to go home?

It's 2:00 A.M. as the passengers file into the airport to form lines shuffling toward customs. I say a quick goodbye to De and Long, hoping to get far enough ahead of them in line so that I won't be drawn into the inevitable, but at an escalator, Long catches up to me and grips my arm firmly. "Please help me, Older Brother," he says in Vietnamese.

He can hardly speak any English at all. I say I'll try.

We wait together in line. De gets in behind us, and when a customs guard motions me forward, I take Long with me, explaining his circumstances to the Thai official examining passports at a desk. He looks up in annoyance and rings a bell by his knee. "Tell him to wait over there," he says, pointing to a place against the glass maze we have just wound our way through. "Over there," he shouts at Long, when he sees him hesitate.

Before the police come to take him away, Long tells De the telephone number of a Vietnamese friend at a tailor shop in Bangkok and asks De to call him. De takes out a ballpoint pen and writes the number in the palm of his hand.

Later, past the passport authorities, hauling our luggage out of customs, I see that the numbers have already sweated into blue blotches. "There's nothing anyone could have done," I say to Mr. De as we shake hands goodbye. He tells me that Long told him that the U.S. authorities in Seattle made him sign a paper never to return to the States.

Hanoi, December 2, 1989. It is my forty-sixth birthday. I am walking in a darkened city whose streetlamps have been cut to conserve electricity; only bare bulbs hung on wires outside shop fronts cast dull glows onto the sidewalks. In this period of "new thinking," families have been allowed to turn their doorways into food stands, offering meals from little boiling pots, heated by charcoal chunks, firewood, and, in some cases, by butane pots. An old woman is hacking up boiled, yellowy whole chickens on a streetside plank. Nearby, a younger woman pulls soap suds through her long hair over a tin basin near a sidewalk spigot. In the fading evening light pricked by those dim spasms of electricity, I pass streets where vegetables have been put out by the curb. All around me, I can hear the murmur of hundreds of souls sitting behind the plaited trays of onion, shallots, tangerines, and Chinese apples. Hardly any vehicles are moving through the city to drown this murmur of voices, the shrieks of children playing in the dark, and the whooshing of bicycle tires sweeping by as this city of several million pursues its quiet affairs. An addled rooster crows. A buffalo bellows off in the dark, somewhere near the levee of the Red River.

Hanoi: "Inside the bend of the river." The Vietnamese have lived here for three thousand years, and yet this impoverished city through which I have walked all afternoon looks as if it had been borrowed from the French and the Vietnamese couldn't figure out what to do with it. If there is any money to be spent on public works, the victors have not spent it on their capital. The drains and gutters are rotting off the eaves of buildings, buildings that haven't seen paint in fifty years, buildings from which the stucco is flaking away in blotches down to the bricks. Cement sewer-caps have crumbled. Rats run out the doorway of the Unification Hotel. Plodding on, I step on something squishy, and look down to see a dead rat. Sewage rills along the curb, flecks of animal this and vegetable that chugging by. Everywhere in the crumbling, untended city, one senses a huge exhaustion and depletion. This is the city that General Curtis LeMay wanted to "bomb back into the Stone Age." The city where American bomber

after bomber went down trying to demolish the Dragon's
Jaw bridge, which never fell. The city that had to send its
children to the countryside to escape our bombs. This is
the tiny country on which we dropped more bombs than
we unloaded on all of Europe, Africa, and Asia *in all of
World War II*. If not bombed into the Stone Age, this
dilapidated *ville* has been ravaged out of the twentieth century. Hanoi—warped by time and decades of warfare—
looks more like a city in 1890 than at the end of 1989.

These are the victors and their sad fruits of victory: in
a side street, stacks of dried, flattened fish; farther on, piles
of pounded pig-bladders, corn on the cob roasting on sidewalk grills, and dried squid. I am the only Westerner walking these back streets. When I turn a corner and come out
of the shadows, people look at me as if they've seen a
ghost. Then I am pointed out for children to see. Someone
calls out *"Lien Xo,"* "Russian." An old man, evidently not
right in his head, walks up to me and starts talking in
Vietnamese. He's not the least bit surprised when I answer
him. In one hand he has a large onion; in the other, a dead
fish. He holds them up to my face and asks me to buy
them. I say I'm not interested and start to laugh, seeing
the scene in my mind's eye. Whatever he sees in his mind's
eye, he starts laughing too. There are no police anywhere.
Although I am walking alone on darkened streets filled
with desperately poor people, I feel safe. Somehow a mugging is out of the question. Back in the United States—
say, in New York or Philadelphia—we'd call in the National Guard if the streets suddenly went as dark as this.
But walking about here, among these people who have
gotten along with one another in close quarters for three
thousand years, the darkness is merely a kind of conve-
nience for the shadowy figures relieving themselves against
the walls of the downtown prison, for the lovers leaning
off their bikes to smooch discreetly.

For all my jet lag and sleepless exhaustion, I am driven
to walk and walk, to listen in on the chatter, to study the

doings in the dark. The back streets still bear the names of their medieval origins—Tho Nhuom, Dyer's Street; Cho Gao, Rice Market; Hang Buom, Sailcloth Row—as well as the names of Vietnamese men and women whose famous battles against invaders preserved independence: the Trung sisters (42 A.D.), Ngo Quyen (939 A.D.), Ly Thuong Kiet (1076 A.D.), and Le Loi (1428 A.D.) who wrote a poetical proclamation the year he drove out the Ming: "Over the centuries / We have been sometimes strong, sometimes weak / But never yet have we been lacking in heroes / Of that let our history be the proof." Walking through Hanoi is like walking through history. I keep on until I hear the strains of amplified music, and then I follow the screechy arpeggios of, yes, a rock-and-roll guitar, until I see a crowd huddled before the vast steps of the Soviet-style National Bank, the whole front of which is draped in a portrait of Ho Chi Minh.

Below the Chairman's avuncular gaze, in the chilly river air, the band is cranking out American tunes in shaky English. The volume's up; the amps are weak; the mikes, screechy, but a huge crowd is turned out: *bộ-dội,* ordinary soldiers, some in Chinese-style ear-flapped caps with red stars over the brims. Some, in pith helmets, stand literally open-mouthed at the rock show spilling from the imperial steps under the smile and wave of their departed Chairman. A large crowd is gathered, leaning on bicycles or huddled together to keep warm. One man in uniform has wrapped his arms around another soldier as they stand listening. A boy and a girl are kissing in the midst of the throng as old ladies with betel-stained lips hawk peanuts, cigarettes, and tangerines. People stare at me as I come close. They look at me to see if I approve of the music. *"Lien Xo,"* I hear again, and this time, taking a chance, I say, "No, American." The result is as if I had said, "Say cheese." I am enveloped by smiles. A soldier offers me a cigarette. Someone says, "America, number one."

It's evident that the band has been practicing to an old

Creedence Clearwater Revival tape. The crowd close by watches me listen to a mangled version of "Born on the Bayou." In their poverty, in their public pleasure in this once-forbidden music, in their weary faces, I sense that something huge is waking up in them, a powerful yearning to live a plausible life after so much sacrifice, so much duty, so much regimentation. "See us," their innocent stares seem to say, "see how special this is to us."

24

THE INSTITUTE
OF LITERATURE,
HANOI

The Institute of Literature is a Marxist incarnation of a more ancient predecessor, the Temple of Literature, established in 1010 A.D. in Thang Long, or Soaring Dragon, as Hanoi was then called, to train especially talented young men of all social classes, from peasants to nobility. Over the centuries, the graduates of the Temple of Literature became the mandarins who upon graduation went on to govern Vietnam at all levels. The names of these young graduates are engraved on stone stelae set on the backs of mammoth stone turtles that still squat in a courtyard in the old Temple's precincts, surrounded by stone walls, and containing moats, bathing pools, poetry-reading pavilions, dark-raftered study halls, and an altar sanctuary dedicated to Confucius. The last of the graduates' names were carved in 1919.

The new Institute is in an old French villa which was undergoing a furious repair as I entered—across a catwalk being used to wheelbarrow in cement mixing—through tall doors sticky with green paint. (The year 1990 marks the hundredth anniversary of the Chairman's birthday, and he was, quite remarkably, a poet and lover of poetry, a Marxist mandarin.) My visit was originally proposed by the American Friends Service Committee after the Director

of Vietnam's International Relations Institute (where its
foreign service officers are trained) remarked to one of the
Quakers' regional representatives, "It's clear we don't
know how Americans think. Maybe you should send
someone to talk about literature."

But since that original suggestion, world events have
shaken Vietnamese confidence in opening up to visitors.
In the past two years, as Vietnam's relations with the
United States have bettered a bit, then worsened, my trip
has been canceled twice. Now I have come at a bad time
anyway: the Djakarta and Paris talks to end the Cambodian
war have produced nothing; the Vietnamese troop withdrawal from Cambodia has not produced an end to the
fifteen-year U.S. trade and diplomatic embargo. And most
disturbing of all for the aging or hard-line leaders of the
revolution are the storm of events in Tiananmen Square,
in Poland, in Czechoslovakia, and now in East Germany—
all of which have been reported to Vietnamese via a television satellite that sends them the *Vremya* broadcast from
Moscow, the Gorbachev Moscow, the *glasnost* Moscow,
the Moscow that insists on shaking things up by a bizarre,
fair reporting of the news. In other words—although I am
supposing this only by the near quarantine that I have been
kept in for the first few days of my visit—my hosts don't
want any further provocation. All my requests to meet
various Vietnamese outside the Institute of Literature are
refused. I am the first American to address the Institute of
Literature in its post–World War II history. That in itself
is courting enough trouble.

After the obligatory tea and cigarettes and tangerines
with the Institute's Director and his staff, I am taken to a
large seminar room packed with the Institute's researchers
and some visitors. I am asked to sit down at the head of
a very long table, next to an older man, a bit round with
his age, perhaps fifty-five, with thinning hair and thick
glasses, a Mr. Binh who once studied at Yale. Mr. Binh

will translate for me; his English is impeccable; his manner, nervous. He is not part of the Institute staff and my sense is that he doesn't want to chance having to answer for anything stupid that I might say. Perhaps, I rather suspect from his reluctance to tell me his name, he has had political trouble in the past.

I begin with a gaffe—I stand up to speak, as if I were their teacher, not a comrade colleague.

"Please take your seat!" Mr. Binh calls up from my left.

The audience is stony-faced. As I sit down, I say, "The habits of a teacher."

Mr. Binh laughs, to my relief, and repeats my apology to the assembly, which doesn't laugh but seems to take note—if one can tell this by a slightly mirthful twist in the molecules overhanging the seminar table. Then we're off. Before actually beginning a description of American literary events, I talk about the separation between Americans and Vietnamese. I use the phrase *bạn tri âm:* "friend," literally, "the one who hears your sound." I suggest that for Americans and Vietnamese to know one another better they need some knowledge of one another's best thoughts in their best expressions. Some of my audience—as any experienced teacher can tell by the blink of eyes—can follow me in English, but when I use the Vietnamese phrase and apply it to my talk and to the present awful state of affairs between the two countries, I sense some real interest and a relaxation in the room. I go on to talk about American continuity and change in some characteristic ideas: John Winthrop's exhortation to the Puritans assembled on the deck of the *Arbella* in 1630, his "City on the Hill" sermon: "Consider that we shall be as a City upon a Hill, the eyes of all people are upon us." I describe how early Americans fled to freedom in the New World which they thought prepared for them by Providence. How Winthrop saw in the founding a chance for a social and moral model to the world which, if the model were neglected or corrupted by arrogance, would become a calumny. (This is the part of Winthrop's sermon that modern politicians never refer to.) I tell my audience—who must by now be wondering where this line of history will lead—that for our early leaders, like Washington and Jefferson, Americans enjoyed "a peculiar situation" in a "chosen country." I mention Manifest Destiny, and now my listeners start to fidget. I talk about conflicting American views of other peoples, of Indians as "imps of Satan" and also as "children of God." With Mr. Binh tracking wonderfully well in his instant translating, I show how the idea of a city on the hill changes in the twentieth century with interpreters as diverse as John F. Kennedy, to whom America was "a beacon to the world," and Ronald Reagan, who after losing his first bid for the presidency told his supporters, "We who are privileged to be Americans have had a rendezvous with destiny since the moment, back in 1630, when John Winthrop, standing on the deck of the tiny *Arbella* off the Massachusetts coast, told his little band of Pilgrims, 'We shall be as a City upon a Hill.' "

I go on to describe the contents of each volume of the anthology: Philip Freneau, "the Poet of the American Revolution" (who died alone in a blizzard at eighty, forgotten and at the time a poor tinker on the back roads of New Jersey), Benjamin Franklin's *Autobiography,* Native American songs and speeches, and Jefferson's Declaration of Independence (which the Vietnamese know from Ho Chi Minh's incorporation of it into the country's own declaration of 1945). I jump ahead to the magnificent five-year stretch from 1850 to 1855 when Emerson, Melville, Whitman, Hawthorne, and Thoreau brought into complex creation their definitions of America. In translating my description of the anti-imperial argument in some of Emerson's and Thoreau's writings, Mr. Binh hits his first and only snag. He can't say aloud: "Civil Disobedience." He just stops. He's embarrassed. He'd rather not say the words.

Covering for him as if he does not know the words, I

explain something about the essay in terms of the Mexican war and early exhibitions of the military aspect of Manifest Destiny. Mr. Binh looks at me and sort of chuckles, then goes ahead and translates these proscribed words, picking up our earlier momentum as we plunge ahead into the early twentieth century and the astounding accomplishments in poetry brought about by Imagism. Jogging on, I quote Philip Roth on the contemporary novelist's difficulty in making "credible much of the American reality." I recommend Saul Bellow's *Humboldt's Gift,* for a portrait of a poet burned up in the stratosphere of Roth's bewildering American reality. By the time I reach realism, black humor, hyperrealism, postmodernism, and "the literature of exhaustion," we have been going for an hour. If it seems impertinent to describe such cultural enterprises to this audience—every member of which almost certainly has lost a relative or loved one to American bombing—I consider my recent look into the Institute's card catalogue, where the only American entries are John Steinbeck, Jack London, Mario Puzo, and assorted mysteries left behind by OSS officers in the 1940s, when our countries were briefly allied against the Japanese.

Questions?

"What is postmodernism?" an intense man of about thirty-five asks. I describe Barth's essay as well as I can and say that I am leaving both "The Literature of Exhaustion" and "The Literature of Replenishment" with the Institute in his *Friday Book*. I am also leaving complete sets of the Cleanth Brooks anthology at the library of the Social Science Committee, at the National Library, and at the library at the University of Hanoi. If my trip accomplishes nothing else, at least some of America's best representations will be available.

"We have heard that students can choose their own education in your country. Is this true?" a university student asks.

I describe how choosing your own major works and

what also are the risks, both for the individual and his or her family as well as for the nation, which gets its doctors, lawyers, teachers, engineers, space scientists, economists, M.B.A.'s, etc., by some odd function of supply and demand, not by any central planning. Then there are questions on how books get published in the United States— i.e., "who decides"—and a question about "the situation of the poet in the United States" which leads us into a long talk, full-circle, all the way back to Philip Freneau, who at the very start of his career wrote a prophetic valedictorian speech at Princeton predicting how rough it would be for poets to make their way in America.

Finally, an older woman asks me what I see in the poetry of Ho Xuan Huong, an early-nineteenth-century poet that I have said I am translating. Ho Xuan Huong is one of the few women in the long tradition of Vietnamese poetry, which is largely male and Confucian. She has survived because of her sharp wit and her stunning ability to compose strictly metrical poems on the spot. Almost all of these beautiful poems were also, in their entireties, shocking *double entendres*. She wrote on forbidden topics: on sex, on male abuse of political power, on the abuses of the concubinage (both she and her mother were *vo lẽ,* or "second wives"), and on the corruption of the Buddhist church. The second "meanings" of her poems are indecent even by modern standards; her craft is beyond anything achieved in contemporary poetry.

I recite one of her poems, which is without double meaning, that I know by heart, and my audience is delighted, even though I mangle the pronunciation.

AUTUMN LANDSCAPE

Drop by drop rain slaps the banana leaves.
Praise whoever's skill sketched this desolate scene:
the lush, dark canopies of the gnarled trees,
the long river, sliding smooth and white.
Tilting my wine flask, I am drunk with river and hills.

My bag, filled with wind and moonlight, weighs on my back,
sags with poems. Look, and love even men.
Whoever sees this landscape is stunned.

It is a fitting end to a two-hour survey of American literature. It also makes clearer the intention of my survey. *Bạn tri âm:* "someone who's heard your sound." Friend.

25

THE LAKE OF
THE RETURNED SWORD

Hanoi, cradled in the delta of the Red River, is a city of lakes and ponds. The Lake of the Returned Sword—bordered by temples and restaurants, overhung by massive trees, dotted by the Ngoc Son islet, where the tiny pagoda is topped like a Christmas tree with a huge red star—lies in the heart of the old city. Centuries ago, around 1425 A.D., when Le Loi led a popular uprising to drive out foreign invaders (this time, the Ming), a fisherman named Le Thanh cast his net out into the Lake and pulled up a sword from the depths. The legend says that the sword, which belonged to Long Quan, the Dragon Lord of the Lake, had a magical glow. Later, when Thanh joined the rebels who were faring badly in their struggle against the superior Ming forces, he gave the sword to Le Loi . . . who seemed to be the first to notice that the sword was engraved with the words "By the Will of Heaven." With this sword, Le Loi routed the Chinese Army.

About a year later, after Le Loi was King, he went boating on the lake. Suddenly the surface started to boil and a golden turtle rose out of the depths. "Please be so kind," the turtle said, "as to return the sword which my master has loaned you." The devout King, who knew his mandate derived from sources more powerful than his own merely personal capacities, unsheathed the sword and threw it into the water, where it was snatched up and taken down by the turtle.

In my travels to and from the Institute, I was often pedaled past the Lake by a cyclo driver whom I had hired by the day. His father had been in the military police, his mother had been killed by American bombs, his wife was pregnant. He wore rags. Often his face was flushed pink, apparently because he drank a lot of *bia ly,* the cheap, flat draft beer sold in various places about the city, including a couple of cafés just by the Lake. Since my diplomat guide from the Foreign Ministry did not have either the time or the predilection (or, maybe, the instruction) to spend much time with me, I was usually on my own, unattended. I could get by on the little Vietnamese I spoke. I often took my pedicab driver to lunch with me, doing so the first time just tò get some food into him to offset his hangover. On subsequent days, I would simply lean back in my seat as we rolled along to ask this skinny man in his thirties where were the best places for *bún bò,* beef and noodles, or *phở,* the popular soup. He'd then smile and wheel us off down the alleys to some hole-in-the-wall without any sign, where we'd sit on little benches six inches above the sidewalk, brushing shoulders with ordinary folk and trying to understand each other's speech.

He wanted so much to talk. He *liked* Americans. He did not like Russians. The war was just *sai lầm,* a mistake. When we rolled past the Polish Embassy, he tapped me on the shoulder, pointed, and indicated thumbs up. He spat in the direction of the Cuban Embassy. I was suspicious at first. Was he an informant? All this welcome to Americans was curious, even though in the United States over the years I had heard report after report from returning Americans affirming the friendliness of Vietnamese, their lack of rancor. Back in Pennsylvania, the stuff about Vietnamese not liking Russians but liking Americans just seemed to me so much wish-fulfilling misjudgment of

Vietnamese politeness by Americans who tend to need the love of other peoples. One of the *ca dao* I had recorded in 1972 began, "Hatred for Diem-Americans will last a thousand years" (*Hận Mỹ-Ngô ngàn nam còn nho mãi*). Yet in Hanoi, barely fifteen years after our war, a woman who ran a coffee shop tried to explain it as she overheard me quizzing my driver. "We hated your government, not the people," as if the war were simply the concoction of a few evil men. I heard this all over Hanoi.

Paul Mus, the French *colon* and scholar who came to teach at Yale, wrote once of how he had been parachuted into Vietnam at the close of World War II to work out a deal for the French return. His parachute landed him near the mountains some sixty miles from Hanoi where Ho Chi Minh had retreated with his Viet Minh Army after the French had retaken Haiphong Harbor. After his short audience with Ho Chi Minh (in which no compromise was given), Mus asked for transport so that he could carry his report to the French command.

"We have no transport," he was told.

"How can I get to Hanoi?" he asked.

"Walk."

"But I'm a Frenchman," Mus protested. "They'll kill me."

"I would doubt it," Ho Chi Minh replied.

Mus describes his trek as the eeriest walk of his life. As he trudged down the roads filled with people, some still fleeing the results of the awful bombardment at Haiphong, he said no one paid him the slightest attention. He might have been a cricket hopping along.

Mus was already part of the past. For the Vietnamese whom he saw but who did not seem to see him, a revolution had occurred, a *cách mạng,* literally a "change of mandate." They were done with hating Frenchmen, with even thinking about Frenchmen. Mus made it to Haiphong completely unmolested.

Similarly, fifteen years after our war, wandering the city

that had suffered so much at American hands, it seemed to me that *it is only Americans who dwell on the war,* that the Vietnamese have undergone a "change of season," that they look to their futures not to their pasts, even though their present lives, marked by extreme poverty, are of course burdened by the past.

In fact, the Vietnamese may be quietly readying their minds for another change of season. On one occasion, my pedicab driver and I stopped for a beer at a ratty little Lake restaurant where two women were ladling out beer into big glasses while grilling food on charcoal stoves at the water's edge. We pushed past the metal chairs all jammed with men to an empty table with a view of the Lake. No one seemed to pay us much notice until an older man, holding a newspaper with bony, nicotine-stained fingers, looked up from his paper and was quite startled to see a Westerner there by the lakeside, drinking beer with a cyclo driver. He smiled, and his smile revealed a few browned snaggly teeth. Then he asked my driver where I was from, and my driver, who was very proud of his American possession, told him and added, "Go ahead and talk to him. He speaks our language."

The old man chose to speak in French, struggling with his lapsed use. He was pleased that I was a university professor. He had once run a bookshop. "The Vietnamese people," he said at one point, "are active and intelligent, but our leaders . . ." He pointed to his head and laughed.

Just then, another man whom I had not previously noticed got up from his seat to come over to the lakeside railing and stand next to us. This made the old man so frightened that he immediately started trembling and folding up his newspaper to leave. "Goodbye," he said. "Good luck. And"—glancing nervously over his shoulder—"don't forget us."

Near that café by the Lake of the Returned Sword is the *đền thờ,* the memorial shrine of Tran Hung Dao, the Gen-

eral who drove out the Mongols in the early thirteenth
century. The spirits of Vietnam's revolutionary leaders—
the Trung sisters, Lady Au, Ngo Quyen, et al.—have been
honored in tombs and shrines up and down the length of
Vietnam throughout the centuries, for these ancestral leaders are not really dead but have merely become *thánh,*
spirit-saints hovering in the continuum of departed souls
who inform contemporary life. They are the *bo cái dai
vuong,* the "great father-mother kings." Perhaps Ho Chi
Minh's Stalinesque mausoleum can be best understood this
way. More Confucian than Marxist, belonging more to
the past, more to the nation's centuries-old aspirations for
independence, than to the postcolonial, postcommunist
world at "the end of history," as Fukuyama would have
it. "Nothing is more precious," runs Ho Chi Minh's
slogan—blazoned on the entrance to his mausoleum,
on monuments everywhere, and even on ancient lintels
that once bore royal mottoes—"than independence and
freedom."

Independence *and* freedom. The Chairman's revolution—in the hands of his successors—has not brought
much of the latter. Though there is no denying that the
survivors—the men and women who now guide that revolution—sacrificed their lives and the lives of their families
to save the country from extermination and from foreign
subjugation, the results are no longer sufficient. They have
given the Vietnamese back their nation, but at such a price
in fervid obedience and individual constraint that one
senses now that mere nationhood isn't enough, that another "change of season" is brewing in the hearts of the
sixty-two million commonfolk, who have had enough of
war and bravery and nobility of sacrifice. Inside Tran Hung
Dao's *den tho,* in a small room off the main shrine room
housing the General's vermillion effigy, there is a curious
thing: the body of a huge turtle that surfaced in 1968 during
a period of fierce aerial bombing. A plaque reports that
the mysterious turtle was dragged ashore and taken to

biologists. It weighed 550 pounds and was nearly five feet long. The scientists estimated its age at between four and five hundred years. It could have been the turtle that took back Le Loi's magical sword. It was at least its cousin. "By the will of Heaven."

26

FINDING THE SKY
REFLECTED IN RIVERS

How immense the high sky is!
Lòng lộng trời cao
—The Tale of Kieu, *XXII, 93*

At last, I am once again traveling a dusty road into the Mekong Delta, the Mekong that I first saw, twenty-two years ago, from the bow of a CIA speedboat roaring to Sadec. And now, once again—after all the years of remembering and of trying to reassemble both my actions and my witnessing into some kind of truth—I am traveling down a road like the one I was kidnapped from in my first misadventure, a road crowded by shrill green paddy and muddy canals, canals like the one Gitelson was dumped into after he was shot. This is the road to My Tho, where Lieutenant Trung and his family now live surrounded by his father's communist enemies. My Tho, where we will ferry across the first big branch of the Mekong, just a bit upstream from Phoenix Island, not far from where the Coconut Monk (a CIA collaborator, my guide informs me with dead seriousness) resides somewhere under house arrest. Seeing Ong Dao Dua is out of the question, but I spend some time telling my guide and our driver of the Monk's sane comedies, trying to convince them of the absurdity of the charge. Probably the new government doesn't even believe it; probably they just feel threatened by the obstreperous, bent man and his lethal humor.

Traveling the road under a brilliant sky, this time, instead of banging along in a tin can of a public bus, I am whizzing past the rice paddies in an air-conditioned Toyota with a guide-translator from the Ministry of Foreign Affairs and a driver. All of this—guide, car, and driver—adds up to an obligatory seventy dollars a day, a fee that I am happy to pay; though I think I could get where I want to go on my own, journeying alone would take too much time, and I only have a week on my visa to visit the children (the children who, if they are there to be found, are now in their late twenties and mid-thirties). Travel isn't easy in contemporary Vietnam. Even my authorization from the North American Department of the Ministry of Foreign Affairs isn't enough to get me out of Ho Chi Minh City and into the provinces—*four* provinces besides that of the former Southern capital. The fact is, I really couldn't get anywhere without my guide, Le Hong Nguyen, a handsome, bespectacled, apparently no-nonsense man who as a dissident university student in the sixties spent six years in a Diem prison, though he was not a communist at the time, who must now negotiate my trip with the various People's Committees that run the Southern provinces as if they were independent principalities. Although we radioed ahead both a synopsis of my mission and the addresses of those I wish to meet, no one in Ho Chi Minh City could say if the various People's Committees will approve my visits, or even, if the *province* People's Committees do approve, whether the *district* Committees will cooperate.

The road is itself a revelation to any American who has come to see what his country has left behind. Whatever we left, nothing remains. If the Vietnamese are forgetting the war, their land has nearly forgotten it. Instead of endless miles of military camps, bridge bunkers, mine fields, convoys, and thickets of barbed wire—instead of Vietnam as I have pictured it all these years—it's now all green and vibrant and filled with peasants going about their simple tasks of tending the fields, herding ducks along waterways, scrubbing down buffalo, and getting their goods to market. The ARVN and U.S. camps are completely gone. The usable hardware—the tanks, the APCs, the warehouses of guns and ammo, the bombs, the planes, the choppers—were all sold for hard cash to other angry Third World countries soon after the war. Even the moonscapes of raw, puckered earth left behind by B-52s, and the dead zones soaked in defoliants, and the miles of red gashes scraped by Rome plows—all have been filled in, reclaimed, or replanted in acres of eucalyptus and by whatever scrubby species of bamboo the Vietnamese could succor in the ravaged land. The defoliated acreage is coming back, even if the toxic residues still lurk in the food chain. The bulldozed land is flourishing in green, even if the weak laterite soils sprout a sparse flora. Coconut palms and eucalyptus rim the roadsides. Clumps of bananas and water palms crowd the bridges along with viny tangles trumpeting yellow blossoms. We speed past men and women walking behind ox carts, past boys riding water buffalo, past roadside vendors of jackfruit, mango, and papaya, our car sweeping over half-mile stretches of eucalyptus leaves laid out to dry on the macadam as the villagers prepare to make incense.

At a long line of buses, trucks, and motorcycles waiting for the My Tho ferry to come back, Mr. Nguyen shows the police my ministry papers and we are waved through to the head of the line. Now the crowd moves in: the gawkers, who are just curious to see a Westerner, and the girls balancing on their bandanaed heads trays of 555 cigarettes, Juicy Fruit gum, and local green-skinned oranges. They too assume I'm a Russian, a Czech, or an East German, and we let them believe that, for in this press of people it would cause too much hullabaloo to be identified as an American. A whole generation has grown up that has not *seen* an American. Merely with my European looks, I am already stared at like a zoo creature let out with his keepers, so Mr. Nguyen doesn't reply when they call through the window and tap at the glass to ask him what I am.

Nonetheless, a middle-aged man strewn with necklaces of *nem,* cubes of fermenting pork wrapped in banana leaves, studies me from the edge of the crowd and comes over when Mr. Hung shuts off the engine to give it a rest and we leave the cool Toyota to stretch our legs in the dense tropical heat.

"Hello, sir," he says, tentatively.

"Hi," I say, tentatively. But his story unravels fast.

He says he was an office manager for RMK-BRG, the big American-owned construction firm that built roads and bases throughout the country, the bases that have now been stripped to their cement foundations and left to the jungle. His English is good, although his conversation is largely a roll call of his former American bosses, one of whom he says he has written to. I ask him if he knew Steve Erhart, who was an office manager at RMK.

"No," he says. "Sorry, sir."

A legless man—from the Hoa Hao Buddhist sect, to judge by his long hair tied up in a chignon—hops through the crowd on his way to the ferry landing. His knees are padded in burlap just above his stumps. He wears leather pads on the heels of his hands which throw him forward.

"This is what you do now?" I say, looking back now at the strings of meat cubes around the RMK guy's neck and slung over his arms.

"Yes, sir," he says. He looks at Mr. Nguyen and then turns back to me. "Do you think the Americans will come back?"

At Vinh Long, the river capital of Binh Minh Province, Mr. Nguyen has a People's Committee pal who gives us the go-ahead to inquire at the People's Committee at Tan Quoi District about continuing our journey. I am trying to get to Tan Phu, a small village that cannot be reached by road. There I hope to see Dao Thi Thai, the fifteen-year-old who was completely scalped by boat propeller blades when she was knocked into the water during a mortaring that forced her family to flee their river village. In 1968, when we discovered her in the Can Tho hospital, she had open, infected sores all over her head, and cranial osteomyelitis—polio of the skull, as it were. She was the girl that Miss Khuy had looked after in Boston, and when Thai was well and came home with two long wigs of Chinese hair, it was Khuy who took her into her own home in Saigon to teach Thai how to read and write and sew. Thai was one of the few who made it out of the grasp of the right-wing lunatics at the Can Tho hospital. As I hand her before and after pictures to Mr. Nguyen, who is sitting in the back seat as we bump along a dirt road to Tan Quoi, I realize she must now be a woman of thirty-seven years.

Tan Quoi is just a dot on a muddy river in the middle of the Delta. The People's Committee official who greets us is a young man; he hardly says anything as Mr. Nguyen, whose job, after all, is to send his foreign clients home pleased, rattles on at him in Nguyen's central dialect with all the maneuvering of a city-smart party apparatchik. The young man doesn't say anything but continues to lean one cheek against the fingertips of an upraised hand. "Say something nice to him in Vietnamese," Nguyen says, and I do, hoping that I've got a guide who knows what he's doing.

Soon we are sitting in the district headquarters, a brick-and-stucco affair, part of which is raised up on concrete pylons over the river. The blue pastel walls are splashed with mildew. We are seated around a dark teak table in the cult room for the village ancestors. Ho Chi Minh's ubiquitous photo is on a wall. A few more of the People's

Committee members show up. It's time for tea and tangerines and Mr. Nguyen gives me a wink as the Committee puts its heads together and mumbles about what to do with me. When they come out of their huddle, the quiet young man in charge smiles and, at last, speaks. He says they want to take me to lunch.

"What's going on?" I ask Mr. Nguyen.

"Eat fir'," he says, smiling.

I figure he thinks it's going well; on the other hand, he may just be happy about getting lunch after our long drive from Saigon. The agreement he suggested I make with him and the driver is that they will not charge me yet another "organization fee" if I pay for their meals and lodging. Meals are a big part of Nguyen's itinerary. Earlier on the highway, he told me that he was so sick when he was let out of jail ("when I getou chair," as he says in his problematic English) in a prisoner exchange program with North Vietnam in 1973 that he could barely walk and could not eat normal food.

"You like snake?" he asks, as an outraged sow squeals across our dusty route to the restaurant, chasing after a scabby mutt that has stolen her food.

Mr. Hung, the driver, smiles at me hopefully. I can tell he likes snake.

"Yeah, sure," I say. "I'll give it a try."

In the empty restaurant (which I am told the People's Committee built for the village) Carlos Santana's "Black Magic Woman" is blaring on the boom box. In the brackish pond off to one side where patrons have been dumping their beer cans, magical fish with bright-green eyes and translucent bodies are chasing one another. Soon, as we talk about what the war did to Binh Minh, we are served whole, head-to-tail eels poached in coriander and mint and scallion; after that come wonderful baked, salted crabs, and then something that I can't identify, but fear is snake. "What's this, snake?"

"No, squish," says Mr. Nguyen, a bit disappointed.

He's popping Heinekens for our friends from the Committee, pulling them out of the cooler he filled with ice back at the Majestic Hotel (or the Cuu Long, as it is now called).

Squish? Through some crossing of the senses, I remember the dead rat I stepped on up in Hanoi. The flesh between my chopsticks is white and chewy and familiar . . . maybe some kind of fish? No, *squid,* he is saying "squid." I smile.

As the beers wash down us in the noon heat, the Committee perks up. The young men who are my hosts were little boys during the war, little boys in this backwater village that must have been run by the Viet Cong. They are the sons of Viet Cong. They like my Southern dialect, which is theirs, and the fact that during the war I taught over in Can Tho at the university. However, as we get up to leave, an older man comes in. "A partisan," Mr. Nguyen tells me.

The older man has wandered by for a drink. He is in fact already drunk and is stunned to find an American sitting with the boys from the People's Committee right there in his watering hole. He's loud and wants to party. I watch the younger group humor him out of respect. The Tet Offensive decimated the local guerrillas. He is one of the few survivors, and it's evident that he's been put out to pasture with whatever small pleasures he needs. It's the young men, the loyal Marxist technocrats, who run things now. The old guerrillas have been pushed aside. Like this grizzled fifty-five-year-old with his cheek and scalp slashed by shrapnel scars, the "partisans"—the Viet Cong who once hunted Americans as Americans hunted them—are members of the various People's Committees, but are more or less *ex officio.* Although we are leaving, he insists on buying us another round, but instead Nguyen snaps open a Heineken for him and says we have to leave because a boat is waiting. This is news to me, but I'm ready.

So we glug our beers and get up to go. The partisan pumps my hand a lot and then simply wraps his arms around me and hugs me. He says, "We never saw an American who was our friend."

Two long homemade canoelike boats, driven by two-cycle engines churning a propeller-rudder assembly fixed to the end of a long pole, are waiting for us back at the district headquarters. The Committee, which provided the lunch, has also decided to donate the ride. With Nguyen, Hung, me, and a boatman in one canoe, and various People's Committeemen in the other, we are about to set off when our engine coughs, dies, and refuses to start, despite all manner of yanking on its cord. The whole town seems to be watching us now from shacks and balconies over the river or from smaller boats rowing by us. Amid laughter from the banks, we steady the boat by grabbing onto the pylons of the district headquarters and then shakily clamber over into the other boat, as some of that crew is forced to disembark.

Then we are off through the inlets of this small river town, past the shops that do their business out over the river from storefronts that offer ceramic vats of fish sauce, grades of lumber, rice bags, baskets of fish, herbs drying from rafters, and even stacked coffins ornamented with tin filigree. The sunlight breaks on us like a splash of hot water. All about us, above the rattle of our engine, we can hear the noise of the village: the pigs and chickens, the children squealing as they cannonball off their porches into the river, the raucous lorikeets scrambling through palms, the clang of a blacksmith pounding some metal, two men sawing planks, and an excited hubbub and babble as mothers washing clothes on boards slanted into the river see me go by and call out to their kids to see the American, for word has gone out from the restaurant that an American is in Binh Minh. I wave back to the smiles and calls from the thatched houses raised out of the river on cement stilts and coconut-trunk pylons. As the villagers watch me go off with the men from the People's Committee, I wonder if I'll end up, in the realm of twisted rumor that percolates out of Southeast Asia, as a sighting of a live POW.

Soon I feel I'm farther out into the countryside than any lone American (except maybe Gitelson) has ever gone. Our shallow boat cuts through a river of ducks parting before our snub, weathered prow in a welter of quack and gabble. We putter up inlets where the only signs of human habitation are big opened nets flounced out over the river on poles, ready to be dropped at high tide. We pass under the nets as a boat piled high with scallions is paddled our way. Then a skiff of Bibb lettuce is rowed past us by a teenaged girl standing in the back and working double oars. Thatched houses come into view, bamboo fish-traps stacked by their sides, along with great stone cisterns. At one house, sheaves of rice paper have been hung out to dry. Shrines and spirit houses dot the muddy banks, and I see platform altars smoking incense at the river's edge. Women are washing their long hair, their children, their pots and pans, their rice, in the silty river. At one landing a man is soaping down a pig with his hands. Farther on, boys have ridden their water buffalo into a deep hole, where the huge bulls stand squinty-eyed, submerged up to their snouts and massive horns.

Cascades of flowers trellis the overhang. We glide through bamboo weirs stuck in the sluggish current. A hay boat glides our way, and then a boat full of rocks. And children, children everywhere: honey-brown skinny-dippers plunging off the banks, tots rocked by their mothers in noonday hammocks, kids sitting patiently on banyan roots as their heads get picked for lice, boys netting fish with their fathers, teenaged girls looking up startled from their pedal sewing machines set out by the river so they can see what's going on. All of these youngsters look whole and healthy. None of them, whatever the scars of their parents, have ever seen fighting. All have been readmitted into the sane continuum of Vietnamese life, which seemed broken forever.

Nguyen keeps turning round to see what I think. I am elated, balmy, rhapsodic. This was the world I could never enter, but could only glimpse. This was the Vietnam almost obliterated by the war. Everywhere about me—in all this dazzle of Delta life—I can see a happiness and a healing, a realm of heaven, earth, and humankind going on with full creative force.

As we approach Tan Phu Village, I search the riverbank and see an old lady with snow-white hair fairly hopping up and down and waving at us. Now she is running along the bank and pointing us ahead. It's Thai's old auntie, whom I last saw twenty years ago in the post-Tet Can Tho hospital where she urged us to take Thai to the United States. She herself had been shot in the leg. I look to see where the old woman is pointing and discover a woman standing at a jetty in bright pajamas and a leaf hat strapped under her chin.

"Is that her? Thai?" Nguyen asks.

When I say yes, he too breaks into a big grin. He has been a guide before (the cooler was given to him by a U.S. Senator) but never a detective, and I can fathom in his smile his fear that our trip might have gone kerplunk.

We moor up, and still other People's Committee personnel come forward to greet us. This must be the local village bunch, but in everyone's excitement we just shake hands all around and everyone turns to Thai, who smiles at me as we too shake hands and I realize she has just remembered me.

Her garrulous old auntie, who probably saved Thai's life in getting her to the hospital as well as getting her to the United States, speaks up first. "Are you the one I talked to in the hospital?"

"Yes," I say, beaming.

"*Trời ơi!*" she says, remembering the intense, skinny youngster that I was. "You've gotten fat." When she laughs, her mouth reveals a snarl of missing teeth; her mirthful eyes, a crease of crow's-feet.

My conversation with Thai will take place at her parents' home, which is a trek from the riverbank. Now our rather large entourage starts out across the raised-up dikes that meander through the shady groves of Tan Phu Village, most of which seems to have turned out to see the American who took Thai away. When we pass by, they join our march, with the local officials leading the way across bamboo-rail monkey bridges over narrow canals that fill when the tide runs back up the Mekong and its tributaries. At the first flimsy bridge, my Pierre Cardin duffel bag shifts on my back and I nearly fall in. At the last bridge, I'm told to stay put until a man comes over for me in a tiny boat that is more like a board, and just as shaky, so that he finally jumps into the mucky water up to his waist to steady the boat across.

Outside Thai's parents' house, her white-haired father is standing by the path, urinating and singing into the hedge of cactus. Gales of laughter go up from the crowd. Auntie smacks his shoulder and says he is disgusting, and I remember that Thai's father was supposed to be insane. (About how many people had I heard that in wartime Vietnam?) He smiles at me like a naughty boy and grasps my hand in his own two hands. (Thai immediately calls to her stony-faced mother to fetch a washbasin.) His *two* hands which means that he wants to show respect. I shake his hands and greet him as Ong, the polite form of "Mr.," and the laughter rises again. I can see that I'm the best entertainment to hit this backwater in a long time.

We go inside. The washbasin which I share with Nguyen is a U.S. helmet. I am sweating like a pig, so I also rinse my face before taking the towel that Thai hands me. In the shadows of the dirt-floor house, huge wasps are circling in the rafters where they have bored their nests. Now, out of the blinding, midday sunlight, I can see Thai better. Her skin is a bit jaundiced, and she is thin. With her hat off, I can see that her Chinese wig looks natural and has held up. She smiles at me again and takes up her hat and starts fanning me, as some other woman from behind pulls out my shirttail and does the same thing.

With Nguyen translating, I learn that Thai has been married twice and has two children, a boy born in 1972 and a girl in 1975. They live with her in Can Tho where she "sells coffee"—i.e., sells anything on the street that will earn some money. When Nguyen rattles on at her in his hurry-up way, she ignores him and goes on at her own speed, giving the answers that she wants to give. She's had a hard life and nobody is going to push her around. When I last saw her, in Boston, I remember being shocked at how the frail teenager that I had removed from the Can Tho hospital had turned into a voluptuous teenager, and I recall how Khuy and I worried that, because of her injury, and because of an older sister who already appeared to be working the ARVN trade, Thai might become a prostitute back in Vietnam. That's why Khuy took her into her home.

Indeed, her first husband was an ARVN soldier. They quarreled when she learned he had a girlfriend. She left him after nine years of marriage, in 1979. Her second marriage ended after five years. Her second husband, a cyclo driver, she says, also had children from a previous marriage, and none of their kids got along. So she lives on her own now. Besides selling coffee and soft drinks, she sometimes does piecework for a bicycle factory, packing bike hubs with cotton. She smiles and says her son will soon graduate from high school. And her daughter too. It's a first for her family. Except for Khuy, it's clear no one has ever given Thai much help.

"Do you remember anything special about the United States?"

"The Mores," she says. Mr. and Mrs. Joseph More who, she adds, she had hoped were the ones coming to see her when the police came and told her an American wanted to visit.

"Anything else?"

"Not really."

But then she takes from her wallet a creased, flattened, and yellowed letter that she has been carrying around since she got it. It is dated August 8, 1968. It is typed and in Vietnamese. It is from me. I am stunned to see my signature at the bottom of the page. Stunned that she would have been carrying about with her a letter that I do not remember having written, but as Nguyen translates back to me the words that I can no longer read, I recall writing Thai after Khuy's death, writing her of how much Khuy loved her, and of how she had wanted Thai to live in her home like a younger sister, of how I thought the best way Thai could remember Khuy was to live a life that Khuy would admire.

"It's a pretty letter," Nguyen says, regarding me in a different light. "Beautiful words."

Thai comes with us on the way back to Tan Quoi in order to hitch a ride with us to Can Tho. In the boat, Nguyen tries to lift up the edge of her wig to see her scarred scalp and Thai ignores him. I whisper to him, "Please don't do that," and he nods okay, but his action makes me marvel at how she has managed to stay on her feet with the life Heaven has given her. When we say goodbye on the street in Can Tho, I give her a Casio watch and a nylon change purse with Velcro snaps that has some money in it. I promise to tell the Mores that she is well. As she walks away into the crowd, her conical hat disappearing into the oblivion that has marked her life for the last twenty years, I am impossibly happy that she still carries my letter with her.

27

CAN THO

That night we eat snake—cobra, to be exact—
with Mr. Loc, a young Turk from the Hau Giang Province
People's Committee. Although the city has had a power
outage, Mr. Hung, the driver, has taken me back to the
chicken-wire cobra cage at the rear of the Colman-lamp-
lit restaurant to prod our main course with a chopstick
until it rises and flares its hood. Later, on our table in a
serving bowl, its flesh looks white and stringy. Nguyen
offers me a strip of the prized ovaries, but I say, "No, you
go ahead," and he wolfs it down. Though I try eating the
cobra, I am relieved when Nguyen and Hung and our
People's Committeeman finish it, put off not so much by
the idea or the taste but by a fact that I picked up in Hanoi
from the physician in charge of Agent Orange research:
the highest levels of dioxin are now being found in reptiles
and turtles, creatures, like humans, with fair longevity that
store the toxin in their fat. Later on our trip, in Long
Xuyen, true to our bargain of their choosing the restaurants, Nguyen, Hung, and I will dine on frogs, wild boar,
and *se sè,* tiny, crisp, browned forest birds whose heads I
flick with my chopsticks into a lagoon circled by two
swans.

Mr. Loc is pudgy, thirty-something, and a chuckler. He

is learning English and has a favorite phrase—"oh,
really"—which he employs something like the French "*ça
va.*" He adds some horror to my growing sense of what
it would be like to live under a People's Committee by
telling me that tomorrow, at my hotel, he has summoned
Dr. Khoa, the former *médecin chef* of the Can Tho Regional
Hospital, along with Nguyen Van O, the boy whose severed arm we saved at the University Hospital in Iowa City,
and the uncle of Bui Thi Kha, the eighteen-year-old
woman whose family and village were erased from the
earth by helicopter gunships and jets in 1968.

"Oh, please," I say, "don't ask them all to come to the
hotel."

"Oh, really? But, Mr. John, it much easier for you."

"Yes, well, thank you, but Dr. Khoa is a distinguished
man. He's old now. I should go to him."

"No, really, he not busy now. *Really.*" He chuckles.
Apparently, Dr. Khoa was removed from running the hospital after the takeover, and is now retired.

"But, Mr. Loc"—I look over to Nguyen for help—"I
can't see them together. I can't interview them all at once.
I want to see where they live, talk to their relatives." I
want to see what Khoa remembers of the incidents at his
hospital, what he might say to me now about the war,
what he thinks of the new government. Dr. Khoa lives in
town not far from my hotel, and Bui Thi Kha's uncle, a
traditional herbalist physician and my only link to her, also
lives in town. Christ, if it weren't for Mr. Loc, I could
walk to their houses. Nguyen Van O, whose name means
"place," is a farmer; he should have a family by now. I
want to see him out in the countryside, the way I saw
Thai.

Nguyen swigs his glass of beer and shrugs his shoulders,
but nonetheless says something to Mr. Loc that I can't
make out.

"They wait," Loc replies. "No problem, really."

Imagine being summoned out of the blue by a young

government official with nearly no education and having to wait in a government-run hotel because some foreigner that you might not even want to see wants to see you. Imagine that, and you're on your way to imagining a life in contemporary Vietnam. I try to focus my mind on the brighter side of this—the scenes of overwhelming beauty and peace that I just saw in the country. On the brighter side, *at least these people are no longer being bombed* and their children have some chance of growing up. I think of the country's long history, its sacrifices, its two thousand years of struggling for freedom, and can't imagine that Vietnamese will govern themselves this way for long.

The next morning, while the authorities have gone off to fetch my interviewees, Mr. Loc takes me around Can Tho. Under a ghastly white colossus of Ho Chi Minh looking out over the harbor and the Ninh Kieu islands, the open market is bustling. But my old town is an impoverished shambles, although Loc tells me that in the last couple of years trade agreements with Thailand and Singapore (the whole Delta is rich in fruits, crabs, and mammoth prawns) promise to bring in some hard cash to get the economy going.

Mr. Hung drives us about in my rented car. Up at the Cai Rang campus of my old university, the language lab is just a maze of dead wires; the English library, an incoherent pile of mildewed volumes left behind by Fulbright and IVS teachers twenty years ago. We pass the hospital, but Loc says we are not permitted to go inside. We pass my old house (where Roger Montgomery rescued me from the roaches, where Chanh and I had our talks, where our cars were blown up before Kennedy's arrival, and where Hintze, Seraile, Chanh, and I held out during Tet); Loc tells me it's now lived in by a member of the People's Committee. Across from the house, in the field where Chanh and I helped build a bridge and where the cops dug in as An Cu village burned, the People's Committee has built a cement-and-ceramic-tile park with potted plants, topiary, and a café. It's completely empty, but soon "to open up." In town, the old tennis-court restaurant— the Ngoc Loi where I first spoke with Gitelson—has been taken over by the People's Committee and made part of their compound. Up the road, the MACV compound is now a soccer field. Out of town, the huge airbase that we fled to at Tet is open rice fields.

Back at the hotel, I am happy to hear that Dr. Khoa sends his regrets but cannot come because his nephew is ill in Ho Chi Minh City and he must tend to him. While Khoa is still his own man, Pham Quang Khiem, Bui Thi Kha's uncle, is waiting for me in the lobby, sitting on a bench next to O, O's older sister, and a boy I don't recognize. I try to say hello politely to all of them at once. Kha's uncle is so old and weak that he has to be helped up the seven flights of hotel stairs to an empty restaurant where we are allowed to talk, while O and his people wait downstairs. Nguyen translates.

Kha is dead. I am so stunned to hear this that I almost start crying, but stop myself to ask how she died. Her frail uncle with his nervous hands and shock of surprisingly black hair, who became her legal guardian after her father and sister were killed and her mother went mad, tells me in his soft, calm voice that shortly after her return from Iowa—he thinks in 1972 or '73—where her hopeless mess of fractures was finally mended, Kha decided to go see her one remaining sister, living in Tra On near their old village. On the way to Tra On, Kha was drowned out on the Mekong in a sudden squall that capsized the boat. She was too weak to swim. Kha's mother, who is Mr. Khiem's sister, is still alive, and he sees that she is taken care of at the Phuoc Hau Pagoda.

"Did Kha say anything about her stay in the United States?"

Mr. Khiem thinks for a moment. I am asking about events that are nearly twenty years past. "Yes," he says. "She didn't say much about the country, but she was moved that Americans would take care of her as if she were their daughter."

Thirty-four-year-old O, who is here with a young cousin and his strikingly handsome older sister, Ngoc An (whom I last saw in 1968 when she looked after her brother in the hospital—she was there with a shoulder wound), is now a father of six, the oldest, fourteen years old; the youngest, four. He came home in 1970 and got married that year to a woman who still does the farming while he does the housework because his arm, though attached and working, was stripped of so much upper muscle that it will always be weak. He doesn't look good. One of his eyes has turned out and both whites are yellowed. He is sweating and nervous. When Nguyen asks him my questions, O defers to his older sister, as he did when he was just a thirteen-year-old boy with his arm hanging to his shoulder by a flap of skin and a plaster cast. I ask him if something's wrong and he says that he got in trouble with the People's Committee for trying to smuggle out a letter to the family that took care of him in Iowa City. Nguyen starts yelling at him, and this, of course, only makes O more nervous and silent.

"Stop!" I finally shout. "What's going on?"

"Don't you see," Nguyen shouts back, "what dumb thing he do?"

"Just what did he do?"

"He try send letter with some frien' who try escape Vietnam. Him frien' get caught and government find O's letter. *That mean him know about escape but not tell.*" Nguyen starts berating O once again, and now both O and his sister, as well as the cousin who is with them, have fallen into a sullen looking-down-at-their-hands.

"Nguyen, please, I don't care about that. You may, but I don't. Now you've gotten them so frightened they won't talk about anything. When did all this happen, anyway?"

"Four year ago."

28

GITELSON

But his name is now forgotten.
Chưa tường dược họ dược tên.
—The Tale of Kieu, *XXVI, 173*

We are upriver, in Long Xuyen. Because of Mr. Loc's "help" in Can Tho, I actually have ended up with an extra day to kill before my exit visa expires and my Royal Thai flight leaves Tan Son Nhut, so I have told Nguyen about Gitelson and asked him if he thought it likely that we could find out anything about Dave's murder. Nguyen thinks we can try, so now we are in yet another office of another People's Committee, but this time the authorities, like the ones in Binh Minh, are helpful.

"It's really a police matter," says Mr. Nguyen Anh Vu, the provincial Director for Information, as he pours us tea from his Chinese thermos. Mr. Vu is a quiet, neat man who goes barefoot in his office and who has smiled patiently throughout my description of the "poor American."

"Mr. Vu. I don't care if the truth is that the Viet Cong killed my friend. I just want to know why he died."

"The easy thing, of course, is to tell you that Americans killed him, which you already suspect. But let's really find out, if we can." He smiles again and calls in an assistant and asks him who is over at the police station that would have been around twenty years ago.

"That's the problem, you see. There was terrible killing in that period. Many of the villages were destroyed. Most of our cadre too."

Nguyen, who is being especially helpful, suggests the name of a senior official whom he knows.

"I'm afraid he's in Ho Chi Minh City," Mr. Vu says. He offers us his 555 cigarettes and lights them with his lighter. "Even I have only been here three years. Come back tomorrow, and maybe we will know something."

The next afternoon, sitting in a conference room with Mr. Vu and members of the local archaeological museum (which displays the artifacts of Oc Eo, a pre-Vietnamese culture that traded with India and the West, judging from an excavated cache of Roman coins), Mr. Nghia, the director of their digs at Ba The Mountain, not far from Hue Duc where Gitelson lived and died, says that once he heard villagers talking "about an American who walked about around here and helped farmers," and that he was killed, but how he did not hear.

We are drinking tea and eating tangerines. Another man says, "A lot of us don't know where our friends are."

29

GOING OUT
AND COMING HOME

Royal Thai Flight 681 is taxiing to the Tan Son Nhut runway, past the empty cement canopies and bunkers that once housed our Air Force. In the distance, a rusting water tower stands next to the remnants of an Army gym, its roof ripped off. Trailing after an old Ford pickup, our jet taxis past a graveyard of U.S. aircraft—Dragonships, Otters, Cessnas, and choppers—cannibalized for their parts. A woman is weeping in the seat next to me. This had been her first trip home in ten years. Now she is a nurse in Australia where she has children who do not speak Vietnamese.

The Thai hostesses in silk sarongs are giving all the women orchids. The plane is mostly filled with Orderly Departure refugees who have jammed all the overhead compartments with cardboard suitcases and string bags—whole families with their names tagged to their lapels: dolled-up little girls in fizzes of chiffon, their black-silk-capped grannies with lacquered teeth, their teenaged brothers with slicked-back hair and shiny *Miami Vice* suits. Soon, for them too, Vietnam will be a memory. Soon they all will be dispersed into the paradises of Anaheim, South Bend, Lyon, Vancouver, and Leeds.

Fifteen years after the fall of Saigon, the big bang of the

war still ripples through the lives of millions: through departed refugees, through Amerasian teenagers loose on
Vietnam's streets, through legless, unemployed ex-ARVN
holding out their Army caps near the foreigners' hotels,
through the maimed and the mad wandering about or
taken in by pagodas. For them, the war is the central memory of their lives. Yet for most of the sixty-two million
who stayed, the war is being forgotten, forgotten in the
rhythm of the rice harvest, forgotten in the raising of children, forgotten in the welter of hopes that peace and a bit
of prosperity are creating, in hopes now fed by events of
the wider world that Vietnam wants to enter. In that kind
of forgetting, there is a sanity, not an amnesia.

How small and sour-grapes seems our postwar punishment of Vietnam, our trade and diplomatic embargoes that
keep the country in economic ruin. How self-punishing
and miserly in American spirit are these policies. How
much better it would be for our national pride if we offered
this country our help, for it is we and those who threw in
their lot with us who seem to dwell in needless quandary,
who live lives punctuated by active resentments and pain.
Go visit Vietnam, I'd tell the troubled vets. Go visit, if
you can, and do something good there, and your pain
won't seem so private, your need for resentment so great.

As our plane revs engines, lurches down the runway,
and finally lifts off into a blank expanse of sky, I watch
the refugees' faces frozen at the oval windows as they leave
their old lives behind. How hard it will be for them to talk
to Heaven as they start new lives in strange lands. At Tet,
when their ancestors will fly up from their apartments and
tract homes to report in at Heaven, will they find their
way? What will they have to say? It is a long way from
Indiana to the sky over Hue.

Perhaps like me these refugees will someday discover
themselves, à la those mysterious dancers in Hue, covering
their faces in a veil of memories to turn and dance them-

selves toward heaven, putting on that red mask of heaven's face, searching for those clarifying moments when they most felt their humanness, their fate, and the force of its decrees. As our plane drones west, high over the Delta which winks back sunlight from its web of river loops and lagoons, I see these new exiles still at the cabin windows already beginning their search of memories. Đi một ngày dàng, học mọt sàng khôn. Go out, one proverb says, and see the sun's face, and the moon's. Go out, says another, and return with a basket full of wisdom. As for me, whatever wisdom I've brought back, my own search, for now, is done.